A Companion to
Survey Research

SAGE has been part of the global academic community since 1965, supporting high quality research and learning that transforms society and our understanding of individuals, groups, and cultures. SAGE is the independent, innovative, natural home for authors, editors and societies who share our commitment and passion for the social sciences. Find out more at: **www.sagepublications.com**

Connect, Debate, Engage on Methodspace

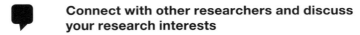 **Connect with other researchers and discuss your research interests**

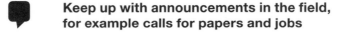 **Keep up with announcements in the field, for example calls for papers and jobs**

Discover and review resources

Engage with featured content such as key articles, podcasts and videos

Find out about relevant conferences and events

Methodspace
Connecting the Research Community

www.methodspace.com

brought to you by

A Companion to Survey Research

Michael Ornstein

Los Angeles | London | New Delhi
Singapore | Washington DC

Los Angeles | London | New Delhi
Singapore | Washington DC

SAGE Publications Ltd
1 Oliver's Yard
55 City Road
London EC1Y 1SP

SAGE Publications Inc.
2455 Teller Road
Thousand Oaks, California 91320

SAGE Publications India Pvt Ltd
B 1/I 1 Mohan Cooperative Industrial Area
Mathura Road
New Delhi 110 044

SAGE Publications Asia-Pacific Pte Ltd
3 Church Street
#10-04 Samsung Hub
Singapore 049483

Editor: Katie Metzler
Assistant editor: Anna Horvai
Production editor: Ian Antcliff
Copyeditor: Neville Hankins
Proofreader: Jonathan Hopkins
Indexer: Silvia Benvenuto
Marketing manager: Ben Griffin-Sherwood
Cover design: Jennifer Crisp
Typeset by: C&M Digitals (P) Ltd, Chennai, India
Printed and bound by: CPI Group (UK) Ltd,
Croydon, CR0 4YY

MIX
Paper from
responsible sources
FSC® C013604

© Michael Ornstein 2013

First published 2013

Library of Congress Control Number: 2012947040

British Library Cataloguing in Publication data

A catalogue record for this book is available from the British Library

ISBN 978-1-4462-0908-0
ISBN 978-1-4462-0909-7 (pbk)

Contents

About the Author

Michael Ornstein teaches sociology at York University in Toronto and since 2000 has been the Director of the Institute for Social Research, the largest Canadian university-based survey research organization. He has been active in the development, design and execution of numerous large scale research projects at the Institute, including the Quality of Life project from 1977 to 1981 and the first Canadian study on knowledge, behaviour and attitudes about AIDS. His recent research is on ethno-racial inequality in Toronto, Montreal and Vancouver, occupational wage differences, age and cohort trajectories of earnings, promotion at Canadian universities and the family strategies for employment and childcare. Dr Ornstein's *Politics and Ideology in Canada: Elite and Public Opinion in the Transformation of a Welfare State*, co-authored with H. Michael Stevenson, was the 2001 winner of the Harold Adams Innis Prize for the best Social Science Federation of Canada supported book in the Social Sciences and English. From 2005 to 2010 he led York's SSHRC-Statistics Canada sponsored Summer Program in Data Analysis.

Introduction

In succession, survey researchers and methodologists have described themselves as practising an art, a craft and a science.[1] In this book, I try to capture all three dimensions.

Quite scientifically, survey researchers define and measure a huge range of material and subjective phenomena and analyse them with statistical models. But even the most factual question involves the indirect measurement of a mental construct and the answer incorporates some measurement error due to respondents, the wording of a question, and the process of data collection.

The first survey researchers thought of question design as an art, first because there were only limited generalizations about how to write good questions and, second, because they understood that their questions incorporated assumptions about how respondents thought about a topic. To a degree, this is still true. The art of survey research also involves subtle judgements about which research questions are worth pursuing and can be answered, as well as technical ingenuity in the design of questions and samples.

Each element of survey research – writing questions, combining the questions in a survey that makes sense to respondents and encourages them to answer, improving the questionnaire by testing, designing strategies to maximize respondents, and accurately and cost effectively collecting data – requires the experience, skill and attention to detail that characterizes a craft. The craft of applied sample design begins with statistical theory, but often it is necessary to compromise between multiple analytical goals and make judgements about spending limited funds.

Chapter 1 describes the invention of modern surveys in the 1930s and their development until the early 1950s, bringing together remarkable advances in questionnaire design, sampling and data collection. Chapter 2 provides a complete account of methodological research on question design and Chapter 3 addresses the practical concerns in writing individual questions and combining them into a questionnaire that is inviting to respondents and encourages them to answer

---

[1] Respectively, for example, see Lazarsfeld (1935) and Payne (1951); Converse and Presser (1986); and Weisberg (2005) and Groves et al. (2009).

carefully. Because many more researchers expect to design and pretest question-naires themselves, these chapters offer quite detailed advice.

Chapter 4 describes the basic types of survey samples and the effects of sample structure and sample size on the precision of survey results, focusing on funda-mental statistical concepts, but with only as much technical description needed to explain them. Chapter 5 deals with practical sample design, such as what kind of sample and how large a sample is needed, in the context of cost and information constraints. Because every sample design can benefit from the advice of an expert, these two chapters are more a primer on the principles of sample design and a catalogue of survey strategies than a practical guide to sample design.

Chapter 6 describes small-scale methods of testing and improving a questionnaire before a larger survey and Chapter 7 deals with collecting survey data, emphasizing the differences between and effects of the mode and process of data collection and the resulting data, as well as strategies to maximize survey response. Chapter 8 discusses the decline in survey response rates over the last 20 years and what it means for the future of surveys.

To learn about the power and limits of survey research there is no substitute for working with a group to design a sample and questionnaire and for using the resulting data to address the research questions that motivated the design. For many such opportunities I thank my colleagues at the Institute for Social Research at York University in Toronto.

For their sage advice and editing prowess I thank Penni Stewart and Jacob and Noah Stewart-Ornstein. Very helpful comments were provided by two anonymous reviewers. At Sage, I thank Katie Metzler for shepherding this entire project, Ian Antcliff for expertly shepherding the manuscript through production and Anna Horvai for much helpful assistance. Any errors, and the likely more numerous failures in judgement, are the responsibility of the author alone.

1

The Invention of Survey Research

Survey research has roots in centuries of census taking, intelligence and psychological testing beginning in the late nineteenth century, research on attitudes from the 1920s, and 'social surveys' of the conditions of the urban poor, pioneered in England by Charles Booth in the 1880s and Joseph Rowntree in the 1890s, and extended to many other countries in the first third of the twentieth century (Bulmer et al., 1991). Modern surveys did not evolve directly from these ancestors, however. Instead, aspiring to represent entire populations, to ask questions on almost any topic, to gather data in a timely manner, and to yield quantitative results, surveys developed out of the public opinion polls initiated in the mid-1930s by American market researchers, notably Archibald Crossley, Elmo Roper and George Gallup (Converse, 1987: 87ff.). Surveys' successful arrival was signalled by their correct prediction of the 1936 US presidential election.[1] In Roper's words, 'advertising men … are to be credited with … the early development of the technique which has been evolved for sampling public opinion' (1940: 325).

Academics were no strangers to the public opinion industry. In 1937, psychology professor Hadley Cantril of Princeton University and Frank Stanton, then research director and later president of Columbia Broadcasting, obtained a Rockefeller Foundation grant to study the psychological and cultural effects of radio. To direct the project they hired sociologist Paul Lazarsfeld, whose first American publication, 'The art of asking why', appeared in the 1935 inaugural issue of the *National Marketing Review*. The first description of longitudinal surveys, by Lazarsfeld and Fiske (1938), is in the second volume of *Public Opinion Quarterly*, established in 1937. During the Second World War, the two US government organizations responsible for surveys were led by Elmo Wilson, an associate of Roper, and academic psychologist Rensis Likert. The monumental surveys of the US Army – over half a million soldiers were surveyed with more than 200

---

[1] For an interesting argument that modern social science *creates* public opinion, see Osborne and Rose (1999).

questionnaires – were led by Harvard sociologist Samuel Stouffer (compiled as *The American Soldier*[2] by Stouffer et al., 1949). According to Lazarsfeld, the development of survey research

> might be dated from the appearance of 'The American Soldier' after World War II. In this work, a large body of data was made coherent and meaningful by careful statistical analysis. 'Survey analysis' … became the language of empirical social research, possessing its own rules for forming basic concepts and combining them into meaningful propositions. (Cited in Rosenberg, 1968: vii)[3]

The next three sections of this chapter describe the development of survey sampling, questionnaire design and data collection until the early 1950s. This work established the conceptual core of modern survey research, but 60 years later no longer serves as a practical guide.

About Survey Sampling

The fundamental idea of applied survey sampling, which is that a properly selected random sample can accurately represent any population, no matter how large and diverse, dates to the late nineteenth century when Anders Kaier employed his 'representative method' to survey the entire Norwegian population. First, Kaier divided the country in two, separating urban and rural areas. In the urban 'stratum' he selected all of the five largest cities and eight smaller cities, to represent medium and small communities; then in each of the 13 selected cities he divided streets into groups according to size and selected a sample of streets; and finally he selected a fraction of the dwellings on each selected street. Counts from the Norwegian Census were used to calculate the appropriate number of selections in each community. In rural areas, a sample of municipalities was chosen on the basis of their main industry. Because Kaier calculated the probabilities at each stage of sampling to give every dwelling in Norway the same chance of selection, characteristics of the population could be estimated directly from the sample without weights (Bethlehem, 2009: 10ff.; Kuusella 2011: 91ff.). In modern parlance, the sample was 'self-weighting'. In other samples selected by Kaier, parts of the population

---

[2]For an extraordinary account of how Elmo Roper convinced General Eisenhower to agree to survey soldiers, see his *You and Your Leaders* (1957: 233–234). Roper is cited by Hyman (1991: 69), who also provides a detailed account of the programme of *Army Survey Research*. For an assessment of the role of *The American Soldier* by one of the researchers, see Williams (1989).

[3]C. Wright Mills (1959) challenged the hubris of Lazarsfeld's assertion that survey analysis had become *the* language of empirical social research, labelling it 'abstracted empiricism'. In his American Sociological Association presidential address Herbert Blumer described it as 'the scheme of sociological analysis which seeks to reduce human group life to variables and their relations' (1956: 683).

had different probabilities of selection and weights were used to produce unbiased estimates of population characteristics.[4,5]

Kaier's sample of the Norwegian population is like a modern multi-stage probability sample, except that the municipalities were not selected at random, but rather 'purposively', on the basis of his knowledge of their characteristics. The key idea is that a representative sample of a complex population can be obtained using two or more *stages* of selection – selecting communities, then streets within the communities, then dwellings on the streets – as long as the probability of selection at each stage is known. 'Systematic selection' is still used routinely, in place of strict random sampling and when the sample size is very small (for example, selecting a small number of communities) there is a good argument for selecting a 'purposive' sample based on a deep knowledge of the units, rather than a random sample. Kaier's methods are close to the modern ideas of 'balanced' samples, discussed in Chapter 5.[6]

Skip forward more than 30 years and modern survey sampling begins with the publication of Neyman's 1934 article, 'On two different aspects of the representative method: the method of stratified sampling and the method of purposive selection', which demonstrates conclusively the risk of bias when a sample is *not* selected at random.[7] Also, he demonstrated the value of sample

---

[4]Kruskal and Mosteller (1980: 174ff.) provide a fine discussion of the concept of representativeness and describe the evolution of Kaier's ideas between 1895 and 1903 and responses at the International Statistical Institute, which was the statistical 'establishment' of the time. To someone schooled only in contemporary sampling statistics, what's remarkable is that the obvious principles of sampling were discovered and not universally welcomed at the time.

[5]Between Kaier and Neyman, the major intermediate figure was Arthur Bowley. In 1906 he argued that the precision of sample estimates could be predicted from Edgeworth's central limit theorem, which showed that sample means were normally distributed, irrespective of the variable's distribution (Converse, 1987: 42). In his 1915 book, Bowley proposed the use of the probable error (rather than the 'standard error' based on the *squared* errors) as a measure of sampling error. Also, he noted that systematic sampling yielded smaller errors than random selection (Kruskal and Mosteller, 1980: 184). Bowley did not, however, conclusively favour random over purposive sampling. Fisher's work was important as well – not because it contributed directly to survey sampling, but because it established the critical importance of randomization. Interestingly, Neyman gives credit only to Bowley, and not Kaier, for the 'representative method'.

[6]The story of survey sampling does not end with the ascendancy of conventional probability samples. Groves and Lyberg (2010) write: 'For years, survey samplers have argued about the merits of deeper stratification permitted in a systematic sample on an ordered list, yielding biased estimates of sampling variance, versus a paired selection design from fixed strata, yielding an unbiased estimator for the sampling variance. Most practical samplers forgo the unbiased estimate of the sampling variance (and error measurement) for the "assumed" lower magnitude of the true sampling variance' (p. 873). In other words, a sample with greater precision is better, even if the error cannot be calculated exactly.

[7]Neyman examined Gini and Galvani's non-random sample of 29 of the 214 geographical units of an Italian national census. Although the 29 units were chosen because they were closest to the overall population average on a number of variables, the resulting sample was shown to be *dis*-similar to the population on other measures. In addition, restricting the selection to units that were close to the average resulted in underestimates of the variation in the population. Neyman's paper is fascinating and not difficult to read.

stratification, whereby the population is divided into two or more sectors or 'strata' and a separate sample is selected in each stratum, not necessarily with the same probability.

Neyman established *the* criterion for the precision of an estimate of a population characteristic: for a random sample, the *confidence interval* is the range of possible values of a population characteristic, with a specified probability. So, the conventional 95 per cent (or any other) confidence interval refers to the range of values, *computed from the sample itself*, that includes the true population value with 95 per cent probability. Important for researchers who need to design a sample before collecting any data, the expected confidence interval of an estimate can be computed from the sample design parameters – the structure and size of the sample – and (except for small samples with non-normal distributions) does not depend on the distribution of the variable of interest.

Neyman also showed how to compute confidence intervals for cluster samples, where the first stage involves the selection of a random sample of *groups*, and then individuals ('elements') are selected within the groups. The most important application of this idea was to 'area probability' samples where geographical areas, such as municipalities, rural districts or city blocks, are selected first, and then a random sample of households is selected in the areas. The huge advantage of area probability samples is that a list of the entire population is *not* required, only a list of all the geographical areas into which the population is found, taken from a census or government records. Neyman's 1937 lectures at the Graduate School of the US Department of Agriculture (published as Neyman, 1938) led to the design of the Sample Survey of Unemployment, the first modern labour force survey, soon renamed the *Current Population Survey*[8] (Frankel and Stock, 1942; Fienberg and Tanur, 1983: 136).

According to Smith, 'The only major features of current survey design that he [Neyman] failed to introduce were multi-stage sampling and variable probability (p.p.s.) sampling, but these followed logically from his work' (1976: 185). The development of area probability samples required two further steps. First, working at the US Bureau of the Census, Hansen and Hurwitz (1943) showed that the most precise estimates of population characteristics were obtained with 'paired selection' – at each stage of a sample where clusters are selected (for example, communities, census tracts or city blocks), *two* clusters should be selected at random, with probability proportional to their size. Second, in the mid-1960s Leslie Kish and his colleagues developed a method called 'balanced repeated

---

[8]The Sample Survey of Unemployment did not employ a strict probability sample. Urban counties outside the largest cities were stratified into 27 cells, based on the cross-classification of three population size groups, three geographical areas and three economic levels. From each cell, one county was selected, except for the largest cell where two were selected (Frankel and Stock, 1942): 'The selection of counties was at random except that a deliberate effort was made to maximize state coverage' (p. 79). Also, the decision to 'maximize state coverage' by selecting just one county (a cluster) per cell did not allow the computation of errors, because the variation between clusters cannot be estimated.

replication' to estimate the precision of estimates of complex statistics, such as differences between means and regression coefficients, from multi-stage samples (Kish and Frankel, 1970).[9]

The first standard texts on survey sampling appeared in the 1950s (Smith, 1976: 186), but the practical methods for estimating errors in complex samples only came into view in the 1970s (Kish and Frankel, 1974) and they were not incorporated in standard survey analysis software until the mid-2000s.

For studies of political attitudes and market research, the adoption of probability samples was much slower. In 1944, Stock wrote:

> A stratified random sample may be entirely selected in the central office, in which case the interviewer's quota will consist of a specific list of names and addresses; or the stratification alone may be determined by the central office, in which case the interviewer's quota will consist of a set number of interviews with each of the various *types* of people. With this method the individuals representing each type are selected 'at random' by the interviewer. The first method, widely used by government agencies, is more accurate but also more expensive. The second method is relatively inexpensive and accurate enough for most public opinion research. It is used by the vast majority of opinion research agencies today. (p. 142)

The 'various *types* of people' from which interviewers were to select specified numbers of survey respondents 'at random' were identified by their 'colour', age, sex and economic status. Bias could arise from mistakes in classifying people on sight, but also there was 'reluctance of the typical middle-class interviewer to approach people in the lowest economic brackets' (Rugg, 1944a: 149).

Berinsky describes the rationale for quota samples in the public opinion research of the 1930s and 1940s as follows:

> Gallup and Roper did not trust that chance alone would ensure that their sample would accurately represent the sentiment of the nation. Through the selection of particular interviewing locales and the construction of detailed quotas for their employees conducting interviews in those locales, these researchers presumed that they could construct a representative sample. (2006: 502)

While this suggests a distrust of the fundamental principles of probability, the strategy has some merit in light of the cost constraints of the public opinion industry, the small sizes of the sample in each community, and the vagaries of survey fieldwork of the time, particularly the interviewers' difficult-to-control avoidance of poorer dwellings and poorer-looking and less cooperative respondents. Without the guarantee of unbiased estimates that comes with probability samples, to a degree the success of non-probability methods relies on luck, which eventually fails.

---

[9]For a fascinating interview with Leslie Kish, who fought in the Spanish Civil War before becoming a leading statistician, see Frankel and King (1996).

Pre-election polls in US presidential elections first legitimized and then undermined quota sampling. After successfully predicting the winners of the four elections between 1920 and 1932, the *Literary Digest* magazine's 1936 poll mistakenly projected the election of Landon over Roosevelt, based on the 25 per cent return of more than 10 million 'ballots' sent out to its readers and to names taken from car registrations and telephone books. The failure is attributed to the over-representation of the middle and upper class among the magazine's subscribers, car owners and households with telephones, compounded by similar bias in the response rates of people who did receive a ballot. Also, changes in political support over the course of the campaign may not have been captured, because many ballots were returned early in the campaign (Squire, 1988; Cahalan, 1989), a problem that plagues election polling to this day. Surveys using quota samples by George Gallup's *American Institute of Public Opinion* and by Archibald Crossley correctly predicted Roosevelt's victory (Crossley, 1937), apparently vindicating their sampling method.

Then in 1948 polls by Crossley, Gallup and Roper all incorrectly predicted the victory of Dewey over Truman in the US presidential election. An investigative committee appointed by the Science Research Council and headed by statistician Frederick Mosteller did not fault quota sampling in principle, although it concluded that: 'It is impossible to separate the error introduced by the quotas set from that arising in the process of selection by interviewers' (Committee on Analysis of Pre-Election Polls and Forecasts of the Social Science Research Council, 1948: 608). The fault was seen to lie in the design of the particular samples – setting quotas that did not match the voting population – or the misapplication of quotas by interviewers. Nevertheless, this Report effectively ended the use of quota sampling for academic studies and led to its slow demise in market research.

About Survey Questionnaires

Long before modern surveys, censuses and the social surveys included extensive questions about individual demographic characteristics and the economic condition of households, and early twentieth-century 'intelligence' tests employed questionnaires of a kind. Modern surveys covered a much broader range of topics, beginning with attitude studies by psychologists, market research and election polling, then extending to a wide range of research on personal experience and perceptions of life.

The first book on question design and the culmination of this period was Payne's *The Art of Asking Questions*; his

> little book was not written by an expert in semantics, not even by a specialist in question wording. The author is just a general practitioner in research … the reader will be disappointed if he expects to find here a set of definite rules or explicit directions. The art of asking questions is not likely ever to be reduced to easy formulas. (1951: xi)

Modesty did not leave Payne short on concrete suggestions, including 'a concise checklist of 100 considerations' for question design, detailed consideration of question formats and an annotated checklist of 1000 common words.

It was recognized that questions on subjective topics were more ambiguous and prone to bias. Abstract concepts and greater detail could make a question more difficult to answer, increasing measurement error and non-response, and the use of response categories with vague boundaries (such as 'agree' versus 'strongly agree') was unavoidable. Also, the validity of answers to subjective questions could not be established by comparison to records or other concrete measures (Cantril and Fried, 1944: 23; Connelly, 1945).

Cantril and Fried's list of the pitfalls of question design is perfectly contemporary. Questions could be 'too vague to permit precise answers', 'obscure in meaning', 'getting at some stereotype or overtone implicit in the questions rather than at the meanings intended', or 'misunderstood because they involve technical or unfamiliar words'. The alternative answers might be too numerous, too long or not exhaustive, or a question might be 'concerned with only a portion of the population and therefore meaningless to many people' (1944: 3).

Payne's book ends with the advice that 'Controlled experiment is the surest way of making progress in our understanding of question wording' (1951: 237). This involved printing two versions of a questionnaire, with some questions worded differently in each version, called a 'split ballot'. Roper included experiments in his surveys from the mid-1930s and Cantril followed shortly. One of the first systematic treatments of question wording, by Rugg and Cantril (1942), is based largely on experiments, although they caution that 'there is seldom any way of determining which presentation is the more valid ... evaluations of the relative merits of different presentations of an issue must rest on *a priori* considerations.'

From their experiments, Rugg and Cantril concluded that:

- '[O]n issues where people were uncertain, it was possible to produce sizable effects by biasing [the formulation of a question], but where opinion was well crystallized, biasing statements had relatively little effect' (1942: 491). Intentionally biased questions could therefore be used to measure the stability of public opinion, on the basis of comparisons to the responses to neutrally worded questions.
- The number and wording of the responses to a question affect the distribution of responses. Respondents tend to choose only from the responses offered to them explicitly, even if this resulted in bias: 'Where a genuine intermediate step exists ... distortion inevitably results when answers are forced into a dichotomy' (1942: 479).
- The tone of a question could affect the answers. For example, Rugg (1941) found that 62 per cent of Americans would 'not allow' speeches against democracy', but only 46 per cent would 'forbid' them. For other topics, however, a comparison of the same two words could result in a smaller effect of wording, or no difference at all.

For more complex topics, there was extensive debate over the use of 'open' and 'closed' questions. 'Closed' questions had respondents choose among fixed answers, while 'open' questions did not offer any answers and the verbal response was recorded verbatim. An example might be a question about the most important problems facing the country. The issue was whether the greater cost of open questions, in terms of time required to answer, the need for better trained interviewers, and the need to classify the responses after the interview resulted in better answers.

This became a dispute between the two groups conducting surveys in the wartime US government. Naturally, the division led by Elmo Wilson, whose background was in commercial political polling, favoured closed questions, but it is harder to understand why psychologist Rensis Likert strongly supported open questions (Converse, 1984; Hyman, 1991). Indeed, based on his earlier research on scales, Likert's name is given to questions asking for respondents' opinions on statements, using a scale from 'strongly agree' to 'strongly disagree'. For reasons of cost and timeliness, the commercial polling firms and their associated academics, including Lazarsfeld and Cantril, firmly sided with closed questions.[10]

This carried over into support of open questions at the University of Michigan's Institute for Social Research (ISR), which was Likert's post-war academic destination, and for closed questions at the University of Chicago's National Opinion Research Center (NORC), which was tied to the political polling firms. Eventually, the conflict was resolved decisively in favour of closed questions, although Converse observed that: 'The open/closed debate was shaped in good part by institutional needs and capacities, and by ideologies *about* research, remaining largely untouched *by* research' (1984: 279).

Cantril and Fried's view, from 1944, is close to the current consensus:

> The major advantage of the open-ended or free-answer question is obviously its ability to record opinion which is catalogued to the minimum degree by the investigator. When issue has become fairly clear-cut, however, or where common sense and experience have shown that meaningful alternatives can be posed, there is little advantage to an open-ended question from the point of view of its faithfulness in reporting opinion. There is even, on the contrary, a considerable disadvantage in the open-ended question from the point of view of reporting precise trends, keeping costs down, and avoiding bias in the coding of answers for statistical treatment. (p. 10)

Perhaps this makes a virtue of necessity, because the development of national public opinion polls in the 1930s was predicated on the ability to sell timely reports

---

[10]Lazarsfeld (1944) attempted to mediate this dispute by proposing a division of labour for major survey projects. First, an open survey would be used to develop closed questions – so that the answers offered in the closed questions included the full range of responses. Those questions would then form the basis of a larger survey using closed questions. Third, a more qualitative survey using open questions would be used to confirm the interpretation of results from the larger survey. As a general practice, this lengthy and complex strategy was simply impractical.

of the findings to major newspapers and magazines, which was much easier using closed questions.

Researchers of the time understood the potentially multi-dimensional character of attitudes and they distinguished between the answers to individual survey items and more fundamental traits underlying them. In a survey conducted in the USA in 1941 for example, Harding (1944b) used about 30 questions on 16 separate topics to measure civilian morale, and he employed factor analysis (an arduous manual calculation in the time before computers) to identify three underlying dimensions of morale.

About Data Collection

The method of data collection of the new survey research was face-to-face interviewing, and the main concern was the effect of interviewers on survey response. By the mid-1940s there were studies of:

- non-response bias due to respondent refusals – although it was not perceived as a substantial threat, at this time when response rates approached 90 per cent (Harding, 1944a);
- the effect of interviewer training on the quality of survey response – more training did not seem to have much effect on the quality of the data, perhaps because most interviewers were well educated (Rugg, 1944b);
- the effect on survey response of the presence of an interviewer – it was found that differences could arise between questions answered on a confidential paper 'ballot' and the answers given to interviewers directly (Turnbull, 1944);
- whether the interviewer's own opinions led to bias in responses – evidence of bias was found by comparing respondents' and interviewers' answers to the same questions (Cantril, 1944: 107ff.); and
- the impact of the interviewer's social class and race – for lower income respondents, Katz (1942) found that working-class interviewers found higher levels of support for labour, while middle-class interviewers found more conservative views; also the combination of interviewer's and respondent's race affected survey responses – to questions about the living conditions of African-Americans, black and white respondents expressed different views to black and white interviewers, with a much larger racial gap in a survey conducted in Memphis than in New York (Hyman, 1991: 39).

Conducting surveys required organizations able to conduct face-to-face interviews on a national scale. Although censuses were just huge face-to-face surveys, their enormity, infrequency and restricted content were the opposite of the agility needed to conduct timely surveys on a variety of topics. Government agencies did develop the capacity to conduct surveys, initially labour force surveys to measure unemployment, but market research and advertising agencies were the first to develop modern survey infrastructure and their methodology was ripe for franchising. George Gallup, who founded the American Institute for Public Opinion in 1935, established the British Institute of Public Opinion in 1937 and French, Australian and Canadian affiliates in 1937, 1938 and 1942, respectively.

The two leading American academic survey centres also date from this period. The National Opinion Research Center was established at the University of Denver in 1941 by a close associate of Gallup, before moving to the University of Chicago in 1947, and Rensis Likert left the US government to establish the Institute for Social Research at the University of Michigan in 1946 (Converse, 1987: 305). By the early 1950s, there were dozens of Gallup affiliates. Within each country, at a time when communication was largely by mail, the economies of scale favoured the emergence of large oligopolistic survey organizations.

Conclusion

Modern survey research emerged between 1935 and 1940, with sample designs capable of representing almost any population, questionnaires covering a wide range of objective and subjective topics, and the development of procedures and establishment of organizations for large-scale face-to-face surveys. Each element was necessary, but it was the combination of sampling, questionnaire design and data collection that constituted the invention of survey research.

2

Writing Survey Questions

The 1950s and 1960s saw little advance over the early ideas about survey question design, which were based on the commonsense ideas exemplified by Payne's 1951 volume and on a small body of 'split ballot' experiments that compared pairs of questions. Only in the 1970s did researchers begin to address the three fundamental limitations of the earlier work: a rather fragmentary, and by the time quite dated, body of experimental research on alternative question formats; the lack of a statistical framework both to quantify the effects of question formats on the answers to survey questions and to integrate the findings of disparate studies of individual characteristics of question formats; and the absence of a theory of survey response.

The need for further empirical research on question formats was addressed by the research programme of Howard Schuman and Stanley Presser. In a series of journal articles, revised and much expanded in their 1981 volume *Questions and Answers in Attitude Surveys: Experiments on Question Form, Wording and Content*, Schuman and Presser report on experiments incorporated in more than 30 surveys that examined the classical design questions, including the distinction between open and closed questions, the effect of 'no opinion' and middle response options, and the value of offering balanced alternatives. Many of these findings are incorporated in Converse and Presser's *Survey Questions: Handcrafting the Standardized Questionnaire* (1986).

New experiments were facilitated by the development of computer-assisted telephone interviewing, or CATI, surveys. Instead of printing two versions of a questionnaire with the questions to be compared, the alternatives were inserted by programming, which allowed more numerous and complex experiments. Also, because there were not just two fixed questionnaires, each experimental comparison was independent of all the others. This robust methodological tradition continues to this day. Of the 78 articles on question design in *Public Opinion Quarterly* between 2000 and 2010 reviewed by Schaeffer and Dykema (2011), about three-quarters employed experiments, not including comparisons of the same questions used in different surveys, which are similar in spirit.

Second, there was a need to quantify and bring order to the disparate findings on question design. Even when the better alternative was clear from an experiment, the conclusion was based on common sense and not the statistical characteristics of the alternative questions. For example, a format that resulted in fewer 'don't know' answers might be superior, but only if respondents with no opinion are not just being encouraged to guess. Also, the experiments compared *individual* characteristics of a question and there was no unified framework to assess the relative impact of different elements of a question on the quality of response.

Andrews (1984) addressed these problems by analysing the results of many question experiments simultaneously. There were two steps. First, he used *structural equation models* (SEMs) to analyse 'multi-trait, multi-method' (MTMM) correlation matrices developed by Campbell and Fiske (1959) to assess convergent and discriminant validity. Those matrices give the correlations between a set of survey questions asking about three or more topics (the 'traits') each with questions in at least three different formats (the 'methods'). So there were correlations between at least nine (3 × 3) survey questions. The SEMs made it possible to divide the total variation *in each question* into three components: the effect of the desired trait, called the 'true' or 'valid' variance or 'validity'; the *method effect*, due to the format of the question; and residual error.

In the second step, Andrews conducted a meta-analysis to separate the effects of the various attributes of a survey item on its statistical characteristics. Treating all the survey question included in the MTMM matrices as observations, he regressed the estimated validity of each question, obtained from the SEM analysis, on variables describing the attributes of the question, such as the question topic, the question format, the number of response categories and whether a 'no opinion' response was offered. The regression was repeated for the two other components of the survey response, the method effect and the residual error. The regression coefficients indicate which attributes of a question result in better measurement, indicated by higher validity, a smaller method effect and a smaller residual error. This approach and the findings are considered in detail below.

In the late 1970s, researchers conducting and analysing large US government surveys developed a more fundamental critique of the craft tradition of question design. Initially they were concerned with the quality of subjective measures, including attitudes, self-identification as a member of a group, and perceptions of everyday life. These gained new importance from the recognition of the limitations of the conventional measures of employment and income that formed the basis of national statistical systems and of purely economic indicators of social progress.[1] The establishment of the *Panel on Survey Measurement of Subjective Phenomena* in 1980 by the US Committee on National Statistics was prompted by

---

[1]These challenges gave rise to the new social indicators movement, beginning in the mid-1960s (Sirgy et al., 2006). The journal *Social Indicators Research* was founded by Alex Michalos in 1974, and Campbell, Converse and Rodgers' definitive *The Quality of American Life* was published in 1976.

the discovery of several instances in which seemingly equivalent survey measurements made at approximately the same time produced surprisingly different
results ... [which] raised questions initially about the reliability, and ultimately
about the meaningfulness, of commonly used survey data. (Turner and Martin,
1984: xii)

There was also a new appreciation of the limitations of institutional statistics and
a realization that surveys could provide alternative measures. For example, crime
victimization was found to be radically underestimated by police statistics, and
health was imperfectly measured by medical records. The new area of population
health combined subjective evaluations of a person's health, survey measures of
exercise, diet and other aspects of daily life, and cultural and socio-economic conditions, with traditional indicators of illness and the need for and use of medical
services. This created new interest in what became known as 'autobiographical
memory', the term given later to the recollection of personal experience, including everyday activities such as shopping and physical activity, sporadic events
such as illnesses and criminal victimization, and lifecourse events, such as changes
in household composition, employment and place of residence. Also, it was recognized that longitudinal surveys were needed to analyse sequences of events, in
order to understand the causal pathways between and among life experiences and
the different aspects of subjective well-being.

These concerns culminated in an initiative to develop a general theory of how
respondents answered survey questions and a parallel programme of empirical
research. Called *Cognitive Aspects of Survey Methods* or the CASM movement, this
rapidly became and continues as *the* dominant perspective on survey response.
Jobe and Mingay describe its beginnings:

Scientific collaboration between cognitive scientists and survey researchers was
initiated during the 7-year period from 1978 to 1984, when university scholars
and government scientists in both fields came together ... Government agencies in three industrialized countries [the UK, the USA and Germany] took
a lead role in promoting most of these scholarly conferences and helped to
support much of the subsequent scientific research. They continue to exert a
leading role, largely because of the potential long-term improvements that this
research appears to promise to the overall quality of data produced by national
statistical agencies. (1991: 176)

The founding 1984 CASM seminar was an initiative of statisticians Stephen
Fienberg and Myron Straf of the *US Committee on National Statistics*, whose man-
date is the evaluation and improvement of US government data collection (Jabine
et al., 1984: 149ff.).[2] The idea was to apply the insights of cognitive psychology to
survey research. Although a number of central figures in the foundation of survey

---

[2]In the same year, ZUMA, a government methodology centre in West Germany, held a conference on social information processing and survey methodology (Jobe and Mingay, 1991: 177),
reported in Hippler et al. (1987).

research were trained in psychology, their contribution had more to do with the basic concept of attitudes and ideas of psychological measurement brought from paper and pencil surveys, and they worked with and were not so different from sociologists such as Lazarsfeld and Stouffer. At the time there was no field of cognitive psychology, whose beginning is commonly dated to the 1967 publication of Ulric Neisser's book by that name.

The CASM movement made the development of survey questions into a problem in cognitive psychology. The CASM model specified the sequence of mental processes involved in answering a survey question, including comprehension, retrieval from memory and generating an answer. Judged by the volume of research on survey design that resulted, the CASM movement has been astonishingly successful, and current thinking about questionnaire design is almost completely dominated by those ideas (see Schwarz, 2007a). The defining text of this era in survey research is Roger Tourangeau, Lance J. Rips and Kenneth Rasinski's *The Psychology of Survey Response*, published in 2000. Although it has some brief but useful and wise advice, unlike the earlier volumes by Payne and by Converse and Presser, this is more an academic study than a guide to questionnaire design; and Sudman et al.'s (1996) *Thinking About Answers: The Application of Cognitive Processes to Survey Methodology* is similar. The last section of this chapter describes and provides an assessment of the contributions of the CASM movement to question design. Strategies for survey pretesting motivated by CASM are described in detail in Chapter 6 and the effects of the mode of data collection in Chapter 7.

──── Experiments on Question Form ────────────────────────────────

Open and Closed Questions

In her 1984 article 'Strong arguments and weak evidence: the open/closed questioning controversy of the 1940s', Converse shows that the widespread adoption of surveys based on closed questions was not based on empirical research. Indeed, there is still not much research on this topic and Schuman and Presser's (1981: 79ff.) experiments in surveys conducted between 1976 and 1978 remain the definitive statement. They compared open and closed versions of three questions concerning 'the most important problem facing this country at present', what the respondent would 'most prefer in a job', and 'the most important thing for children to learn to prepare them for life'.

These three questions are difficult because the respondent must select one answer from a web of interconnected ideas, and so creating equivalent closed questions required some arbitrary choices. For the first question, respondents were asked to choose among eight problems facing the country: food *and* energy shortages, crime *and* violence, inflation, unemployment, decreased trust in government, busing (of children to schools outside their neighbourhoods in order to achieve racial integration), the breakdown of morals *and* religion, and racial problems. Even with so many alternatives, some of the answers are quite ambiguous and three of the eight are undesirable 'double-barrelled' responses that combine two answers in one. Not everyone would agree that the 'breakdown' in 'religious observance and influence' and 'declining morals' are related; nor would they define 'racial problems' in the same way. Fixing these problems, however, requires a longer and longer question that would be still more difficult to answer.

Comparing the open and closed questions on the same topic, Schuman and Presser found that:

- The response distributions are quite different. In the open and closed questions similar proportions of respondents choose the simple, less emotional responses, such as 'inflation' or 'unemployment' as national problems or 'good pay' as the most desirable characteristic of a job. 'Affective' responses were much more likely to be selected, when included among the responses in the closed question. 'Crime and violence' was reported as the most important national problem by 35 per cent of respondents when the answer was read to them, compared to 16 per cent who gave that answer to the open question (1981: 83).[3] In another experiment, 59 per cent of respondents chose 'work that gives a feeling of accomplishment' as the most important attribute in a job when it was one of five options read, compared to about 15 per cent who gave this answer to the equivalent open question (1981: 89, 95). No exact principle, however, seems to govern the differences between forms.
- Changing the alternatives presented in a closed question in order to match the most frequently chosen *open* responses still does not result in equivalent open and closed questions. While a second version of the closed question about work values reduced support for 'work that gives a feeling of accomplishment' from 59 to 31 per cent, this was still twice the 15 per cent who gave that answer to the open question.
- Non-response was around twice as high for the open questions; they elicited significant numbers of tautological or ambiguous answers; and a few respondents gave multiple answers to the open question and refused to choose between them.
- When a closed question is used, allowing or even encouraging the respondents to give an answer *other than those explicitly listed* did not remove the discrepancy between open and closed questions – respondents are far more likely to choose one of the answers presented, rather than 'thinking outside the box'.
- The correlation between the responses to the open and closed questions on the same topic and other survey variables was not necessarily the same.

For questions with a wide range of possible responses, there are no equivalent open and closed questions. Rather than serving as bins into which respondents put their answers, the responses offered in a closed question are integral to its meaning. The responses presented discourage inappropriate answers, but to a degree they artificially confine the range of responses and bring to mind considerations – effectively arguments in favour of a particular response – that are not there with the open question. Open questions suffer the opposite problem.

---

[3] In the hands of a motivated politician, the appropriately framed closed question could be used to provide evidence of public alarm over an issue.

Without the suggested answers, some respondents have difficulty deciding what constitutes an appropriate answer and they are more likely not to answer at all to give ambiguous or unintelligible answers.

For research on a complex topic, where inadvertent framing of the issue may result in bias, there is a strong argument for using open questions in a pretest or pilot survey to design closed questions for a larger survey that follows. If this is not feasible, for topics where a very wide range of responses is possible it makes sense to put one or more open questions *before* the closed questions, so they are not subject to any inadvertent influence on the choice of response categories. This is problematic in printed self-administered questionnaires, however, because the respondent is able to look ahead at a later closed question. In internet surveys, the open and closed questions should be on separate screens.

Two classes of open questions were not considered in this discussion. First, questions asking for a numerical answer, such as how often, when, or with what frequency an event occurred, are considered below in the section on the results of SEM models. Second, for questions about experiences, such as remembering the names of magazines a person has read or the kinds of exercise they have done, there is strong evidence that providing respondents with a checklist yields larger and more accurate counts than an open question, because people forget (Schaeffer and Presser, 2003).

A cognitive approach would stress the sheer difficulty of *both the open and closed versions* of Schuman and Presser's three questions about problems facing the country, job attributes and children's needs. Aside from the difficulty of imagining the range of alternatives for the open questions, with either format the respondents will have difficulty deciding between nearly equally answers. There are also contingencies that cannot be captured by a single choice. For example, someone might say that the best job is a 'meaningful' one, but only if the pay is adequate and the job is safe. Regardless of format, the answers to difficult questions are more likely to be affected by the question form. For questions with a wide range of reasonable answers, a more time-consuming but less risky strategy is to ask respondents to *rate* a number of attributes and then, if a ranking is absolutely required, ask the respondents to choose only among the top-ranked items.

Tone and Balance

In a 1976 replication of Rugg's experiment, Schuman and Presser (1981: 277) found that 48 per cent of Americans would 'forbid' 'public speeches against democracy' and 79 per cent would 'not allow' them – an astonishing 31 per cent difference that is even larger than Rugg's 1941 figures of 54 and 75 per cent.[4] While the direction of the difference is always the same, exactly what is being forbidden or not allowed dramatically affects the difference. Schuman and Presser find a 17 per cent

---

[4]Schuman and Presser report figures from three separate surveys in fall 1974 and in February and spring 1976, which vary a bit.

gap if the question is about 'public speeches in favour of communism', but just a 5 per cent gap for 'showing of X-rated movies' and 4 per cent for 'cigarette advertising on television'.

The size of the forbid/not-allow difference is strongly and negatively related to a respondent's education. For 'speeches against democracy', the difference was 30 per cent for respondents with up to 12 years of education, 17 per cent for 13–15 years of education, and just 7 per cent for respondents with 16 years of education or more. The worrying implication is that the *strength* of the relationship between education and support for this measure of free speech depends on the wording of the question.

The size of the forbid/not-allow difference depends on the topic because the different words are interpreted in terms of the implied action. Forbidding speeches conjures images of police intervention, while 'not allowing' them has the flavour of polite observance of some public consensus. Whichever euphemism is used, education or other characteristics of respondents are likely to affect the interpretation. For cigarette advertisements, on the other hand, the distinction is of no consequence. Whether they are forbidden or not allowed, preventing the advertising of cigarettes merely involves government regulation. This points to the general problem that differences in political sophistication, related but not reducible to education, potentially affect the relationship between education and attitude measures, the subject of the 1950s' debate over the F (for fascism) scale (Brown, 1965: 477ff.).

The variety of things that can be forbidden or allowed has spawned a minor research industry and Holleman (1999) was able to conduct a meta-analysis of no less than 52 such experiments. On average, respondents were 14 per cent more likely to not allow than to forbid, although the standard deviation of the difference, 10 per cent, is quite large.[5] Four different factors increased the size of the forbid/not allow difference, each by about 5 per cent: the complexity of the issue; the combination of abstractness and complexity of the issue (but not abstractness on its own); the number of sentences in the question; and whether the topic involves morality. This is consistent with the idea that more difficult questions lead the respondent to idiosyncratically interpret ambiguous terms as clues about its meaning.

One might think that respondents who are less concerned about an issue would be more influenced by the tone of a question. But, after accounting for education, Schuman and Presser find that the magnitude of the forbid/not allow difference is *un*related to attitude strength. More general evidence comes from analysis of a number of US surveys by Krosnick and Schuman (1988) who find that the intensity of an attitude, the topic's importance to the respondent, and the respondent's certainty of his or her attitude generally *have no effect* on the degree to which

---

[5]This overestimates the true standard deviation, however, because it also incorporates sampling variation, and some of the experiments included in the meta-analysis have quite small samples.

changes in the form of a question affect the answer.[6] The only exception is that respondents with less intense attitudes and for whom a topic is less important are more likely to select a middle answer.

While using emotionally charged words such as 'forbid' in survey questions is not a good practice, this research also points to the consequences of ambiguity and differences in the sophistication of respondents. If the idea is that the police will arrest anyone who makes a 'public speech against democracy' or that it should be 'against the law' to make such a speech, then the question should say so. Otherwise, variation in respondents' interpretation of the question – related to their education, literacy and familiarity with the issue – undermines the validity of their responses, and this cannot be detected or fixed in subsequent data analysis. Moreover, experimental comparisons between two or more formulations of an inherently ambiguous question cannot tell us which version is better. While the the comparisons between questions using the terms 'forbid' and 'not allow' tell us how respondents answer, *neither* wording is good practice.

The lessons of the forbid/not allow debate extend beyond individual words and phrases to the wording of entire questions. Schuman and Presser take this up in the context of question 'balance', though it is now more common to refer to the broader idea of 'framing', adopted from psychology. Framing effects are also contingent and potentially unexpected. For example, Schuman and Presser (1981: 186) find very small differences in the answers to questions asking about 'abortion' and 'ending the life of an unborn child', and support for a law requiring a permit to buy a gun falls by just 6 per cent if (in the USA!) the question mentions that 'such a law would interfere too much with the right of citizens to own guns'. Support for a law requiring people to lower the heat in their homes in the event of a fuel shortage, however, dropped by 13 per cent in two surveys and by 4 per cent in a third if the question mentioned the alternative that 'this should be left to individual families' (p. 193). A similarly large effect of wording is found for questions about whether workers newly hired in a unionized workplace (or 'union shop') should be required to join the union. Finally, what Schuman and Presser call 'formal balance' in a question – asking if the respondent agrees with some statement *'or not'* – has no impact on responses.

Consider a more recent example of framing from Sniderman and Theriault, who compared the questions:

> Are you in favour of or opposed to a big increase in government spending to increase the opportunities for poor people *so they can have a better chance of getting ahead in life?*

---

[6]Perhaps the effect of question wording on interested and informed respondents involves a more accurate understanding of the implied meanings of subtle differences in the formulation of a question, thus creating differences not intended by the question designer. While less interested and informed respondents cannot make those distinctions, they are influenced by, again unintended, differences in the tone of alternative wordings. The effects could cancel out.

Are you in favour of or opposed to a big increase in government spending to increase the opportunities for poor people *even if it means higher taxes*? (2004: 143)

Although they describe exactly the same policy, the two statements had 87 and 52 per cent support respectively. Neither question is balanced, as the first invokes a redundant cliché and the second emphasizes the potential cost of the measure. A balanced formulation of the question would just stop after 'poor people', leaving respondents to make what they wish of the idea's desirability, cost and effectiveness. A single question that combined the last phrases of both questions would appear to be unbiased and might have the advantage of producing more thoughtful answers than a short question with no argument on either side. But because there are often a variety of arguments on each side of an issue, whether any two particular arguments are balanced and do not result in bias cannot be known without prior empirical research.

Because the effects of question wording observed in these experiments are so unpredictable and vary so much in magnitude, there is no general theory of the effect of words and arguments on survey response. Indeed, the substantive interpretation of the differences is more interesting than the few methodological generalizations that have emerged. The findings also raise the question of what constitutes an attitude and what surveys are doing when they measure attitudes, which are considered in the last section of this chapter.

Response Categories

The type and number of response categories to closed questions has been the subject of research since the 1920s when psychologists began to measure attitudes (Krosnick and Presser, 2010). Response scales can differ in a variety of ways, including the number of categories, whether the categories are numerical or verbal or a mixture of the two, and whether 'middle' and 'no opinion' categories are offered. Of course, often the choice of response categories follows from the format of the question. For example, a verbal scale with four of five categories ranging from 'strongly disagree' to 'strongly agree' is used only to rate statements, while 'sentence completion' items ask respondents to choose from among verbal answers closely tailored to the topic, rather than agreeing or disagreeing with anything. Comparison of these alternative question formats, which require statistical modelling, are considered in the next section on SEMs.

One simple question about response scales involves assessments, for example a person's rating or their neighbourhood or the performance of government, where it is assumed that the underlying evaluations are smoothly distributed. A question with more categories allows the respondent to answer more exactly, but not beyond the precision of his or her underlying judgement. In order to measure the intensity of feeling about an issue, Katz (1944: 60) asked: 'How strongly do you feel on this question?' and provided respondents with an illustration of a 100-point 'thermometer' – with zero labelled 'don't care', 50 labelled 'fairly strongly' and 100 labelled 'very strongly'. A version of this 'feeling thermometer' is still used in election surveys to gauge respondents' views of candidates. With this scale, most answers are the round numbers 0, 10, 20, up to 100 and a few numbers in between, such as 25, 75 and 95. Psychometric studies show that there is little improvement in precision beyond nine categories (Lozano et al., 2008). It is necessary to label the top and bottom of a numerical scale and good practice to attach a verbal label to the midpoint. Typically four or five categories give adequate measurement, but a longer scale avoids risk if the underlying distribution is highly skewed and most respondents could choose just one or two categories of a shorter scale. For topics about which respondents have highly differentiated views a longer scale captures the greater precision in their minds.

A second consideration is whether to use mainly numerical scales, say a seven- or nine-point scale labelled at each end and perhaps in the middle, or a fully labelled scale with an adjective for each category. In a study of job satisfaction Conti and Pudney (2011) showed that the response distributions of labelled and unlabelled scales can differ markedly. The mainly numerical scale has better psychometric properties because the respondents think of the categories as dividing the continuum uniformly, whereas verbal categories such as 'very good' and 'excellent' induce respondents to make absolute judgements, based on their interpretation of those adjectives. The risk is that a large proportion of respondents will choose just one or two of the verbal categories. In that job satisfaction study more than 40 per cent of respondents were 'mostly satisfied' (p. 1089)[7] and it is not possible to differentiate within that 40 per cent, even though they cannot possibly be equally satisfied. Also undesirable from a statistical perspective, the fully labelled scale yielded a highly skewed response distribution. Responses to the mainly numerical scale were also skewed, but not nearly as much. Because job satisfaction is something that respondents can estimate in sharp detail, using a scale with more points, say 9 or 11, is a good idea.

Fully labelled scales provide more transparent survey results. It is easier and more meaningful to report the percentages of, say, 'very good' or 'excellent' responses than to describe the distribution of ratings on an unlabelled scale. Even if the individual items are used only as constituents of an additive scale or when analysis is focused on models and not description, the results are more concrete and more easily explained with a fully labelled scale. This is balanced by the usually superior statistical properties of numeral scales, a point considered in the next section.

Naturally, more people choose a middle answer to a question when it is offered explicitly. Asked in a series of telephone surveys whether US 'penalties for using

---

[7]Conti and Pudney (2011) show that the difference between the partly and fully labelled questions is a function of gender and racialization. They observed differences between interviews and self-administered questionnaires, and the presence of other persons during interview also affected responses. The interaction between gender and measured job satisfaction affected the gender differences in the predictors of job satisfaction, and this also depended on the mode of data collection and the question form.

marijuana' should be more or less strict, in various surveys only 6–9 per cent of respondents *volunteered* that penalties should stay the same, and about 4 per cent had no opinion; offered the explicit option that marijuana policies could stay about the same, however, support for that middle position rose to about 25 per cent, with about 3 per cent no opinion (Schuman and Presser, 1981: 165). Thus respondents are reluctant to give an answer that is not offered, even when it is a logical and distinct option. Almost all respondents who take a middle position do so only when it is offered explicitly, otherwise they choose a substantive answer, rather than indicating that they have no opinion.

When the answers to a question are inherently numerical, nothing is gained by grouping the responses. Schwarz et al. (1985) have a lovely and often-cited demonstration that the response *categories* can affect the response distribution to a remarkable extent. German respondents were asked, 'How many hours they watched TV daily'. One version of the question had six categories with 30-minute intervals (under ½ hour, ½ to 1 hour, etc.) and a highest category of 'more than 2½ hours'; the second version of the question also had six 30-minute intervals, but ranging from 'up to 2½ hours' to 'more than 4½ hours'. With the first version, 16 per cent of the population said they watched more than 2½ hours of television per night; with the second version the figure was 37.5 per cent! Rather than a passive, convenient way to record their answers, respondents used the categories as information about the range of outcomes in the population, which affected their answers.

A different but equally serious problem arises when the survey answers employ what are known as 'vague quantifiers', words such as 'several', 'a few', 'sometimes', 'often' and 'constantly'. Not only are their answers affected by respondents' varied definition of these categories, but also they are affected by respondents' ideas of appropriate or average answers (Bradburn and Miles, 1979). Also, the meanings attached to the vague quantifiers are related to respondents' age and education, creating artefacts when those groups are compared (Schaeffer, 1991). Again, it is better to ask for a numerical answer.

'No Opinion' Responses?

Perhaps no aspect of question design has had more attention than whether to include an explicit 'no opinion' answer (or 'don't know', which is more pejorative). By an unpredictable but often substantial degree, the proportion of 'no opinion' responses is higher when a 'no opinion' response is mentioned explicitly and the difference is even greater when the respondent is first asked separately if he or she has an opinion on the topic. On a question about a popular topic in public policy it would not be unusual to have 15–20 per cent non-response if 'no opinion' is an explicit answer, compared to 5–7 per cent if it is not.

Presumably, respondents who give an opinion when they are offered a 'no opinion' response are unaffected by the format. At issue is what happens to the 'reluctant' respondents, who give a substantive answer if the question implies that they can and should answer, but answer 'no opinion' if that response is legitimized.

One possibility is that they actually have no opinion and, pressed to answer, merely choose randomly. But abundant evidence, summarized by Krosnick et al. (2002), indicates that this is not true. If the reluctant respondents had no opinion at all, *excluding* their random responses should increase the correlations between that question and other survey measures, but Schuman and Presser (1981) find this does not happen. More sophisticated analysis using SEMs by McClendon and Alwin (1993) reveals that the reliability of questions is *not* improved by removing the reluctant non-respondents. Also, it is frequently observed that *including* the reluctant respondents has little effect on the relative frequency of substantive answers.

While reluctant respondents do not answer randomly, on average they are different from respondents who give a substantive response, even when a 'no opinion' answer is offered. Reluctant respondents are typically more ambivalent, less informed about the topic, and have less education. Also, offering a 'no opinion' response is not completely effective in discouraging substantive answers from respondents with very weak or non-existent opinions. An extensive review of research leads Krosnick and Presser to conclude that 'no opinion' responses 'often do not result from genuine lack of opinion, but rather from ambivalence, question ambiguity, satisficing, intimidation and self-protection' (2010: 284).

The implication is that questions generally should *not* include an explicit 'no opinion' option, but that a follow-up question asking about the strength of a person's attitude is useful, though costly in questionnaire time. This depends on the question topic, however. If there is room for only one question, an explicit 'no opinion' response should not be offered for questions when a strong majority, say at least 80 per cent, of respondents can be expected to answer. If there is reason to think that more than 20 per cent of respondents cannot answer, however, there is a substantial risk that the opinions of a minority will be represented as 'public opinion', so an explicit 'no opinion' response should be used.

In part the debate over 'no opinion' response is actually about how much the answer to just one question can tell us. For topics where there is wide variation in respondents' knowledge and interest, no single question can adequately measure both the engagement of respondents and their substantive positions,[8] and a separate question about engagement in the topic is needed to supplement one or more questions about respondents' positions. A nicer, but more complicated solution is to use an experiment to measure the proportion of reluctant respondents and how they answer when a 'no opinion' response is not offered.

Question Order

There are three ways in which the order of questions in a survey may affect responses. 'Semantic' order effects involve the influence of the specific content of

---

[8]For discussions of the dimensionality of attitudes see Krosnick and Abelson (1992) and Alwin (1992).

a question and the respondent's answer on his or her answers to subsequent questions. 'Serial' order effects involve broader trends as a survey proceeds, for example respondents may become more comfortable or competent after answering a few questions, and later on fatigue and declining motivation may lower the quality of their responses. These effects are considered below, based on results of SEMs.

A third, intermediary category involves the effect of *general* content of the survey topic on later answers. The common example is that respondents say they are more interested in a topic after they have answered a series of questions about it. Questions about interest in and information about a topic should therefore appear *before* substantive questions about their attitudes. Cowan et al. (1978) found that respondents are more likely to recall incidents of criminal victimization if those questions followed a series of more general questions about crime. Thus the 'priming' effect of non-factual questions about a topic can increase the accessibility of biographical memories.

There is very little research on whether the serial position of items – just their location in the sequence of questions in a survey – can result in directional effects. Regarding this question, it is common to cite just one analysis of surveys conducted in one community (Detroit) around 1970, also by Schuman and Presser (1981). For only 8 of the 113 items that appeared in different positions in two different surveys was there a significant difference in the response distributions. Three of the differences resulted from semantic effects that involved the specific changes in question order, leaving just five significant changes, which the authors concluded 'seem quite inexplicable and are probably due to sampling error' (p. 26). While it would still be nice to have some more recent research, there is no reason to believe the placement of questions within a survey affects the answers, except when there are explicit connections between their content.

Schuman and Presser (1981: 27) distinguish two types of semantic order effects: *part–part effects*, which affect questions *at the same level of generality*; and *part–whole effects*, which affect the answer to a general question that follows one or more specific questions. An example of a part–part effect comes from a 1948 US survey that asked:

> Do you think that the United States should let Communist newspaper reporters from other countries come in here and send back to their papers the news as they see it?

> Do you think a Communist country like Russia should let American newspaper reports come in and send back to America the news as they see it? (Hyman and Sheatsley, 1950: 29)

Thirty-seven per cent of respondents answered 'yes' to the question about Communist reporters if it was first, compared to 73 per cent if it was second; 65 per cent said 'yes' to the question about American reporters if it was first, versus 90 per cent if it was second. There is nothing mysterious about this tendency for respondents to shift their answers so they are more consistent.

What is more interesting is that the order effect implies that respondents did not answer the questions by retrieving a fixed attitude from memory. Nor does it make sense to think that some respondents have contradictory attitudes on the same topic, and that the one elicited depends on the order of the questions. These order effects imply that respondents actively consider each question in the few seconds it takes to answer.

Whether respondents invoke a rationale of consistency when they answer two or more related questions, giving rise to a part–part order effect, is not a theoretical issue but depends on whether or not respondents see the questions as connected. So Schuman and Presser (1981: 31) found no order effects for a pair of questions about public distrust of doctors and of lawyers or for a pair of questions about the fitness of women and of Jews to be US president. One might think that the first pair of questions would invoke ideas about professions and the second one ideas about equity, but this was not so in the minds of respondents.

The classic example of a part–whole effect, again from Schuman and Presser, involves two questions about abortion. The first question refers to the legal right to abortion if a woman is 'married and does not want any more children' – this is the 'whole' because it describes the more general circumstance; the second question asks about access to abortion 'in the case of a defect in the unborn child' – this is the 'part' because it describes a specific circumstance. Asking the general question first has no effect on responses to the specific question, but asking the specific question first lowers support for legal abortion measured by the more general question by 12 per cent. The logic is that when the general question is second, some respondents interpret it as referring to abortion in what is known to be a healthy pregnancy. In other words, if the 'part' is mentioned in an earlier question, that instance is *excluded* from consideration of the whole.

This effect is often interpreted in terms of the four principles of conversation set out by Grice (1975). His 'maxim of quantity' states that contributions to a conversation should not be redundant. So, having given his or her opinion about abortion in the case of a birth defect, the respondent takes the subsequent question to exclude this circumstance. This is an appealing explanation, but cannot be distinguished from the idea that mentioning a birth defect suggests that this should be a consideration in deciding about access to abortion. Consistent with this alternative explanation, Schuman and Presser (1981: 40) find the part–whole effect is much larger for respondents who describe this as 'a difficult issue' than those who are 'very certain' of their position.

A part–whole effect is also found with two questions that ask about a person's satisfaction with 'life as a whole' and satisfaction with their marriage. When the general question is second it may be construed as a request to rate aspects of a person's life *excluding* marriage, on the grounds, *pace* Grice, that the information about marriage would be redundant. This is what Schwarz et al. (1991) find.

Now consider putting the question about 'life as a whole' after a *series of questions* covering a number of domains of life, such as a person's job, financial situation, health and family relationships. Having rated all of these favourably, it makes no sense to say that your 'life as a whole' is miserable. In fact the ratings in individual domains more accurately predict overall life satisfaction – a correlational effect – when the general question *follows* the individual ones (McClendon and O'Brien, 1988; Schwarz et al., 1991; Mason et al., 1994). Thus, when many 'parts' are mentioned before a general question, rather than excluding them from consideration of the whole, the respondent infers that the whole consists of those parts.

The implications of these experiments are straightforward. When there is a possibility of a part–whole order effect, ask the general question first.[9] For potential part–part effects, however, there is no optimal order and comparing questions asked in a different order can be revealing. If possible, the order of the questions should be randomized; if this cannot be done, an alternative is to introduce all the different 'parts' *before* asking any of the questions. The latter option will have the 'correlational effect' of enhancing the consistency between the questions, as might occur if the respondent was to hear a debate on the issue before answering.

The magnitude of semantic order effects is affected by the survey mode. Order effects are more likely to appear for questions asked by interviewers because respondents do not know which questions are coming up and cannot change their previous answers. Order effects will diminish when respondents can see the related questions on the same printed page or screen before answering.

The Order of Responses *Within* Questions

A natural concern is that the order of *responses* to a question could affect responses. Unlike *question* order effects, these are likely to arise from the short-term cognitive processes involved in answering individual questions, rather than the question content. The evidence is that surveys with interviewers tend to result in *recency* bias – favouring the *last* response – and, less consistently, self-administered surveys result in *primacy* bias – favouring the *first* response (Krosnick and Alwin, 1987; Bishop and Smith, 2001; Krosnick and Presser, 2010: 278ff.).

Analysing over 500 experiments on questions with two responses in Gallup telephone surveys, Holbrook et al. (2007) found that 19.2 per cent of the items exhibited statistically significant recency effects, whereas a negligible 1.8 per cent had significant primacy effects. Averaging all the experiments, a particular response was chosen with 2 per cent greater probability if it came second. If the true value is the mean of the two response orders, the average bias is just 1 per cent. Response order effects were more common for more difficult questions, when the responses

---

[9]In principle, there is the possibility of a 'halo' effect, whereby the following domain ratings are positively affected by the initial general rating. The idea is that a respondent who first rates his or her 'life in general' very highly will tend to overestimate the quality of life in its constituent domains. An alternative to putting the general question first is to randomly assign it a first or last position. Placing the same general question before and after the domain ratings will artificially raise consistency between the before and after ratings, because respondents will tend to remember and want to repeat their initial rating.

were longer and for respondents with less education – consistent with the general principle that method effects are larger for questions that are more taxing and for respondents with weaker cognitive skills. Also the effect was greater for questions where there is no clear break between the 'stem' of the question and the answers. These are quite small differences, but might be a concern for multi-mode surveys that combine self-administered questionnaires and interviews.

Some unusually large response order effects have been reported. Schuman and Presser (1981: 60) and Bishop and Smith (2001) find questions where it exceeds 10 per cent. Usually, the questions that exhibit these large effects are complex and/or unanswerable. A question from Schuman and Presser, for example, asks whether there will be sufficient petroleum supplies *in 25 years*, and one from Bishop and Smith (1997) asks, 'Do you think that, in the long run, atomic energy will do more good than harm?' But Schuman and Presser (1981: 67) find a very large recency effect for a simple question about divorce and Mingay and Greenwell (1989) find a small, but significant primacy effect for one about health status.

This research suggests that small response order effects arise from subconscious cognitive characteristics and habits that involve perception and memory. So in interviewer surveys it is slightly easier to remember the last answer, and with visual presentation in a self-administered survey the eye is drawn to the first response. These might result in changes in responses of 1 or 2 per cent and, like the entirely inadvertent choices in the wording of almost any question, are hardly worth worrying about. Potentially much larger effects appear when a question is very difficult for the respondent, which is a function of the question topic and the respondent's ability to answer. Items that exhibit large order effects, a form of bias, are also likely to have high levels of random measurement error.

Rather than any features of the question, Krosnick and Alwin (1987) argue that a significant cause of response order effects is satisficing, whereby respondents choose an acceptable answer, rather than giving their most considered response. That respondent motivation and attention can reduce unwanted method effects is demonstrated by Malhotra's (2009) finding that there were almost no response order effects for a complex but interesting ranking task in an Internet survey, but substantial recency order effects for simpler but less interesting questions. Thus, the motivation of respondents and the quality of respondents' experience are as important as the quality of the questionnaire.

Response order effects are usually quite small and arise from an unpredictable combination of the survey mode, the question topic and difficulty, and the respondent's cognitive skills. If an unbiased estimate of the response distribution is needed, the only certain solution is to randomize the order of responses and take the average response as the estimate. Unless this variation is introduced, it is not possible to measure or take account of order effects. The questions that are most prone to sizeable response order effects are the ones that respondents have the most difficulty answering and then it is always better to simplify the questions or screen out respondents with no answer, even if it is also possible to do an experiment.

Social Desirability and Acquiescence

'Social desirability' is bias that results when respondents give answers that are designed to put them in a good light. It includes over-reporting of 'good' things like voting and doing exercise, and under-reporting of 'bad' things like drug use and prejudice. If social desirability is an individual psychological characteristic, one alternative is to measure it in the survey and use its value to adjust the responses to other questions; the best known scale was put forward by Crowne and Marlowe in 1960. There is no agreement that this is a good idea, however. Not only does attempting to measure social desirability consume valuable questionnaire space, there is no consensus on how to measure it (DeMaio, 1984). Instead, for topics where social desirability is a problem, researchers try to design questions that minimize it. One strategy is to de-stigmatize the behaviour or insert details in the question to encourage the respondent to focus on the facts. A question about voting, for example, might mention that many people do not vote because they are too busy. For a more elaborate example, see Belli et al. (1999).

While social desirability can also affect the answers in a self-administered survey, the concern is much greater for surveys with interviewers. In a face-to-face interview a common strategy to avoid the problem is to put some of the questions in a booklet that the respondent completes in private and returns to the interviewer in a sealed envelope. In a face-to-face survey using a laptop the interviewer can turn over the computer to the respondent.

Another strategy, invented by Warner (1965) and discussed at length by Fox and Tracy (1986), is called *randomized response*. The idea is to pair a question that is prone to social desirability bias with an innocuous question whose response distribution is known from another survey. The respondent answers only one of the two questions at random, *without telling the interviewer which question he or she answered*. For example, the respondent might be asked to flip a coin and then answer one question for heads and the other for tails. For a meta-analysis of applications of the technique see Lensvelt-Mulders et al. (2005). A potential difficulty, encountered by Holbrook and Krosnick (2010), is that measurement error arises because some respondents make mistakes in implementing the choice of questions.

A similar idea is the *item count* or *unmatched count* technique invented by Raghavarao and Federer (1979; also see Mutz, 2011: 27ff.), whereby the item that is subject to social desirability is concealed in a list of innocuous attitudes or behaviours. At random, a respondent is given either a list with or a list without the stigmatized item and asked to indicate the number of attitudes she endorses or behaviours she engaged in, without saying anything about the individual items on the list. The desired estimate is obtained by subtracting the counts obtained when the item prone to social desirability bias is and is not included in the question. Coutts and Jann (2011) provide a nice comparison of random response and unmatched counts.

Randomized response and item counts yield unbiased estimates of the incidence of the socially desirable behaviour or attitudes *for the sample*, but a major drawback is that they do not provide the responses of *individual* respondents. Group comparisons, say between age groups, can be made by subdividing the sample, but the resulting increase in sampling error is a serious analytical limitation because there is no individual response to the sensitive question to incorporate in conventional data analysis.

Acquiescence, also called *agree response bias*, is the tendency of a survey respondent to answer positively, *regardless of a question's content*. This can be thought of in terms of satisficing (Holbrook et al., 2003) or responding with minimal effort, especially if the question is difficult or the respondent has no opinion, or can be seen as a personality trait, called *extreme response style* (Billiet and Davidov, 2008). While it can also arise for factual questions, acquiescence is typically a problem in measuring attitudes and there is quite consistent empirical evidence that it exists (Kankaraš and Moors, 2011). The magnitude of acquiescence is unpredictable and it cannot be measured if every respondent answers the same questions.

The traditional strategy is to reverse the direction of some of the items, so that respondents who answer consistently agree with some statements and disagree with others. This has significant drawbacks, however. A reversed item may sound unnatural and so the answers are prone to response error, and the need for the respondent to spot short words that change the question's direction may also increase error. Although changing the direction of about half the items removes bias in an additive scale, the bias in *individual* items is unaffected. A complicated way to deal with this is to randomize the directionality of *each* item individually. If acquiescence is a serious concern, a better solution is to change the questions to a format where the response does not involve agreement.

Meta-analysis of Question Characteristics Based on Structural Equation Models

In their seminal 1959 article, Campbell and Fiske showed how a 'multi-trait, multi-method' (MTMM) matrix of correlations between measures of two or more 'traits', each measured in at least two different ways, could be used to determine the measures' validity. They realized that the observed correlation between measures of two traits would overestimate its true value if the traits were measured in the same way and the method of measurement affected the answers. Thus the reliability of an additive scale tends to be overestimated from the correlations between the items that are measured with questions in the same format. It is only possible to measure and account for this bias if there is additional information, provided by the MTMM approach, to estimate the effect of the measurement.

When Campbell and Fiske did their work, there was neither the statistical theory nor computation tools to analyse an MTMM matrix in numerical terms, and so they relied on informal inspection of the correlations. With the development of structural equation models (SEMs)[10] and software to estimate them by Jöreskog

---

[10]A nice history is provided by Matsueda (2012). For a lovely overview of SEMs with historical notes see Skrondal and Rabe-Hesketh (2007).

(1970; 1978) it was possible to cast MTMM matrices into a latent variables framework and to estimate the parameters of a statistical model. A latent variable, in this sense, is just a theoretical construct that cannot be measured directly but affects the answers to survey questions that are observed 'manifest' variables. For example, support for the welfare state might be measured by combining the answers to questions about support for a number of different government policies, because even with some explanation a direct question about 'the welfare state' would be subject to varying interpretation and some degree of incomprehension. Similarly, job satisfaction and support for nuclear power are latent variables that could be measured by a group of questions in a survey.[11]

As applied to an MTMM matrix of correlations between survey items, in the SEM each survey item is affected by three latent factors:

- the *trait* that the item is intended to measure;
- the *method* of measurement, which is just the format of the survey question; and
- the *residual error*, which includes all the remaining variance, due to random error and the 'unique variance' measuring the influence of any other substantive factors affecting the response but not conceptualized, said to be 'exogenous' to or 'outside' the model.

The total variance of the survey item is divided into three corresponding components: the valid variance or 'validity', the method effect and 'the error'.[12]

Jöreskog's LISREL program and a number of others developed since the 1970s can be used to estimate the parameters of the SEM. Figure 1, adapted from Andrews (1984: 419), is an example. It shows three substantive questions about drinking beer, eating too much and watching TV 'to get away from it all' in the previous month; each measured with a yes/no question, a four-category measure of frequency (almost every day, every few days, once or twice, or not at all), and by the number of days the activity was done in the month.[13]

---

[11]This is not to deride the interest in measuring a person's self-understanding of their position with regard to more abstract concepts such as support for the welfare state or liberalism or nuclear power. The point is that to a degree self-identification in these dimensions involves variation in the definition of the categories presented. Rather than choosing between self-identification or a single, general question, it is much more interesting to ask both a general question and more specific questions, in order to gain insight into the substantive bases of self-identification or the reasoning behind adopting a broad position. Even more interesting: consider randomizing the order of the general and specific questions.

[12]This is a confirmatory factor analysis model, where the factors of each of the traits and each of the methods are used as measures. If four traits are measured with three methods, there are seven factors in all and estimation of the variance is based on the 66 correlations (or covariances in an 'unstandardized' model) between the 12 (4 × 3) survey items. The fit of this 'confirmatory' model can be measured because the 66 independent correlations among 12 items are larger than the number of model parameters.

[13]A statistical complexity of the problem, not addressed until later, is that the error distributions of the binary measure, the ordinal variable and the 'count' are different.

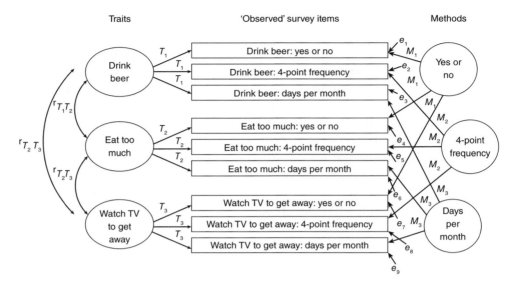

Figure 1   Multi-Trait Multi-Method Model from Andrews (1984: 419)

As Figure 1 shows, there are six latent variables, three for the traits, T_1, T_2 and T_3, and three for the methods, M_1, M_2 and M_3, and there are nine residual error terms, e_1 to e_9, one for each of the individual survey items. Each item is exactly equal to the sum of three components: a contribution of the trait it is intended to measure – its 'valid' or 'true' variance; a contribution of the method; and some degree of residual error.[14] A 'good' survey item consists mostly of valid variance (so T_1, T_2 and T_3 are close to one – where one is the maximum value since it is conventional to estimate a 'standardized' model, based on the correlation coefficients), with small method effects and a small residual error (M_1, M_2 and M_3 as well as e_1 to e_9 are small). Rather than the T, M and e values themselves, it is common to focus on their squares, which are variances. Since the total variance of each item is one, any two of the validity, method effect and error determine the third value. For each item, x_{ij}, which measures trait i using method j, $T_i^2 + M_j^2 + e_{ij}^2 = 1$. T_i^2, the proportion of the variance accounted for by the 'validity' of the measure T_i, varies between zero and one (so, 0–100 per cent) and can be interpreted as the percentage of 'true variance' in the variable; M_j^2 is the effect of method j.

---

[14]It is common to estimate 'standardized' MTMM models from their correlations, in which case the equations for the observables do not include a constant and the item variances are assumed to be one. It is possible to estimate SEMs in metric form using their covariances instead of their correlations. There is an extensive literature on the specification and estimation of models of MTMM matrices, for example Byrne (2010: 275ff.), Eid et al. (2008) and Höfling et al. (2009). The most important assumption – for otherwise it is impossible to obtain independent estimates of the method effects – is that the covariances between traits and methods are zero.

Now the problem is to measure the impact of the various characteristics of survey items – the general format of the question, the number of response categories, whether a 'no opinion' response is offered, and so on – on the validity, method effect and error of a question. A single MTMM analysis cannot separate the various characteristics of survey items because the number of question formats of the variables analysed in each SEM is usually just three or four, while questions can vary in many more respects. Andrews' ingenious solution was to conduct a meta-analysis where the observations are individual survey items, each characterized by its format, number and type of response categories, and so on, *and* by the MTMM-based estimates of its validity, method effect and error estimated from the SEM. Regressing the validity, method effect and error on the characteristics of the items yields estimates of how the different characteristics of a survey item affect its quality.

Andrews estimated MTMM models for no less than 2115 survey items from six surveys, five of which were US national population surveys. From the meta-analysis he found that, *on average*:

- about 65 per cent of the variance of a survey item is valid or 'true' that measures the intended concept;
- just 3 per cent of the variance is due to the methodological characteristics of the survey items; and
- 30 per cent is residual error.

Thus, *comparing reasonable ways of asking a question*, there is relatively little difference in the quality of items with different formats, compared both to the true variation *and to the residual error*, which by definition is unrelated to any of the systematically measured characteristics of the question. Of course, the question formats being compared in the models are not chosen at random, but constitute plausible ways of asking a question about a designated topic. This implies that there is much more to be gained by decreasing the residual error variance, improving the effort and concentration of respondents, and refining the substantive topic of a question, than by improving the format of a question.

Unless they are accounted for, method effects and error affect the covariances between survey questions and so result in bias. The reliability of a scale computed from the correlations between questions with the same format is always *overestimated* because those correlations combine the effects of the common trait *and the common method*. Ignoring the residual error leads to *underestimates* of the covariance between items measuring different traits and results in bias in regression model coefficients. On the positive side, for typical survey items where two-thirds of the variance is due to the trait, a scale of four of five items has an acceptable level of reliability.

It is reasonable to be concerned about the generality of Andrews' findings, which were based on surveys conducted only in the USA in the mid-1970s. The extraordinary effort and quantity of data required for an MTMM-based meta-analysis mean there are few comparable studies. It is therefore very encouraging that Scherpenzeel and Saris (1997: 360) find that four more recent studies yield quite similar estimates of the relative magnitudes of the three components of item variance. Measured in the recent European Social Surveys (ESSs) in many European nations, the mean validity of survey items is 0.639 per cent, with a standard deviation of 0.175 (Saris et al., 2011: 63).

Any estimate of the effect of the question format on its statistical characteristics requires some kind of multiple measurement and MTMM matrices obtain those multiple measurements *in a single survey*. An alternative is to use a longitudinal survey in which the same respondents answer the same question on at least three occasions. Because the repeated item employs just one 'method', longitudinal data provide an estimate of reliability only, which is equal to the sum of the valid and method variance. From the MTMM analysis it is known that the method component is quite small, on average.

Alwin (2007; also see Alwin and Krosnick, 1991) used longitudinal surveys with at least three waves separated by two years or more to estimate the reliability of 426 survey questions. The critically important result is that average reliability, 0.634, with a standard deviation of 0.157, is very close to the value obtained by the MTMM studies. Because the methodology is completely different, this is very powerful confirmation of the basic findings of the MTMM analysis.

Alwin found interesting differences in the reliability of questions on different topics. Questions about a person's financial situation had a mean reliability of 0.592, compared to 0.671 for questions about the perceived quality of life and 0.594 for measures of self-esteem. Also, he found that longer questions were *less* reliable, that the inclusion of an explicit 'don't know' answer had no effect on reliability, that the labelling of response categories increased reliability, and that questions with three response categories had much lower reliability than questions with either two or four responses.

The figures above for the validity, method effect and residual variation are averages, and the role of the meta-analysis is to determine how they are affected by the characteristics of each question. Andrews measured the effects of 13 variables divided into four groups, as follows:

- characteristics of the response scale, such as the number of response categories and whether a 'no opinion' response was offered;
- other non-substantive characteristics of the item, such as its length (just counting the number of words);
- the topic of the question, including its sensitivity to social desirability and salience; and
- attributes relating to the entire survey, such as the mode of data collection and the position of the item in the survey.

Respectively, the 13 variables explained 66, 72 and 67 per cent of the variance in the validity, method effect and residual error of the survey items.[15]

Andrews found that the number of response categories had the strongest effect item on item validity. Questions with 20 or more categories or which asked for an exact number had the highest validity, followed by questions with 9–19 categories and 4–8 categories. Scherpenzeel and Saris (1997) and Saris and Gallhofer (2007a) obtain somewhat different results. They find that beyond 10 categories there is no increase in validity. The logic is that with longer scales, for example thermometers labelled 0 to 100, random variation in interpretation of the scale increases error, but there is no increase in the precision of responses. Scherpenzeel and Saris (1997) find that answers in the form of exact counts have lower reliability when the range of possible answers is very large and there are high outliers.[16]

Consistent with Alwin (1992: 93), Andrews found that three-category measures had *lower* validity than response scales with two categories (yes/no, effectively) or with four or more categories. So, if the intent of the question is not to obtain a yes or no answer and there is a logical middle category, using five response categories will provide more precise answers.

For a group (or 'battery') of items in the same format, Andrews found that the validity is highest for the first five items, drops somewhat for the next five items because residual error increases, and is much lower thereafter, when method effects and residual error both increase. This suggests that short-term boredom and difficulty of maintaining concentration set in quite quickly when respondents are asked to answer many questions with the same format. If the topic requires many questions, minimally they should be divided into groups with separate introductions, and if possible different question formats should be used.

Over the length of an entire questionnaire, validity is highest from about the 25th to 100th questions; it is somewhat lower at the beginning of the interview before the 25th question; and it is significantly lower beginning around the 100th question, but does not decline after that. For a typical questionnaire this means that responses are a little more erratic in the first few minutes as the respondent learns about the task, then he or she concentrates well until fatigue starts to sets in around the half-hour point. More difficult questions should be put near the beginning of a survey, but not in the first few minutes.

Comparing questions of different length, Andrews found that longer questions (defined as 16 words or more), following an introduction of medium length (16–64

---

[15]Because the validity and error account for almost all of the variance and their total is close to one, each can be predicted from the other – high-validity items have low error and vice versa. As a result, the regressions for the validity and error give very similar results, which is why their explained variances are similar. What is more interesting is that the explanatory power of the regression for the method effect is also very similar, which is not an artefact because the method effect accounts for only a small part of the total variation in the typical survey item.

[16]Perhaps the solution is not to use grouped categories at all, but to collect direct counts and deal with the outliers in data analysis by rescaling or employing robust statistics.

words), had higher validity than shorter questions and questions with a short or very long introduction. This suggests that the risk of short questions and short introductions is that they may not provide enough information for a precise response, while a very long introduction provides more information than a respondent can retain.

Beyond these few generalizations, the findings of the different MTMM meta-analyses are somewhat inconsistent. For example, Andrews found that including an explicit 'don't know' among the response categories increased validity, but Rodgers et al. (1992) found the opposite, and Scherpenzeel and Saris (1997) and Saris and Gallhofer (2007a) found no effect. Andrews found that labelling some but not all of the response categories increased validity, while Scherpenzeel and Saris found that labelling all the categories is better. Some features of questions, such as the topic, whether the question is 'sensitive' and the mode of data collection, have consistent effects, but they are not considered here because, from the viewpoint of the question writer, they cannot be changed.

In addition to comparing a wide range of question topics and formats, MTMM models can also be used to compare different measurements of one trait or just one methodological difference. For example, Alwin (1997) compared different response scales for measuring life satisfaction and Saris et al. (2010) used the ESS to compare agree–disagree questions to questions with 'item-specific' response categories that use a 'sentence completion' format.

Two of the questions compared by Saris et al. asked:

> whether the respondent would agree strongly, agree, neither agree nor disagree, disagree or disagree strongly, with statement that her country 'should allow more people from the poorer countries outside Europe to come and live here' – the 'generic' response categories;

> to what extent do you think [the country] 'should allow people from the poorer countries outside Europe ... to come and live here?' Rated: allow many to come and live here; allow some; allow a few; or allow none – the 'item-specific' response categories.

The second question, with item-specific responses, was much more reliable and valid (p. 71). Similar results were obtained for a number of other paired comparisons and these findings were confirmed in separate analyses of data from each of the more than 20 countries with ESSs. So Saris and his colleagues conclude that survey responses tailored to the question provide better measurements than the generic rating of statements with agree–disagree responses.

This contrasts with Saris and Gallhofer's (2007a: 24) MTMM-based finding that, on average, 'indirect requests', such as agree–disagree questions, and 'direct requests', such as the item-specific questions above, have about the same reliability and that the former have slightly higher validity. Probably this is because the comparisons of agree–disagree and 'item-specific' questions by Saris et al. involve substantively different questions. The first question above asks about 'allowing more people' to enter the country, while the second asks *how many* people should be allowed to enter the country. The item-specific response categories are better because the question topic lends itself to answers phrased in terms of the numbers of immigrants, rather than agreement with a statement.

The meta-analyses demonstrate the limits of generic formulae for question design. Definitely, they offer useful guidance about the length of questions, the number of response categories and other features of questions. But these considerations should be secondary to and must align with the substantive content of a question. The finding that questions with three response categories are less reliable on average than questions with two or four or more responses, for example, is no reason to avoid questions for which there are exactly three reasonable answers.

While statisticians have made remarkable progress in understanding measurement error and how to account for it in survey data analysis, providing the necessary data remains a major challenge. Estimating errors in one survey usually requires at least three measures of a trait *and measures of two other traits* with the same three measures.[17] This takes up considerable space in a survey, squeezing out other content, and it is a repetitive and potentially discouraging burden on respondents. An attractive but complicated alternative is to use *estimates* of measurement error from *other* surveys or to predict the measurement from the type of question, which is the strategy being pursued in the ESS by Saris and his colleagues (2011). In measuring the statistical characteristics of survey questions, longitudinal surveys with three or more waves have a tremendous advantage, because reliability estimates can be obtained for any repeated individual variable.

The Cognitive Model of Survey Response ────

Rather than any general understanding of how respondents answer questions, interpretation of both the simpler survey experiments and MTMM meta-analyses relied on a variety of ad hoc, commonsense explanations. The cognitive model of survey response provided such a model, which is why the CASM movement has had such a powerful influence. Formulated by Roger Tourangeau in 1984,[18] the model breaks the process of answering a question into four steps:

1 Comprehension – understanding words in the question, identifying the concepts, determining what the question is asking, and deciding what information is needed.
2 Retrieval – recalling the relevant information from memory.
3 Judgement – formulating an answer based on the comprehension and retrieval.
4 Response – fitting the answer into the response categories.

---

[17]To decrease the response burden, Saris et al. (2004) show that it is possible to have subsets of the survey sample answer questions in just two of the three formats, and then combine covariances obtained from different subsets in the SEM. There is significant additional statistical complexity and greater error, however, because the covariances are not all based on the same respondents.

[18]For a more recent and definitive formulation see Tourangeau et al. (2000) or the briefer statement by Tourangeau and Bradburn (2010).

A respondent may not go through the steps in sequence and may double back. If the information specified in step 1 cannot be retrieved in step 2, for example, the respondent may reinterpret the question in terms he or she can answer. Also, in the few seconds that respondents need to answer a typical question, the steps may overlap.

Rather than an empirical model with measurable parameters that can be falsified, the cognitive model of survey response is a conceptual model, or maybe a paradigm. In a more qualitative style, cognitive researchers have used supplementary questions to ask respondents whether they understand the question, what information they retrieved, and how they form judgements. Also they developed the use of 'think aloud' interviews, whereby the respondent is asked to say what goes through his or her mind when answering a question (for more detail see Schwarz and Sudman, 1996). But these methods are too slow and costly to use in actual surveys and so this empirical side of the CASM enterprise is considered in detail in Chapter 6, on survey pretesting, which is where the methods are used.

The development of the cognitive model shifted the focus of question design from the researcher's purpose in writing a question to the ability of the respondent to answer and the quality of the answer. It provided the concepts and language to describe how respondents answer questions and to bring order to the disorganized multitude of experimental findings. Like the craft tradition of survey design that it attempted to supersede, however in practice the cognitive model and cognitive methods were more effective at diagnosing problems with existing questions than indicating how to write new questions.

Two limitations of the cognitive model are that it does not explicitly incorporate the effect of an interviewer on a respondent's answers or the respondent's cognitive skills and motivation. Not only do interviewers vary in the way that they read questions, deal with respondent queries and prompt a slow or reluctant respondent, the mere presence of an interviewer may affect the responses, as we see in Chapter 7. The respondent's skills and motivation affect how well she understands the question, and her effort to retrieve relevant information, as well as the process of judgement. Effects of social desirability could be seen as expanding step 4 of the model to include modifying the response in light of an interviewer's presence or, even in a self-administered survey, to appear in a better light (see Cannell et al., 1981).

CASM and Attitudes

Cognitive researchers raised the fundamental question of what it means for a person to express an attitude and they shed new light on why responses are affected by wording and question order. To a degree this has unified and made sense of the earlier behaviourist explanations of wording and order effects, and the CASM framework has also provided a way to think about question design.

Traditionally, an attitude is thought of as a relatively permanent evaluation, which is retrieved from memory in response to a survey question. This 'dispositional' model of attitudes has been developed in an extensive research programme by Russell Fazio (beginning with Fazio et al., 1982; for a review see Fazio, 2007). The idea is that an attitude is an association between an 'object' and an evaluation, where the object might be a person, group or organization, material object, experience or idea. Attitudes vary in strength on a continuum from the strongest attitudes, which are said to be 'automatically activated' when the object is brought to mind; to weaker attitudes, which require more time and effort to bring to mind; and to non-attitudes, when there is no evaluation attached to an object. Attitudes that are not activated 'automatically' become more accessible if they are brought to mind by earlier questions on a related topic – the process of 'priming'. Weak attitudes result in more measurement error, because the respondent cannot retrieve the answer with consistency, and when there is no attitude to be retrieved the respondent must construct one on the spot.

This harks back to Converse's (1964) distinction between attitudes and non-attitudes – called the black and white model of non-attitudes – and to his view that many people have no attitudes on important public issues. To avoid embarrassment, respondents with 'non-attitudes' answer anyway, but more or less randomly. Achen (1975) attacked Converse's view with an analysis of longitudinal surveys. By examining individuals' responses to the same question repeated over time, Achen showed that measurement error is responsible for much of the observed temporal instability in opinion and for the low correlations between logically related questions. The implication is that scales formed by combining a number of individual questions are much more stable, as Peffley and Hurwitz (1985) showed. While there is also strong evidence that the reliability of attitude questions is lower for respondents with less knowledge and understanding (Zaller, 1992; Zaller and Feldman, 1992; Bartle, 2000), this is not the same as saying that those respondents have no attitude at all. This again raises the issue of whether questions should include an explicit 'don't know' response, and it lends support to the argument *against* doing so.

The cognitive model can describe the dispositional model of attitudes, as follows:

- If there is an attitude corresponding to the question, judgement (step 3) is omitted and respondents just comprehend the question (step 1) and retrieve the corresponding attitude (step 2); then they may have to fit the retrieved attitude into a response category (step 4), for example by deciding whether the attitude is closer to 'agree' or to 'strongly agree'.
- If there is *no* attitude corresponding to the question, the respondent skips steps 2 *and* 3 and, at step 4, chooses an answer at random.

This truncated scheme, however, is fundamentally at odds with the way that cognitive researchers conceive of survey response.

For the dispositional model of attitudes, the key difficulty is not that there is some measurement error, but the evidence that wording one side of a question, the order of questions and apparently small changes in question wording – think of the forbid/not allow difference – can substantially change the attitude expressed, *even for well-informed respondents with high cognitive skills.* If attitudes are merely retrieved, why would they be affected by question formats and order?

The alternative, four-step cognitive model of survey response can be characterized as a 'construal' or 'attitude construction' model. In response to the attitude question, the respondent begins with comprehension of the question, in step 1; then retrieves the relevant memories, sometimes called 'considerations', in step 2; and forms a judgement, in step 3 (see Tourangeau et al., 2000: ch. 6 and Schwarz, 2007b). Rather than being retrieved from memory, the survey responses *are formed only as the respondent answers*. Differences in the wording of a question and the contents of previous questions change the memories retrieved and potentially also the process of judgement.

Tourangeau et al. (2000: ch. 6) have different names for the dispositional and construal models. The former they call the 'file drawer' model, based on the idea that answering a question involves retrieving a pre-existing attitude or 'file' from storage. Their version of the construal model, labelled the 'belief-sampling model', has as its 'key assumption … that retrieval yields a haphazard assortment of beliefs, feelings, impressions, general values, and prior judgments about an issue'. Exactly which memories are retrieved is 'affected by a large number of determinants, some chronic and some temporary' (p. 179). In the third, judgement step of the model, respondents take the average of the memories that they retrieved in step 2. This, they say, 'is a simplified version that assumes the assignment of equal weights to each consideration' (p. 181), and they suggest that a more complex model would allow the respondents to assign different weights to the various considerations retrieved in response to a question. In the belief-sampling model respondents have a stock of memories from which their answers are constructed, but there are no mental 'things' – persistent links between an object and an evaluation – that can be called 'attitudes'.

To provide empirical support of the cognitive model, Tourangeau et al. (2000: 183ff.) asked respondents to report the 'considerations' that came to mind as they answered questions. Many respondents, they found, mentioned more than one consideration, which implies that their response was not a report of a single attitude. The attitudes of respondents who brought to mind more considerations in answering a question and whose considerations are more mixed were less stable over time.

The cognitive model provides parsimonious explanations of question order effects. For 'part–part' effects, which involve two or more questions at the same level of generality, an earlier question changes the comprehension of the later question, which alters the memories retrieved in step 2 and so the judgement process in step 3. For 'part–whole' effects, which involve the exclusion of the 'part' mentioned in a first question from the 'whole' considered in the second question, the changed comprehension of the question affects which memories are retrieved in step 2. When a number of 'parts' are the subjects of earlier questions, for example various domains affecting the overall quality of life, the response to a following general question tends to rely on previously retrieved memories, because they are more accessible.

The dispositional model cannot account for the systematic effects of question wording and order because it does not distinguish mental facts (my office is in a tall building) from attitudes (my office is unpleasant) and because attitude *in*consistency is merely considered as error. Construal models, on the other hand, seem to overemphasize the impact of the context of questions and the unsystematic nature of the retrieval of memories that feed into respondents' judgements. Still, it does not make sense to think that a person who repeatedly and without hesitation describes their office as unpleasant is merely retrieving the same mental images each time and combining them in the same way to get the same answer.[19] Even if this does describe the response process and exactly the same considerations are brought to mind every time a question is asked, then those considerations must be fairly stable attitudes.

A reasonable compromise between the two positions would be to say that among the memories that can be retrieved in response to a question about attitudes, in step 2 of the cognitive model, some respondents tap a fairly stable link between an object and an evaluation, or an 'attitude'. If among the considerations retrieved, there is an 'attitude' that corresponds closely to the question, the respondent discards any other retrieved memories and reports that answer; if none of the memories corresponds closely to the question, the belief-sampling process comes into play and the respondent answers by summarizing the various memories he or she has retrieved.

Other models of attitudes also address this conundrum. Eagly and Chaiken (2007) distinguish between the *expression* of an attitude, which they see as constructed in response to a question and so potentially affected by changes in question wording and context, and the attitude itself, which is a more stable 'inner tendency' or 'latent property' of a person. Compared to the belief-sampling model they grant more permanence to attitude-like memories and recognize that the process of answering a question alters the expression of an attitude, but they do not give as much emphasis to the effects of context and chance on which memories are retrieved. Petty et al. (2007) explain variability in attitudes by allowing the possibility that two or more, potentially contradictory, attitudes are associated with a single object. Which attitude is expressed in response to a question depends on the situation. Conrey and Smith (2007) describe still another alternative: the 'connectionist' idea that attitudes are constructed from the pattern of links between mental representations at the time a question is asked.[20] The implication is that the considerations brought to bear in answering a question are connected and not independent, as the belief-sampling model suggests.

---

[19]Contradicting their more general 'construal' model, when describing context effects, Tourangeau et al. consider the circumstance when a 'question automatically triggers the retrieval of a highly accessible attitude' (p. 217). This sounds like Fazio's definition of an attitude as a persistent object-evaluation link that is 'automatically activated'.

[20]A good introduction to the literature on attitudes in social psychology is a 2007 (Vol. 25, No. 5) issue of the journal *Social Cognition*, used as the main source here. Also see Bohner and Dickel (2011).

If to some degree attitudes are constructed only when a survey question is asked and the response might be affected by the wording and question order, the answers to an unbiased question are unaffected by arbitrary choices of words and by previous questions. But this is not at all how we express our opinions to friends or decide how to vote. Instead, it is common to think about the candidates and their policies over a period of time, and maybe talk about it with others. In other words, we bring to mind the considerations that would arise with a longer, more rambling survey question with a number of alternatives and we make use of the answers to previous questions. This argues for measuring attitudes with a group of questions that raise points on both sides of an issue and for measuring respondents' interest in a topic. Also, it lends support to the use of experiments in order to determine the effect of question wording and order. More on this in the next chapter.

Autobiographical Memory

If there is any aspect of question design that belongs in the realm of cognitive psychology it is the memory of past events. Three of the 11 chapters of Tourangeau et al.'s definitive *Psychology of Survey Response* (2000) are devoted to autobiographical memory, dealing with questions measuring the number, time and duration of events, and their factual characteristics. Still, the contribution of the cognitive model is not so clear. For questions about autobiographical memory, the focus is first on comprehension – identifying what qualifies as a relevant memory – and second on retrieval. While the efforts of researchers inspired by CASM have told us a lot about biographical memory, the model itself has not played much of a role.

The fundamental and simple problem is just that: 'By far the best-attested fact about autobiographical memory is that the longer the interval between the time of the event and the time of the interview, the less likely that a person will remember it' (Tourangeau et al., 2000: 82). In designing survey questions, a common problem is that the period of time for which information is desired is longer than the period that respondents can remember reliably. It is especially difficult to measure the frequency and other characteristics of activities that are affected by seasonality, since respondents must cover an entire year. A better, but usually more costly alternative is to spread data collection over a year and ask respondents about shorter periods.

Think about measuring movie attendance. Over a short period, say two weeks, responses will be reliable, but many people will answer 'zero' and the estimate will have a large error because the 'zero' category lumps together respondents with a wide range of true frequencies. Lengthening the reference period to a month or more will decrease the proportion of 'zero' answers, resulting in more precise estimates, but also more error because:

- some respondents will mistakenly locate earlier events as closer in time; called 'forward telescoping', this leads to overestimates of movie attendance;
- others will mistakenly locate more recent events as earlier in time; called 'backward telescoping', this leads to underestimation; and
- some respondents will forget about a movie entirely, also leading to underestimation.

So an estimate is unbiased if, by luck or design, the underestimation due to backward telescoping and forgetting is equal to the overestimation due to forward telescoping. This can happen because empirical studies show that forward telescoping is much more common than backward telescoping. Ideally, the question should ask about a period for which all three errors are small, but accepting some error in order to cover a longer reference period. The ideal period depends on the experience in question. In consumption surveys, for example, respondents can quite accurately recall automobile and major appliance purchases for a year or more, but for food and small daily expenditures such as buying a coffee, the period is much shorter (and even then, asking respondents to keep a diary or save receipts is much better than depending on free recall).

For common events and when the recall covers a longer period, respondents will tend to switch from attempting to remember individual events to some sort of averaging or calculation. For example, a respondent might estimate that he or she goes to the movies about once a month, so 12 times a year, but not in the summer, so, say, 10 times in the last year. Depending on the topic and period of recall, estimation of this kind may be *more* accurate than direct retrieval because respondents can discount unusual events. The large body of research on strategies for remembering discrete events and on when respondents switch to estimation is nicely summarized by Tourangeau et al. (2000: 126ff.; also see Friedman, 1993).

Interest in this topic long predates CASM. Indeed, *the* classic study and constant presence in this literature is Neter and Waksberg's (1964) analysis of home repair and renovation expenditures in the USA. Using a panel survey, they demonstrated both substantial forgetting over a period of just three months and considerable forward telescoping, though recall was much better for major than minor repairs. In subsequent research, forward telescoping has been found to predominate over backward telescoping, so the usual bias is towards overestimating frequencies.[21]

In order to improve recall, Neter and Waksberg invented a strategy called 'bounded recall', which involved asking respondents the same questions at two points in time. They demonstrated that reminding respondents of their answers in the first wave of the survey decreased forward telescoping and increased the accuracy of reports for the period between the first and second interviews. This strategy, known as 'dependent interviewing', is commonly used in longitudinal surveys. Rather than asking if the respondent changed jobs since the last

---

[21]The phenomenon has no widely accepted explanation. It makes sense that the precision of dates of events declines as the event becomes more distant; the question is why this typically leads to forward telescoping. Tourangeau and Bradburn's (2010: 332) not-entirely-convincing explanation is that 'Even though there is no systematic bias in the perceived time of occurrence, telescoping seems to reflect a combination of this increasing uncertainty about when the events occurred and the imposition of a boundary on the earliest reports. The effect of this bounding is to truncate reports of events that are remembered as having occurred before the beginning of the reference period. Since there is a greater uncertainty about when the events occurred the further back in time they actually took place, a larger number of events will be telescoped forward.' Also see Tourangeau et al. (2000: 126ff.).

interview, for example, the question 'feeds back' the respondent's description of his or her current job from the previous interview and asks if there was any change.

It is not always possible to conduct a longitudinal survey, not to mention the greater cost. Sudman et al. (1984) showed how to use bounded recall in one interview, by first asking respondents questions about events over a longer period and then asking the same questions about a shorter period. So an initial set of questions might ask about purchases in the last three months and, immediately following, the same set of questions would be asked about purchases in the last month. This improves the quality of estimates for the second, shorter period. Usually the answers for the first, longer period are discarded, though with statistical adjustment they are sometimes used.

Another strategy, invented by Loftus and Marburger (1983), is clear from the title of their article, 'Since the eruption of Mount St. Helens, has anyone beaten you up? Improving the accuracy of retrospective reports with landmark events'. The idea is that significant world events can provide a natural 'reference period'. Gaskell et al. (2000) caution, however, that the date of the reference event must be firmly in respondents' minds, because it too is subject to telescoping. A generalization of this strategy is to use more personal landmarks, for example by asking students about events during a university term or academic year. Sudman and Bradburn (1973) describe a strategy called 'aided recall' to reduce forgetting. The idea is to break down abstract classes, say purchases of clothing and footwear, into the categories of everyday experience, for example purchases of a coat or shoes.

Pessimistically, Sudman et al. (1996) conclude that: 'There is little to suggest that the questionnaire designer can have much impact on which method the respondent chooses [to recall events over some period], except through the offer of an appropriate time period' (p. 223). They advise that the quality of recall is improved by slowing down the pace of an interview, by lengthening the question in order to give respondents more time to think, and by adding an instruction designed to slow the response (p. 225). Also, they recommend that questions should request exact numbers rather than present respondents with grouped categories.

Finally, to aid in the recall of complex events over a long period, Freedman et al. (1988) developed the 'event history calendar', subsequently elaborated by Belli (1998; also see Belli et al., 2009), who describes the method as follows:

> The event history calendar method incorporates two features: (1) a calendar covering important life domains (residence, schooling, work, marriage) that serves as a common reference point for interviewers and respondents, and (2) a 'flexible' interviewing style that allows discretion in the use of information from each domain to aid recall in others. The method was developed to facilitate recall of autobiographical events, some of which may have occurred years prior to the interview. Respondents are introduced to the calendar and first asked to recall and place in time major (salient) life events (e.g., school graduations, residential moves, marriages, employment). Then respondents are asked

to recall and place on the timeline other events of particular interest to the survey, using the previously reported salient events as recall aids. The major life events may facilitate both the simple recall of less salient experiences and their placement in temporal space. (Belli et al., 2007: 604)

A New Science of Question Design?

The traditional mantra is that there are no rules of questionnaire design, only a collection of advice, mainly about what not to do. Payne (1951: xi) laments: 'The reader will be disappointed if he expects to find here a set of definite rules or explicit directions.' Almost 60 years later, Groves and his colleagues (2009) devote just 10 pages of their survey methods text to question design, compared to 18 pages on respondent *problems* answering questions. Rather than asking if there are sufficiently exact rules for writing questions, a more reasonable criterion is whether there is now a sufficient and coherent body of *proscriptive* advice on writing survey questions. Based on this chapter, the answer is 'almost', or maybe even 'yes', which is also the view of Schaeffer and Presser (2003).

Following a lull in the 1950s and 1960s there was a revival of experiment-based research, which became a significant programme of research by the 1970s, and continues to this day. There is substantial empirical research on every aspect of questionnaire design and consensus on many issues. A fair criticism is that in pursuit of general principles of questionnaire design, too little attention has been paid to variation over time and between localities and cultures. Studies using records for external validation are small in number and often use small and local samples. In recent years, however, the field has benefitted from the availability of large international surveys, from researchers with methodological interests around those surveys and from increasingly sophisticated analytical methods, especially SEMs.

What this impressive body of research cannot do is predict the *magnitude* of the effects of question format on response. For example, there is good evidence for the existence of acquiescence – bias in favour of positive responses that is unrelated to the question's content – and we expect the effect to be larger for respondents with less knowledge and interest in the topic, and for topics in which there is less public knowledge and interest. But the size of the effect is not predictable and all that can be said is that it is not a good idea to rely heavily on agree–disagree ratings of statements for research on a new or low-salience topic. Really large response order effects typically occur when questions are too complex, and then the appropriate remedy is to clarify and simplify the question or break it into parts, not change the format.

Meta-analysis of MTMM experiments shows that on average about two-thirds of the variance in a survey question is attributable to the question *content;* just less than one-third is residual error resulting from variation in respondents' understanding of and way of answering the question and only a few per cent is attributable to the method. This suggests that researchers should concentrate on the substantive content of questions more than their format and that decreasing residual error by encouraging the respondent to answer carefully will do more to improve the quality of data than using any particular question format. Also, it points to the value of including multiple measures of key concepts in surveys and argues for using SEMs to account for measurement error. If this is not possible and good estimates of measurement error can be obtained from another survey, analysts should consider 'errors in variables' approaches, which incorporate the external estimates of measurement error.

A leading light of the CASM movement has lamented the failure of 'the large amount of questionnaire pretesting done in the cognitive laboratories of major survey research centres and statistical agencies ... [to] contribute to a cumulative body of knowledge about principles of questionnaire design' (Schwarz, 2007a: 284). Even for questions about attitudes and autobiographical memory, where CASM has a lot to say about how respondents answer questions, it does not say much about how to write better questions. Indeed, in those areas designers have taken their lead from a robust body of conventional, incremental, experiment-based research. This goes back to the fundamental limitation of the CASM model, which is that it is a paradigm and not an empirical model with defined and measurable parameters. Equally important, there is significant variability in how respondents answer a question, due to variation in their knowledge and interest and cognitive skills.

3
Designing a Questionnaire

While methodologists have focused on the design of individual questions, the success of a survey research project depends more on strategic choices about which questions to ask in a limited time. This constraint has become more acute because it has become increasingly difficult to obtain acceptable response rates with longer surveys. Telephone surveys of the general population are now generally limited to about 20 minutes, which allows for about 70 closed questions, and each open question takes the space of about three closed questions. While the limitation depends on the mode, the target population, costs and many other factors, survey length is always a major constraint.

Effective questionnaire design requires a conceptual plan, and the first section of this chapter addresses broad issues in the planning and development of a survey questionnaire. The second section sets out three general principles of questionnaire design, complementing the more technical considerations in the last chapter, followed by brief discussions of the measurement of identity and socio-economic position. The next section is about the use of experiments, originally devised for methodological research, for substantive research on attitudes and social judgements. The chapter concludes with a discussion of 'total survey error', a unified approach to the quality of survey data that incorporates every step in the research process.

Drafting the Questionnaire, Consultation and Pretesting

An academic visitor to a national statistical agency will be impressed by the complexity and very long timetable – sometimes years – required to plan and implement a new survey. This requires time and money, and often it is motivated by a high degree of risk aversion and slowed by painstaking decision making, but even small and quick surveys benefit from an explicit development plan. Once a draft questionnaire is completed, plan to: (1) have experts, or at least colleagues and friends, review the questionnaire, since ideally some will be familiar with the subject matter and some will have survey expertise, and then revise; (2) perhaps ask co-workers or friends to complete the questionnaire and provide comments – but remember that they are likely to be more informed and perhaps better educated than the typical respondent, and then revise; and (3) pretest with respondents similar to the intended survey population, and then revise. Chapter 6 deals with pretesting in detail. Remember that consultation and questionnaire testing is not a democratic process and it is the role of researchers to make decisions. At each stage of consultation and revision, the draft questionnaire should be as complete and finished as possible. Attention to detail is critical. Even a short questionnaire has many details and it is easy to make mistakes.

The Internet provides vast and free resources for survey design dealing with almost every imaginable topic. Besides censuses and labour force surveys, there are large-scale national surveys on many topics, especially continuing academic surveys, such as the US General Social Survey; the national household panel surveys, particularly the German Socio-economic Panel (GSOEP) and the British Household Panel Survey (BHPS) and its successor the UK Household Longitudinal Study; and the major comparative surveys, especially the European Social Survey (ESS), the World Values Survey (WVS) and the International Social Survey Programme (ISSP). All have websites with questionnaires and technical reports. Also useful is the Survey Question Bank (SQB), coordinated by the UK Data Archive at the University of Essex.

——— How Many Items to Measure a Concept? ————————————————

An important distinction is between questionnaires designed to measure just a few concepts precisely, often using standardized scales, and questionnaires with a variety of items, many of which are designed to be analysed individually. This goes back to the time when psychologists developed measures of concepts like intelligence and authoritarianism, while 'pollsters' focused on individual questions about voting intentions and support for particular policies. To this day, there is more emphasis on single items in more sociological fields, including political science and geography, and more emphasis on multi-item scales in more psychological fields, especially health. In fields where researchers rely on multi-item scales, the question is whether some sacrifice in the precision of measurement and loss of comparability with other studies is worth the potential gain of more diverse survey content.

Sometimes a decision about how many items are used to measure a concept involves the difference between more descriptive and more analytical analysis of the resulting data. It is easy to think of 15 or 20 separate aspects of the evaluation of a university course; for example: Was the lecturer clear, easy to hear, responsive to questions and well organized? Was the choice of topics and course readings appropriate? Was evaluation fair? To a degree each rating is unique and might help improve the course, but a factor analysis will reveal that just a few questions are needed to measure the overall quality of a course.

Survey researchers often face the opposite question, of whether a single item is adequate. Good research is done with individual items, for example the ubiquitous health measure that asks, 'In general, would you say that your health is excellent, very good, good, fair or poor?' and single-item measures of personal happiness (Layard et al., 2008). Of course, a lot is known about these particular measures from their use in many surveys.[1] It is more difficult to decide what constitutes adequate measurement when no previously tested measure is available. With a single item, the risk is that an apparently sensible question will be unreliable or invalid. Even one additional question on the topic provides some evidence on that score. Also, it is often valuable to measure respondents' knowledge about or interest in the topic.

Consider the problem of measuring a more general concept, for example support for nuclear power generation. A person's attitude might combine a number of considerations, such as the cost, safety and environmental impact and the risks of fuel disposal. What is the minimum number of questions that should be devoted to this one element of a survey in which a number topics were competing for space? Just two items are required to provide some idea of the quality of measurement, but they yield only one covariance and so there is no quantitative basis for choosing between the two items if they disagree. Three items yield three covariances and four items yield six covariances. For short scales in sociology and political science, the reasonable convention is to employ between four and six items. If more space is available and the topic has a large number of distinct attributes, for example the qualities of a job, the number of consecutive items in the same format should be limited to about 10, beyond which item reliability declines.[2]

There is a highly technical literature on test development, but for a nice introduction more appropriate to general surveys see DeVellis (2012).

Writing Survey Questions

A good questionnaire provides the respondent with a coherent experience. There is more to be gained from maximizing the respondent's ability to give good answers

---

[1] On the health measure see Crossley and Kennedy (2002), and on life satisfaction see Krueger and Schkade (2008).

[2] Often one can hear this problem in face-to-face interviews when, for example, respondents are asked if they strongly agree, agree, etc. with a series of statements. After the first few statements it is common for respondents to restrict their answers to only 'agree' or 'disagree'. This leaves the interviewer in a bind. He or she senses that the respondent is just ignoring the 'strongly agree' and 'strongly disagree' answers, but reminding the respondent of the problem affects the 'standardization' of the interview, and usually is against the rules. Two solutions are to restrict the number of questions in a group or to have the script instruct all interviewers to remind respondents of all the response categories midway though a longer battery of questions.

than testing his or her alertness with rapid changes in topics and questionnaire formats. A survey should begin with easy questions that familiarize the respondent with the task and increase confidence in his or her ability to answer, then move to the hardest questions, then go back to easier questions at the point where the respondent may begin to flag. For a group of questions on one topic, it is better to ask consistent questions than to change the direction of items to reduce bias.

In Payne's 1951 volume and in textbooks over the years, advice on writing questions is not in short supply and the basic ideas can be described in just a few pages; for example see Groves et al. (2009: 242–252) or Krosnick and Presser (2010). Writing good questions involves just three basic principles: questions need to be understood; they need to be answerable; and the response categories should fit the question.

The first concern is whether respondents understand the question in the intended way, and the most important problem is ambiguity. Consider some examples of:

- *activities and events*: Have you been shopping if nothing was purchased or if you picked up groceries on the way home from work? Is a brisk walk 'exercise'? Is a person watching television if they are caring for a child who is watching? Does 'seeing a doctor' include visits to a hospital emergency department or being treated by a nurse?
- *nouns*: Does 'income' include all income or just employment income, before or after tax? Does the 'year of immigration' refer to when a person first visited a country, when they came to settle, or when they assumed the legal status of a would-be immigrant? Is a truck a vehicle? What about a snowmobile?
- *adjectives*: Is 'annual' income for the last calendar year, or the past year from the time of the survey? What is the dividing line between part-time and full-time employment?

Correcting these ambiguities only requires more detail. Keeping questions short and simple is good, as long as they provide respondents with enough information to answer reliably. Survey designers may not see ambiguities because their training and knowledge lead them to fill in the missing details without their being aware of it.

Second, suvery questions should be answerable. One question from the ESS (Saris et al., 2010) asks respondents if they agree that, 'Before doctors decide on a treatment, they rarely discuss it with their patient.' How could a lay person answer this question? Rather than being factual, the question appears to tap a dislike or distrust of physicians or the medical system, or perhaps respondents generalize from their own limited experience, though what a respondent makes of the question cannot be known from their response. Rather than a subtle means to measure attitudes, ambiguous questions and questions making untested assumptions about what respondents' know merely have a high level of measurement error.

There are also technical criteria for answerable questions: a question should deal with one issue, rather than being 'double-barrelled'; a question should not be so long or detailed that the respondent is unable to remember all the details – but it should provide sufficient detail to be clear. In interview surveys, the respondent should be given enough time to answer thoughtfully.

Third, the response categories should fit the content of the question and the metric and precision of respondents' natural way of answering. For questions with inherently numerical answers, recording the exact value makes the question easier and decreases measurement error. It is easier to answer '2' or '3' or '4', than to choose the category '2 to 4'. When the potential answers include large numbers or it is difficult for respondents to answer exactly, grouped categories can make sense, but first consider whether it would not be better to ask for a rounded answer. For example, a question about expenditures or income could ask for an answer to the nearest 100 or 1000, or 10,000, depending on the topic and currency.

For questions where the answers are divisions of an abstract continuum, such as agreement with a statement or ratings of various kinds, the number of response categories should correspond to the respondent's ability to differentiate. Four or five categories are sufficient for most topics. Nine- or eleven-point scales are appropriate for ratings of central aspects of life, where respondents can have highly differentiated responses. Respondents can give answers for longer scales, with 20 or 100 or even 1000 points, and there may be reason to use them to allow comparisons to another survey, but the greater range does not increase the precision of measurement. Three-category answers should be avoided if the middle category indicates neutrality or ambivalence; depending on the topic, it is better to ask the respondent to choose between two categories or to expand the number of categories to five.

Questions about Identity and Behaviour ———

In the 1980s when the HIV pandemic grew, surveys were developed to count the numbers of male same-sex contacts. Researchers found that significant numbers of men who had sex with men did not regard themselves as 'gay'. Referring to sexual orientation or identity when posing questions about sexual behaviour resulted in underestimates of the numbers of same-sex sexual contacts and especially of the number of *opposite-sex* contacts of men who also had sex with men. These are called surveys of men who have sex with men, or 'MSM surveys'.[3]

There is a corresponding distinction between persons who say they 'have a disability' and people whose everyday lives are affected by disability. So surveys about disability focus on and are often called studies of 'activity limitation'. Still another aspect of disability concerns accommodation from state and private institutions, for example accommodation in submitting university coursework and writing exams. Indeed an index of the effectiveness of programmes of accommodation is the degree to which their intended beneficiaries come forward. Thus 'disability' involves complex relations between identity, behaviour and claims for recognition by voluntary, state and governmental institutions.

---

[3]For example, see the European MSM Internet Survey at http://www.emis-project.eu/project.

These conceptual distinctions arise in other areas: a person's ancestry is not the same as her racial identity; a person may think of herself as unemployed, when by official definition she is not, and vice versa; a person's sex may differ from her gender identity; and voting for a political party is different from identifying with the party. When both are measured, the relationship between the more objective and subjective measures can be very revealing.

Education, Labour Force and Economic Position

Except to economize on the number of questions, almost always it makes sense to measure education, labour force characteristics and economic position by using questions from major government surveys. Because they are used for the national accounts and other national and international economic standards, these questions are designed with great care. Also, using a standard question provides usually free comparisons to high-quality official surveys. The same logic applies to demographic measures, such as age, gender, relationship to other members of a household, place of birth, ancestry and year of immigration.

For education, more detailed surveys measure years of full-time schooling, all degrees and diplomas and often the fields of apprenticeship and post-secondary credentials as well as *incomplete* post-secondary attendance (substantial numbers of people attend college or university without completing a degree). Although the number of years of education was once the economists' standard measure, completed degrees and diplomas have a substantial impact on earnings and other outcomes, net of years in school. If there is space for just one question, the logic is to ask for the 'highest level of education' with detailed categories that include incomplete levels, such as 'some university'. Because of differences between educational systems, international comparisons of the effect of education are not simple (see Schneider, 2010). For persons educated outside the country of a survey, it can make sense to use an open question, record the answer verbatim and code the answer later.

In measuring income the two biggest problems are the refusal to answer and respondents who do not know their income. Also, underestimates result from respondents' tendency to interpret a question about income as a question about earnings only and to report take-home pay, rather than earnings before taxes and deductions. If there is time for only one question, an example of good practice, from Statistics Canada, is:

> What is your best estimate of your total personal income, before taxes and deductions, from all sources during the year ending December 31, 2010?

People who cannot or refuse to answer this question are asked if their income is under $30,000 and, if they answer, a further question gives them a choice of six or seven more detailed income ranges – a method known as 'unfolding'. Somewhat better answers, though for most surveys it is not worth the additional time, are obtained by first asking if the respondent had any income from a number of sources, reading a checklist that includes sources other than employment, such as rent and interest.

To ask about *household* income, Statistics Canada first asks how many members of the household other than the respondent received any income from any source in the previous calendar year and then asks a version of the question above that refers to 'your total household income, received by all household members', with a similar unfolding strategy if the respondent does not answer. For surveys that focus on income, much more detailed questions may be included, for example the GSOEP (2008) asks about 11 sources of income, and also measures some job benefits. Even the most careful questions about income are prone to significant measurement error – Moore et al. (2000) provide an extensive review. In surveys conducted by government agencies, an attractive alternative to measuring income in a survey directly is to ask respondents to give permission to access the income figures reported in their tax returns.

While income is a fundamental dimension of the distribution of rewards in society and it is related to almost every aspect of how people live, a person's level of 'consumption' more directly describes their level of welfare. Consumption is less variable than income because people save extra income and, if they are able, dis-save when their income is not sufficient. Especially for poor people, there is strong evidence that consumption is a better measure of well-being than income (Brzozowski and Crossley, 2011; Meyer and Sullivan, 2011). Measuring only income also ignores the benefits of wealth, of which the most important is home ownership. The value of owner-occupied housing can be conceived in terms of the 'imputed rent' that would otherwise be spent on that accommodation. As well as smoothing variation in income, liquid assets are insurance against unexpected misfortune, such as job loss, illness and marital separation.

Governments conduct regular surveys of consumption in order to measure changes in the cost of living, which requires information on both the prices and purchases of goods and services. The measurement of wealth is less institutional-ized, although many countries have regular surveys. Accurate measurements of both consumption and wealth require long and complex surveys devoted to only those topics. Consumption is measured with spending diaries and/or by asking the respondent to recall spending on exhaustive lists of goods and services. The detail reminds respondents of purchases they may have forgotten, but results in very high respondent burden. Assets and liabilities are measured with long lists enumerating the huge variety of possible possessions, investments and forms of debt.

Measuring consumption and assets with a few questions in a larger sur-vey can significantly improve the understanding of material conditions and the many aspects of life they affect. The difficult challenge is to identify the types of consumption that are critical to well-being and develop a small number of questions that respondents can reliably answer. Clearly the place to begin is with housing and related utilities, then perhaps to continue with questions about transportation (especially if it is required for work) and food, and maybe obligatory repayments for student loans. For one such effort see Browning et al. (2003).

For assets, the place to begin is with home ownership, also asking homeowners to estimate the approximate value of their property and the amount outstanding on any mortgage. Second most important, perhaps, is a measure of financial assets, but a simpler alternative is to ask whether a household could cope with the emergency need for a large expenditure and, if it could, how the money would be found.

Measures of consumption can also be used to measure material deprivation. The idea is to determine whether people can afford the necessities of life (an OECD review is Boarini and d'Ercole, 2006). An example from Statistics Canada[4] begins by asking, 'Do you and your family eat fresh fruit and vegetables every day?' If the answer is 'no', the next question asks, 'Is this because you cannot afford it, or for some other reason?' Other questions ask if the respondent and his or her family are able to:

- obtain dental care if needed;
- replace or repair broken or damaged appliances;
- get around the community, either by having a car or by taking the bus or an equivalent mode of transportation; and
- buy some small gifts for family or friends at least once a year.

In a similar vein, there are good measures of 'food security', which measure hunger and malnutrition (see Wunderlich and Norwood, 2006).

In order to classify occupations accurately it is necessary to ask for a respondent's exact (usually called 'detailed') occupation in an open question, and then manually or with some automated help classify the responses into one of several hundred occupations. The classifications of detailed occupations used by national statistical agencies[5] to some extent incorporate industry, so it is common for questionnaires to include that question, which also requires coding an open response into one of several hundred categories; sometimes there are also questions about a person's main work tasks.[6] This is very costly in terms of questionnaire time and effort required for classification. The problem is that

---

[4]The questionnaire for the *Ontario Material Deprivation Survey* is at http://www.statcan.gc.ca/imdb-bmdi/instrument/5161_Q1_V1-eng.pdf.

[5]As well as national and multinational occupational classifications, the International Labour Organization has an international classification. Look at http://www.ilo.org/public/english/bureau/stat/isco/isco08/index.htm.

[6]The GSOEP (2008) wording, which is typical, reads:
What is your current position/occupation? *Please give the exact title. For example, do not write 'clerk', but 'shipping clerk'; not 'blue-collar worker', but 'machine metalworker'. If you are engaged in public employment, please give your official title, for example, 'police chief' or 'Studienrat'* [emphasis in original].

respondents cannot reliably describe their jobs in terms of skill or even in terms of the traditional white-collar/blue-collar distinction (where do technicians fit?).

Until the 1980s prestige and socio-economic scales of occupations were a major interest in sociology, the former based on survey ratings of social standing of occupations and the latter on the education and income of persons in an occupation, usually computed from a census (Ganzeboom and Treiman, 1996). This research continues, but has become less central to thinking about inequality, which has come under the influence of economists. Likewise the interest in categorical, Marxist or Marxist-inspired classifications based on occupations in combination with business authority and/or ownership has declined somewhat (but see Bergman and Joye, 2005; Leiulfsrud et al., 2005; Lambert and Bihagen, 2011).

———— Using Survey Experiments for Research on Attitudes ————

Survey experiments, which began as a tool for developing survey questions, have developed into a unique and powerful strategy for studying attitudes and understanding complex social judgements. While the use of experiments to study attitudes is an interesting though incremental extension of that methodological research, the studies of judgement involve genuine innovation.

An example of the former is Schuman and Bobo's (1988) research on support for government enforcement of the right of black families to live in white neighbourhoods in the USA. They found that racial prejudice, opposition to government regulation, and class prejudice each affect attitudes towards housing segregation. The questions in their experiments varied the group potentially subject to discrimination, comparing blacks, Japanese-Americans and Jews, comparing regulation at the community level to regulation by a higher level of government, and measuring the effect of providing the assurance that the black family had the same income and education as other families in the neighbourhood. By asking only one of the experimentally varied questions to different, randomly selected fractions of the sample, they avoided the order effects that would inevitably arise from asking respondents two or more variants of the same question. Kuklinski et al. (1997) explore attitudes towards affirmative action in hiring for African-Americans in similar terms.

Political scientist Paul Sniderman did much to develop and encourage the use of experiments to study racial attitudes (for example, Sniderman and Piazza, 1993; Sniderman et al., 2000) and his research gave birth to the remarkable cooperative survey venture initiated by Arthur Lupia and Diana Mutz in 2001, with funding from the US National Science Foundation. Their *Time-Sharing Experiments for the Social Sciences*[7] provides researchers with the opportunity to apply to have their survey experiments included in a national survey without cost.

---

[7]See http://www.tessexperiments.org/introduction.html.

Sociologist Peter Rossi (1979; also see Rossi and Anderson, 1982) took survey experiments in an entirely new direction. Rossi recognized that experiments could be used to study complex social judgements, for example the appropriateness of earnings, the seriousness of crimes, support for government expenditures and what actions constitute sexual harassment. Sniderman and Grob (1996), Wallander (2009) and Atzmüller and Steiner (2010) provide extensive reviews of the method and results of this research, and Nock and Guterbock (2010) and Mutz (2011) provide discussions on the uses and practicalities of survey experiments. The strategy can be seen as an elaboration of studies of the prestige of occupations in surveys of the 1950s, where respondents were asked to sort occupations, printed on cards, into ordered categories of 'social standing'. A serious limitation was that every respondent was required to rate each of a set of occupations.

Rossi realized that survey respondents could be asked to evaluate 'vignettes' defined by experimental variation in more than one dimension and he christened the technique 'factorial surveys' because the number of possible vignettes is equal to the product of the numbers of categories in all the dimensions. Examples of the vignettes rated in one study of occupational prestige, for example, were for 'Barbara Wells, Stock Clerk' and 'Kenneth Taft, Box Packer', and, for comparison, some occupations were specified without the incumbent's gender (Bose and Rossi, 1983: 319). So, the effect of gender on the rated prestige of an occupation is measured by comparing the average ratings of the same occupation with male and female incumbents.

When the vignettes vary in more than two dimensions the number of unique vignettes easily becomes much larger than any one survey respondent could evaluate. Rossi recognized that it was sufficient for each respondent to rate only a random sample of all the possible vignettes.[8] For example, Alves and Rossi (1988) asked survey respondents to rate the fairness of household earnings on a nine-point scale from 'extremely overpaid' to 'extremely underpaid', where the vignettes described a man or a woman in a one-person household or a couple and give their education, occupation (51 titles were used), gross annual earnings and net earnings (taxed at various rates ranging from 0 to 35 per cent). So there are many thousands of possible combinations. The impact of the experimentally varied factors was measured by regressing the rating of fairness on the characteristics of the vignettes. In respondents' assessments of fair earnings of a couple, Alves and Rossi found that each year of education of the husband was worth almost twice as much a year of education of the wife (p. 553). Also, respondents preferred a more compressed distribution of income because, on average, they judged the highest earners as overpaid and the lowest earners underpaid, accounting for their educational and occupational qualifications (p. 550).

---

[8]Atzmüller and Steiner (2010) consider alternatives to a random selection of vignettes for each respondent.

Because the individual factors are buried in a more complex vignette, respondents may be unaware of how their judgements are affected by the different factors, and certainly they would not be able to quantify their relative effects. Respondents whose answers revealed that they think women deserve lower earnings, for example, might not be willing to express discriminatory attitudes; indeed they might not have consciously discriminatory attitudes.

Analysis of factorial survey data yields *overall* estimates of the effect of each factor on the measured judgement, for example the effect of gender on what constitute fair earnings. Not only is the effect of gender likely to vary across respondents, its magnitude could be affected by the respondents' characteristics, such as their gender, age, education and attitudes, which could also be measured in the survey. In statistical terms, the judgements of all the vignettes rated by each respondent constitute a cluster and the vignette data can be characterized as hierarchical, where the judgements of individual vignettes are nested within respondents. Jasso (2006) provides a complete formulation of vignette experiments in a multi-level framework that measures between- and within-respondent variation in judgements and how this relates to the respondent's characteristics.

Although the validity of the experimental findings rests on the random allocation of vignettes to the survey respondents, not on any particular characteristic of the sample, surveys with experiments are not exempt from the hazards of generalizing to a larger population from a survey of a small locality or from a non-probability sample or a probability sample with a low response rate. For more descriptive research, a drawback of experimentation is that all respondents do not answer the same question and so describing the distribution of responses is not a simple matter.[9]

Total Survey Error ——

Total survey error (TSE), whose name is taken from the title of a 1979 book by Anderson et al., is a conceptualization of the entire chain of survey design and execution between the conceptualization of a measure and the final results. In principle this provides a basis for the efficient allocation of resources in the individual steps of the survey process. The subtitle of Herbert Weisberg's 2005 book on the topic is *A Guide to the New Science of Survey Research*. In the 2010 special issue of *Public Opinion Quarterly* on TSE, Groves and Lyberg conclude that 'For many within the field of survey methodology, it is the dominant paradigm'

---

[9]One strategy is to disregard the experimentally varied form or order of the questions, thus implicitly treating the experimental variations as the natural range of ways of asking the question. An alternative is to combine the responses to the question asked in all the different ways in a single model that includes variables indicating which question was answered by each respondent. But the resulting analysis is neither simple nor easy for another data user to replicate. A third possibility is to consider only the randomly selected fraction of respondents who, analysis showed, answered the 'best' question, but this comes at the cost of reducing the size of the available sample.

(p. 849), and the website of the Program in Survey Methodology at the University of Michigan's Institute for Social Research proclaims: 'Survey methodology is the study of sources of error in surveys.'[10] The textbook on survey methodology by Groves et al. (2009) is organized around TSE.

Although he did not use the label, the TSE is usually traced to statistician W. Edwards Deming's 1944 *American Sociological Review* article 'On errors in surveys'. He goes beyond conventional statistical considerations of the sources of survey error to the idea of the survey in the production of knowledge, including:

- 'bias of the auspices', which arises from respondent reaction to the survey sponsor;
- 'changes that take place in the universe before tabulations are available';
- 'omitting questions that would be illuminating to the interpretation of other questions';
- 'bias arising from an unrepresentative selection of the date for the survey'; and
- 'errors in interpretation', arising from 'bad curve fitting', 'failure to take account of respondents' difficulties' and 'personal bias in interpretation'.

The modern idea of TSE is to treat each step in the design and execution of a survey as resulting in a component of error that contributes to the discrepancy between the research objective and the survey data. In statistical terms, the TSE is a measure of the error in a variable, conventionally just error in mean for the entire sample and so, just like the usual term for sampling error, its value is different for each variable in a survey. Conventional sampling error is just one component of TSE. The statistical model is that the observed value of the variable is the sum of the variable's true value and a number of components of bias, for example due to the lower response of some groups in the target population, wording of the question and the presence of an interviewer, and a number of components of variation, including sampling error, differences in the interpretation of a question and variation in the behaviour of interviewers (for a formal development, see Biemer, 2010a: 44ff.).[11]

The value of the TSE perspective is that it incorporates the effects of every step of the survey process and so it draws attention to the idea that good surveys require effective compromises between the different sources of error. For example, the high cost of persuading reluctant respondents to answer a survey results in a compromise between a smaller sample with a higher response rate, resulting in lower bias, and a larger sample with a lower response rate, resulting in lower sampling error. Another tradeoff is between a longer survey with a smaller sample, resulting in smaller measurement error and a shorter survey with a larger sample, lowering the sampling error. If the different components of TSE can be measured, then its

---

[10]http://psm.isr.umich.edu/overview (accessed on 30 January 2012).

[11]Some of the components of TSE can be estimated using an 'interpenetrated design', invented by Mahalanobis (1946), whereby at each stage of data collection from interviewing through to production of the final data, the sample is randomly divided in two. Accounting for random variation, comparisons between the two halves measure the error introduced at each stage.

proponents argue that the 'paradigm provides a theoretical framework for optimizing surveys by maximizing data quality within budgetary constraints' (Biemer, 2010b: 817).

One direction in the elaboration of TSE has been improved conceptualization of the components of error. A nice idea, due to Groves et al. (2009: 48), is to think of each survey statistic as *a particular measure* for *a particular population*. The measure begins with a concept, which is embodied in a survey question; this evokes a response, which is processed into a survey datum. Representation begins with a population of interest, which might be restricted in designating the 'target population', some of whose members might be missing from the sampling frame from which a sample is selected, not all of whom respond. Errors arise at each juncture. Invality, for example, involves slippage between the researcher's concept and the corresponding survey question, and measurement error captures influences on a respondent's answer, outside a factual reading of the question.

Smith (2011) advocates a still broader idea of TSE, which he christens 'total survey measurement *variation*', to include the impact of both empirical and conceptual features of a survey – such as the different components of a complex concept, such as morale – and necessary (but to a degree arbitrary) decisions, such as when a survey takes place.

What began as a mainly technical consideration of error also led to efforts to think about the value of a survey in the broader terms of 'quality'. Biemer and Lyberg's *Introduction to Survey Quality* conceives of surveys as a form of production: 'To achieve error prevention and continuous quality improvement, a process perspective should be adopted' (2003: 25). This is a fitting legacy for Deming, who is *the* legendary figure in the development of industrial quality control, renowned for his role in Japan's post-war economic recovery.

While TSE brings an important, unified conception to the complexity of the survey enterprise, ordinary surveys do not provide a basis for estimating the many components of error, let alone the totality of bias and variance. For example, to estimate the impact of the survey mode on error requires that groups of respondents with similar characteristics be surveyed in different modes, and often very little is known about sample under-coverage. The truly extraordinary effort and cost of measuring TSE effectively restricts its use to the largest and most important surveys conducted by national statistical agencies.

The idea that a survey is the sum of its errors is not very inviting. Indeed, Deming's (1944) foundational article ends on this wonderfully pragmatic, upbeat note:

> It is not to be inferred from the foregoing material that there are grounds for discouragement or that the situation is entirely hopeless with regard to the attainment of useful accuracy. My point is that the accuracy supposedly required of a proposed survey is frequently exaggerated – is in fact often unattainable – yet the survey when completed turns out to be useful in the sense of helping to provide a rational basis for action. Why? Because both the accuracy and the need for accuracy were over-estimated.

Conclusion

Questionnaire design is deceptively simple. Surveys use everyday language, researchers are usually experienced writers, and there are useful guidelines for writing questions. For the researcher, one challenge is that the ambiguity in everyday language is often not visible to someone who is knowledgeable and immersed in a survey topic. Researchers often write questionnaires for survey respondents who are unlike them in education, interests and culture. Sensitivity to this difference is an important element of the craft of questionnaire design, as is the ability to write questions that truly reflect a theoretical concept and which respondents can understand and answer. Often the most difficult design decisions involve hard-to-quantify judgements about the topics of questions and the number of questions devoted to each, especially for collaborative projects.

4

Fundamentals of Probability Sampling for Surveys

A sample design is an answer to the question 'For this research, minimizing cost, what kind of sample and how large a sample is needed?' In principle this is a statistical question, but only rarely can it be answered precisely. One reason is that sampling error, which is what sampling statistics can predict beforehand, is only one component of error in survey-based results – as the TSE perspective says. While the other components of error are not known with much precision, a more serious concern is that it is quite common to ignore them completely, so that the sample estimates have substantially larger errors than predicted from the standard calculations based on the sample design parameters.[1]

A more difficult and interesting aspect of sample design, however, arises from the inherently multi-purpose nature of almost all surveys. The high cost of mounting a survey and the additional research possibilities resulting from the inclusion of each new measure lead researchers to specify multiple objectives; indeed many surveys involve explicit collaborations designed to maximize their range. Even when the primary goal is to measure a well-defined outcome, almost always the variation between subgroups is also important and there it is much more difficult to set limits. For example, it is common to expect both gender and age differences in a survey outcome – but the age trajectories could be different for women and men, so it is necessary to have a sufficiently large sample in each age category, separately for women and men. To the extent that the design criterion is the sampling error in subgroups of the population, setting limits becomes much more difficult.

Since the size of the sample, and usually to a lesser extent the type of sample, are usually the main determinants of the cost of a survey, a sample design represents a strategy for most effectively spending the money available for data collection as well as a compromise between competing research objectives.

---

[1]For very helpful comments on this chapter I thank my colleage Bryn Greer-Wootten.

Like questionnaire design, applied survey sampling combines theory and the lessons of practice. Although statistical theory is unbending in a way that the rules of questionnaire design are not, survey sample design seldom has the precision of data analysis. The process of designing a questionnaire changes and refines the research question, and sample design is no different. In the words of the statistician Leslie Kish:

> The survey objectives should determine the sample design; but the determination is actually a two-way process, because the problems of sample design often influence and change the survey objectives. (1965: 4)

The defining characteristic of a probability sample is random selection. While each element need not be chosen with the same probability, the selection must be based on chance, and the probability that an element is selected must be known. The probabilities make it possible to calculate *unbiased* estimates of characteristics of the sampled population, which means that the average of all the estimates made from many, many different imagined samples, each one selected randomly, is equal to the 'true' population value. The expected difference between the sample-based estimate and the population value is the *sampling error*. The critical question is how the sample structure and size affect the error.

The title of this chapter is not to be taken as an argument that only probability sampling is legitimate. In Kish's words again:

> No clear rule exists for deciding exactly when probability sampling is necessary, and what price should be paid for it. The decision involves scientific philosophy and research strategy … Probability sampling for randomization is not a dogma, but a strategy. (1965: 29)

This chapter deals with the concepts and uses of survey sampling and the statistical fundamentals and the next chapter addresses the key issues in applied sampling, including the appropriate use of probability and non-probability samples and how to decide on the sample design and the sample. We begin with a general discussion of probability sampling, starting with the three fundamental sample designs of simple random samples, stratified samples and cluster samples. With this conceptual framework in place, the same ground is covered in statistical terms. At the cost of some repetition, this gives a clearer view of the relations between different sampling designs and the overall statistical framework of survey samples.

This introduction draws heavily on Kish's magisterial *Survey Sampling* from 1965, although the key formulae and their derivations[2] can be found in any

---

[2]Unlike the aspects of survey methodology associated with social science, including question and questionnaire design and survey pretesting, in sampling statistics it is not common to provide reference to the origins of basic formulae. Instead, to varying degrees, each author derives them from the underlying mathematical principles. This chapter proceeds in the same manner, so the results may seem to be 'pulled out of a hat'.

basic introduction to the topic. While it remains a fine reference on basic applied sampling, Kish's volume was written long before the advent of large-scale telephone surveys and the invention of Internet and multi-mode surveys, not to mention fast desktop computers and software for analysis of complex samples. Lohr (2010) provides a modern alternative attuned to contemporary statistical thinking and with many examples; a good, more traditional alternative is Levy and Lemeshow (2008).

——— The Target Population, Sampling Frames and Auxiliary Variables ———

The Target Population

Any sample design begins with an idea of the population that the survey is intended to describe, called the *target population*. Each member of the population is an *element*; each element in the sample is a *selection*; and each selected element for which data were gathered successfully is an *observation, case* or *subject*, depending on the discipline. The elements may be persons, such as adults, students, members of a visible minority or workers, or they may be groups or organizations, such as households, businesses and voluntary organizations. Defining the target population often means giving a precise definition to a colloquial category. For example: 'adults' – beginning at what age? 'workers' – even if they work one hour a week? 'students' – full-time, part-time, in degree programme? 'retirees' – even if they returned to work in a new job? businesses – of some minimum size, including unincorporated businesses and self-employed persons without employees?

Coverage

The term *coverage* refers to the proportion of the target population that can actually be selected and surveyed, often expressed as a percentage. Defects in coverage are described as *non-coverage* or *undercoverage*. Practical and cost limitations often lead researchers to restrict the definition of the target population. So it is not unusual for population surveys to exclude persons who are homeless or live in an institution, do not speak a majority language, live in a 'remote' area, or do not have a telephone.

There is a subtle distinction between undercoverage and the exclusion of elements that are not properly members of the target population. It is not credible to think that people without a telephone landline, who in many countries are predominantly young non-parents, are not members of the adult population, but a case can be made for the exclusion of people in institutions. Unless the sample is very large, the exclusion of a small group only affects whether its members contribute to estimates of characteristics of the population, because there are usually not sufficient observations to estimate characteristics of the excluded group.

Undercoverage is problematic only when there is a systematic difference between the covered and not-covered segments of the population *for the variables measured by a survey*. The problem is that the technological, social and organization processes affecting coverage are seldom random. Take the seemingly innocuous omission of new telephone numbers after the publication of a printed telephone directory. The missing listings are disproportionately for people who are more mobile, including tenants and people experiencing changes in household composition, who will therefore be under-represented in the sample. People with 'unlisted numbers', who intentionally exclude their telephone numbers from a directory, are also distinct.

Sampling Frames

To select a sample requires a *sampling frame*, which is just a list of all the members of the population or sometimes a list of groups (such as households) that covers the population but does not identify individual elements. When the target population is defined by an institution, organizational records often provide the list, for example, students at a university, workers of a large firm or members of an association. Private and sometimes government lists can be used as frames for 'establishment surveys', where the unit of analysis is a business or governmental, non-profit or voluntary organization. A sample that is selected from a list of the *individual elements in the entire population* is called a *list sample*.

Except in the small number of countries with a population register, no list of the general population is available to researchers. The usual substitute is a list of addresses from property records or a private or government directory. If the research focus is on household characteristics – such as the household size, composition, and income and physical characteristics of the housing unit – the addresses provide a complete list of the population (other than homeless persons).[3] Then, to conduct the survey, it is only necessary to contact any informed household member. If the intent is to survey individuals, however, the problem is that an address may correspond to one *or more* persons. In order to select an individual at random, someone living at the address must be contacted and she or he must be willing to say how many eligible respondents live there and to identify them in a way that one (or more, sometimes) can be randomly selected. The situation is exactly the same when a sample is drawn from a list of household telephone numbers. In both cases the households constitute clusters.

For telephone surveys of the population, a printed or electronic directory can be used as a sampling frame, but it leaves out unlisted numbers. Printed directories omit new numbers, resulting in undercoverage. So, instead telephone surveys

---

[3]There are still details to be worked out, however, such as whether any person should be associated with a vacation or second home, whether to count residents who are away overnight at a school or job, and how to deal with children who spend some time with each of two parents who live apart.

often employ *random digit dialling* (RDD), where the list consists of plausible telephone numbers – the numbers are selected with some degree of randomness, but they have valid area codes and leading digits known to be in use. Such a list includes telephone numbers that are not listed in a directory, but also numbers that are not in service and working, but non-residential numbers. For RDD surveys, it is common to purchase lists of telephone numbers compiled by commercial organizations, using the numbers in directories to make guesses at numbers that are in service but not listed.

Sometimes one sampling frame does not cover the entire population. For example, there may be separate lists of landline and mobile telephone numbers. Anyone with both types of phone could be selected from either frame and so has a higher chance of selection than someone with only a landline or mobile. A *multiple frame sample* (see Lohr, 2009) involves selecting a sample from more than one frame. If the sampling frames are mutually exclusive, combining the data is straightforward, but if they overlap, to determine the probability that a person is selected it is necessary to ask each respondent whether she has an entry and so could be selected from each list employed for the sample.

Multiple frame samples are often used to lower costs, especially when some members of the target population are on an institutional list and some are not. For example, most practitioners in a profession might belong to a professional association, and they could be sampled from its membership list. Locating practitioners who are not members of the association requires a separate survey of the general population. Because the latter will require many calls to find each eligible respondent, the cost is much higher and so the question is how large each section of the sample should be. Often there is a temptation to live with bias resulting from the exclusion of hard-to-survey respondents to lower costs. Similarly, telephone survey costs can be reduced by combining a directory-based sample, where the numbers are very likely to reach a private household, with an RDD sample that also reaches unlisted numbers and people with new numbers.

Often there are defects in a sampling frame. A list may include *blank* and *ineligible* entries that do not identify population elements, such as vacant addresses, vacation homes and business addresses (when surveying households). These can be ignored, except that it might be necessary to increase the initial sample to make up for the blanks. Second, a list may have duplicate entries that are not detectable beforehand; for example a list of telephone numbers may not provide the information needed to identify two or more numbers reaching the same household. Households with more than one entry in a listing are more likely to be selected, so if this is possible, respondents should be asked if they have two or more numbers and these observations should be given a weight inversely proportional to the number of entries.

The most serious defect in a list sample is missing entries; for example, new members of an organization, people with an unlisted telephone number, and newly built dwelling units. Almost always the missing entries are distinctive in some way and their absence results in some degree of sample selection bias. This can only be remedied by finding a way to add them to the sample.

Auxiliary Variables

Sometimes a sampling frame provides 'auxiliary' information about the entire population, including respondents, non-respondents and elements not selected for the sample. Often this is true of samples of students, workers or service recipients taken from administrative records. If a list of telephone numbers includes addresses, they can be used to obtain information on a person's neighbourhood from a census or property records. RDD telephone samples, of course, do not have this information unless a number can also be found in a directory. The value of *auxiliary variables* is that they provide a basis for comparing the survey respondents to the population and compensating for non-response in data analysis, a process that is called *calibration* (Särndal and Lundström, 2008). Also, auxiliary variables can be used for sample stratification, discussed below.

Simple Random Samples, Systematic Samples and Balanced Samples

Intuitively, a sample is a miniature version of a population and the closest to this idea is a *simple random sample*, in which each element has the same probability of selection. Whether one element is selected has no effect on whether any other element is selected, so the selections are said to be *independent*. The proportion of the population selected is called the *sampling fraction,* denoted $f = n/N$, where n is the size of the sample and N is the size of the population.

Since elements are selected with the same probability, a simple random sample is an *epsem* sample, an acronym for 'equal *p*robability of *s*election *m*ethod'. Statistical computations with *epsem* samples do not require *weights*, since each observation has the same influence on an estimate. Any such sample is said to be *self-weighting*.

If, in the process of selecting a sample, a selected element *cannot* be selected a second time, selection is said to be *without replacement*, otherwise selection is *with replacement*. Except for cluster samples, discussed below, the difference[4] is usually unimportant and both methods yield *epsem* samples. Selection *without* replacement is often more convenient, though slightly more complicated statistically.

Rather than choosing the sample with a table or computer-generated random numbers it is usually easier to select a *systematic sample*. The idea is to choose every nth element from a list of the population, after a random start, where n is computed to give a sample of the desired size. In order to select a 10 per cent sample, for example, a number between 1 and 10 is chosen at random, say 6. Then the

---

[4]A statistical fine point is that for a finite population, selections for a simple random sample selected *without replacement* are not completely independent, because after the first selection each additional selection cannot be a previously selected element. If the size of the sample is small relative to the population the difference is negligible, but it has more consequence as the sampling fraction becomes larger.

6th, 16th, 26th, … observations are selected. If there is a suspicion that the list has some unusual periodicity that could coincide with the sampling interval, or just to be cautious, the list can be sorted randomly before the sample is selected. If the sample has been sorted randomly, to select a simple random sample without replacement it is only necessary to take the required number of beginning at the start of the list. For an interesting discussion of the surprisingly subtle problem of selecting a simple random sample, see Hirodoglu and Lavallée (2009). Systematic selection is used routinely for list samples.

Taking systematic sampling one step further, say that there is an 'informative' auxiliary variable that is strongly related to the survey outcomes of interest. When the sampling frame is a list of addresses, for example, the auxiliary variable could be a measure of the socio-economic condition of the neighbourhood, derived from a census. Now, before selecting a systematic sample, sort the sampling frame by the auxiliary variable. Even though the incomes of the *individual* households are unknown, sorting the list by *neighbourhood* income approximately sorts it by individual income, because the two are related. Then, the systematic selection of every *n*th address in the sorted list means that the selected respondents are spread uniformly through the income spectrum of neighbourhoods and *individuals*. This guarantees that the sample closely resembles the population in terms of neighbourhood and individual income.

If the sample is large, using the auxiliary variable has very little advantage because, *on average*, with a simple random sample the distribution of income in the sample is the same as in the population, and the resemblance increases with the sample size. If the sample is small, say less than 50, selecting a systematic sample after sorting by an informative auxiliary variable can substantially improve the resemblance between the sample and population, compared to a simple random sample.

More generally, a *balanced sample* is a random sample that is selected in a manner that assures it closely resembles the population, in terms of one or more auxiliary variables. While *the average* of all simple random samples exactly matches the same as the population, a balanced sample has less error than the average of all the imagined random samples. For the auxiliary variables measured for the entire population that are used to generate the balanced sample, there is no sampling error at all, while for variables *related to* the auxiliary variables there is less sampling error than a simple random sample.

With only one auxiliary variable, systematic selection can be used to select a balanced sample, but there are more general methods which can be used to align the distributions of sample and population values for many variables simultaneously (Berger and Tillé, 2009: 51ff.). Exactly measuring the statistical advantage of a balanced sample is not simple because traditional *design-based* analysis of survey data, which incorporates the effects of stratification and clustering, does not capture the statistical gains of a balanced sample. Instead it is necessary to employ more complex *model-based* analysis, which uses the auxiliary information employed in selecting the sample (Binder and Roberts, 2003).

Stratified Samples

Stratification involves dividing the survey population into two or more mutually exclusive groups, called *strata*, and then selecting a *separate* simple random sample in each *stratum*. To see the value of this strategy, consider a study of five communities, a large city with 80 per cent of the total population, and four small towns, each with 5 per cent of the population. Say that the budget provides for a sample of 1000. On average, a simple random sample would include 800 selections in the metropolis and 50 from each of the four towns, but because the one, large, simple random sample does not explicitly account for the presence of the five communities, the size of the sample in each community varies randomly, following a binomial distribution. In the four towns, 95 per cent of the time, the sample sizes would range from 37 to 66. The random variation in the proportions in the communities increases the sampling error and limits the ability to analyse and compare the four smaller communities.

Stratification solves this problem. It is only necessary to select five *separate* simple random samples, one in each community, with 800 selections in the city and 50 in each town. This is a *stratified sample*, where the communities are *strata*. Because the size of the sample in each community is made exactly proportional to its population, this design is known as *proportional allocation* and yields an *epsem* sample, and the sampling fraction is the same in each stratum. The sampling error from a stratified sample with proportional allocation is smaller than the error from a simple random sample of equal size because the sample in each stratum is exactly proportional to its population.

If the most important research goal is to compare the five communities rather than estimate characteristics of the entire population, proportional allocation is not optimal. Because the sample in each of the small towns is quite small, estimates of characteristics of the four towns have much greater uncertainty than estimates for the city. To maximize the precision of community comparisons, the sample in each group should be the same size – in this case 200 in each community, regardless of the size of their populations, assuming that the variation in the measures of interest within each community is about the same. Relative to their populations, this under-represents the city and over-represents the towns. The city is said to be *undersampled* and the towns *oversampled*. Of course, the sampling fractions in the five communities are no longer equal.

It is still possible to estimate characteristics *of the population* with this sample of 200 in each community, by accounting for community size. Each observation must be given a *weight* inversely proportional to its probability of selection. Because the city is 16 times larger than the towns, but is represented by the same size sample of 200, observations from the city have weights 16 times larger than observations from the towns.

Maximizing the precision of estimates of the differences between towns by selecting 200 observations in the city and each town significantly limits what can be said about the city dwellers that make up 80 per cent of the population. So, a common compromise that recognizes the importance of the metropolis while facilitating comparisons between the five communities is to select, say, 400 observations in the metropolis and 150 in each of the four towns, or perhaps 500 and four times 125.

When surveying business and other organizations it is common to stratify the population by size. Because size has a major effect on the nature and power of organizations, stratification provides assurances that there are sufficient observations to measure the effect of size. Also, since the largest units often have a disproportionate impact on estimated characteristics of the population, *not* explicitly controlling the number of large units selected can dramatically increase the sampling error. Of course, when stratifying by size it is common to have larger sampling fractions in the strata with larger units.[5]

Any sample design is only best for a specific research purpose. A simple random sample or stratified sample with proportional allocation treats all the observations equally, maximizing the precision of estimates of characteristics of the entire population, but at the potential cost of having too few observations to analyse smaller groups. Stratification allows the researcher to allocate more observations to identified groups, but the unequal probabilities of selection and resulting need for weights may substantially reduce the precision of estimates of the characteristics of the entire population.

Cluster Samples

Clusters are natural groups of population elements, such as households made up of individuals, employers with workers, classes of students and schools divided into classes. A *cluster sample* involves first selecting a random sample of *clusters*, called *primary sampling units* or PSUs, and then selecting a random sample of elements from each of the selected clusters. Within each cluster, it is possible to select just one element, a particular number or fraction of the elements, or all of them. Sampling error arises from both the random sampling of clusters and the random sampling of elements within clusters, which corresponds exactly to the within- and between-group variance in the classical framework of two-way analysis of variance. The difference between cluster and stratified samples is that elements are selected only *from selected clusters*, whereas elements are selected *from every stratum*. In the terminology of data analysis, clusters are *random*, while strata are *fixed*. If every cluster is selected, it becomes a stratified sample.

---

[5]Brewer and Gregoire (2009: 28) suggest that six is the optimal number of size strata, defined so that the strata are equal in total size. When the sample is small or when there are repeated surveys from the same population, a good alternative to stratification by size is one-stage random sampling with the probability of selection proportional to size. Also see Kish (1965: 92ff.).

If every element is selected from the clusters, there is no within-cluster contribution to sampling error. This is common, for example, in longitudinal household panel studies, which select every member of a household, and in surveys of students administered in school, college or university classes.

Elements from the same cluster are almost always more similar than elements from different clusters. For example, adults in the same household have similar levels of education and cultural background, and students from the same school tend to come from the same community and so their parents have similar levels of education and income. The homogeneity within clusters means that a cluster sample provides *less* unique information than a simple random sample of the same size, so estimates from the cluster sample are *less* precise. Of course, this loss of precision is different for each variable.

In order to estimate the within-cluster variance it is necessary to select at least two elements from each cluster, except for clusters with only one element such as one-person households. Surveys of households are often problematic in this regard because it is difficult to conduct more than one interview per household. The usual procedure is to select one person at random, either from a list of eligible members (the 'Kish' method) or with a less intrusive method, such as selecting the household member with the most recent birthday. Sometimes the selected respondent is asked to provide 'proxy' information about other household members.

Despite their greater statistical complexity and higher levels of sampling error, cluster samples have three important uses. First, a cluster sample must be used when there is no accessible list *of the population elements* from which to select a simple random sample or stratified sample, but only a list of clusters, such as household addresses, employers or schools. Selecting randomly *within a cluster* still requires a list of elements, *but only for the selected clusters*, and assembling those lists can be made into a separate step in data collection. So, *area probability* samples of households require, first, the random selection of areas (usually 'enumeration areas' or other areas defined by a census) – these are then clusters – and, second, a random selection of addresses within clusters. If no list of addresses is available, it is necessary to send someone to compile a list on the site, a procedure that is appropriately called 'listing' (Kish, 1965: 301f.). Similarly, in selecting workers within firms, it is only necessary to obtain a list of workers for the selected firms.

Second, cluster sampling often lowers the cost of data collection, because the cost of additional selections within a cluster is usually much lower than the cost of selecting additional clusters. In face-to-face surveys, blocks or other small areas are used as clusters because the proximity of selections makes it possible to visit a number of selected addresses on the same trip and to attempt to obtain an interview where there is no one home at a selected address or a person refuses. Taking firms as clusters of workers, the per-cluster costs include contacting a firm, convincing the managers to grant access to their workers, selecting a random sample of workers within the firm, and travelling to the firm to distribute questionnaires, whereas the much smaller per-worker costs include contacting the worker, administering the survey and entering the data.

The third and most analytically interesting use of cluster samples is for multi-level models (variously called multi-level, hierarchical and mixed models), which analyse phenomena at two or more levels simultaneously. Examples include students in classes in schools, workers within firms, and persons within households within communities (a good introduction is Snijders and Bosker, 2011). Multi-level modelling expands the classical idea of analysis of variance – variation between and within clusters – by explicitly incorporating the characteristics of clusters, measured independently (say the size of a firm or the characteristics of its pension plan) or obtained from the survey itself (such as average age or attitudes of the workers who complete a survey). Multi-level models allow the *relationships* between individual characteristics to vary within groups. Famously, the strength of the relationship between parental status and student achievement could vary between classes. And this variation could be a function of the teacher, the school or the school board.

Clusters need not be selected with simple random sampling. Think of a survey of workers based on a cluster sample of employers, all of which are listed and whose size is known. If a simple random sample of employers is selected and then the same *number* of workers is selected within each employer, in order to estimate the characteristics of the population of workers it is necessary to weight the observations by employer size; and the resulting highly unequal weights can dramatically increase errors. On the other hand, if the same *proportion* of workers is selected from each firm, the samples of workers in the largest employers will be many times larger than the samples in the smaller employers. This is undesirable because, after the first few selections, workers at the same employer provide a lot of redundant information, not to mention the potential difficulty in gaining access to them.

The solution is to select larger employers with higher probability. If employers are selected with a *probability proportional to size*, termed *pps* selection, and the same number of workers is selected at each employer, the result is an *epsem* sample. This is because the probability that a worker is selected is the product of the probability that the firm is selected (which is proportional to the size of firm, N_i for the ith firm) and the probability of selection for each worker in selected firm (equal to n/N_i where n is the *constant* number of selections per firm). Multiplying the two factors, the N_i cancel out, and the overall probability of a worker being selected is proportional to n, which is a constant, and the total sample size is just n times the number of employers selected.

Multi-stage Samples

Another effective strategy to deal with variation in the size of employers or other organizations is to divide them into strata on the basis of size and then select separate samples in each stratum. The result is a *stratified cluster sample* with *three* stages: (1) the strata for employers, based on size; (2) a random sample of employers, one for each stratum; and (3) a random sample of workers from each selected employer. The sampling fractions of the different employer size strata need not be equal and it makes sense to select large employers with greater probability because they have more economic impact and affect more workers. It is common to place very large units in the same stratum and select every one, called *selection with certainty*. Then, there are progressively smaller sampling fractions for the smaller size strata. Further complications can be imagined, such as *pps* selection of employers within size strata or stratification of workers within employers, for example separating management, manual and non-manual workers.

Actually, just such a sample was used for Statistics Canada's Workplace and Employee Survey (WES), described as follows:

> business locations [from a list of all businesses in Canada maintained by Statistics Canada] ... are stratified into relatively homogeneous groups called strata, which are then used for sample allocation and selection. The WES frame is stratified by industry (14), region (6), and size (3), which is defined using estimated employment [and then employees are selected from] lists of employees made available to interviewers by the selected workplaces.[6]

A sample with more than two stages is called a *multi-stage sample*, while the term *complex sample* refers to any design other than a simple random sample. Multi-stage samples involve a hierarchical combination of simple random, stratified and cluster sampling, but always with a simple random sample or selection of all elements at the lowest level.

Major population surveys by national statistical agencies almost always involve multi-stage samples. For example, here is a brief description of the Canadian *Labour Force Survey*, which, among other things, provides estimates of employment, nationally, for provinces and for larger metropolitan areas:

> The LFS uses a probability sample that is based on a stratified multi-stage design. Each province is divided into a large geographic stratum. The first stage of sampling consists of selecting smaller geographic areas, called clusters, from within each stratum. The second stage of sampling consists of selecting dwellings from within each selected cluster ... In each dwelling, information

---

[6]Accessed on 25 October 2011 from http://www.statcan.gc.ca/cgi-bin/imdb/p2SV.pl?Function=get Survey&SDDS=2615&lang=en&db=imdb&adm=8&dis=2. This survey also provides an example of how a target population may involve exclusions because a group is difficult to survey, is so small that it poses disclosure risks to the respondents, or is not governed by the same paradigm as the rest of the sample. The WES excluded Canada's northern territories, primary industry (agriculture, fishing, hunting and trapping), unincorporated family businesses, religious organizations and government. Unfortunately, this imaginative survey, which was the only systematic source of information on the work experience of Canadians and provided unique information on employers and their employees simultaneously, has been discontinued.

about all household members [age 15 and over] is usually obtained from one knowledgeable household member.[7]

Still another example is the design for a survey of high school students in a Canadian province:

- The province is divided into four regions: the dominant metropolitan area, the sparsely populated north, and two areas to the east and west; although the four regions differ in population, about one-quarter of the selections are allocated to each region.
- In each region, a sample of high schools is selected from the list of all schools, with probability proportional to school size.
- In each selected school in each grade, one class is selected at random.
- Within each selected class, every student is asked to complete a survey.

The regions are strata, the schools are clusters, the classes are clusters, and the students are the elements. The smallest geographical stratum is *oversampled* so there is sufficient precision in estimates for that stratum.

Multi-stage sampling is an extremely flexible framework that provides for the selection of a probability sample, provided there is: an initial listing of some kind that assigns the entire population to mutually exclusive units; a means to identify and select individual elements at the lowest level; and a way to select randomly at each of the other levels of aggregation.

Statistical Characteristics of Samples ———

Now we consider the statistical characteristics of the different types of survey samples, beginning with definitions of the two key statistical criteria, bias and sampling error, and then considering simple random samples, stratified and cluster samples in turn. For each of the three main types of sample, the key formulae are in a box. These formulae provide *design-based* estimates, meaning that they incorporate only information used to design the sample – the size of the sample and population, and the specification of any stratification or clustering.

Bias and Error

Because each random sample is different and none is exactly the same as the population, sample-based estimates have some degree of *sampling error*. Conventionally, the precision of a sample estimate is measured by the *standard error of estimate*, often called *the* standard error or just *the* error. Often it is useful to refer to its square, called the *error variance*. The standard error is just the standard deviation

[7]Accessed on 24 October 2011 from http://www.statcan.gc.ca/cgi-bin/imdb/p2SV.pl?Function=getSu rvey&SDDS=3701&lang=en&db=imdb&adm=8&dis=2. For more detail see Statistics Canada, 2008.

of the estimates that would be obtained from repeatedly selecting (in principle, infinitely) many random samples in exactly the same manner and the same size as the actual sample. Given an estimate of some characteristic of the population obtained from a sample (so the population value is not exactly known, due to sampling error), the range of possible population values is known as the *confidence interval*, and usually taken as the range where 95 per cent of the values are found.

Simple Random Samples

Sampling statistics begin with the *central limit theorem*, which says that when a simple random sample is selected from an infinite population, for any variable:

1 The sample mean is an unbiased estimate of the population mean.
2 The standard error of the sample mean is equal to the *population* standard deviation (which is usually not known and must be estimated from the sample) divided by the square root of the sample size.
3 For a sufficiently large sample, the estimates of the mean have a normal distribution.

Since the shape of a normal distribution is completely determined by its mean and standard deviation (the standard error, in point 2 above), the central limit theorem means that it is possible to calculate a confidence interval for the estimate of the *population* mean *from characteristics of the sample only*. Of course, this is the entire point of sampling – to use a sample in place of a population that is too large, too expensive or impractical to measure in its entirety.

As the value of the standard deviation in the population is usually not exactly known, but must be estimated from the sample, the sampling distribution of means has a Student's *t*, rather than a normal, distribution.[8] Except for very small samples – say under 50, though a larger number may be required if the variable has a highly skewed distribution – this has no consequence, because the *t* distribution converges to the normal as the sample size increases. A second distinction is that survey samples are selected from a 'finite' population, which means that as the size of the sample increases, it will eventually include a non-negligible proportion of the entire population.

Box 1 gives the formulae for the mean and standard error for a simple random sample. The *finite population correction* or *fpc* is equal to $\sqrt{(1 - f)}$, where f is the sampling fraction n/N; it accounts for the increased resemblance between a sample and the population as the sample becomes a larger proportion of the entire population. Compared to a sample that is negligible in size relative to the population, if the sample is half the population so $f = 0.5$, the *fpc* is 0.707 and the error is 29.3 per cent smaller; if $f = 0.2$ the *fpc* is 0.894 and the error is 10.6 per cent smaller; and if $f = 0.1$ the *fpc* is 0.949 and the error is 5.1 per cent smaller. For samples less than 10 per cent of the population, it is common to ignore the effect of the *fpc*.

[8]The Student's *t* distribution is similar to the normal distribution except it has bigger 'tails', and is governed by three, not two, parameters: the mean, standard deviation and degrees of freedom. The number of degrees of freedom is just the sample size minus one.

Box 1

Simple Random Samples

N is the size of the population and n is the size of the sample, so the sampling fraction f is n/N.

The n values of some variable y are designated y_i, where i ranges from 1 to n.

The estimate of mean y is $\bar{y}$, equal to the sum of all the y_i divided by n, $\bar{y} = \dfrac{\sum y_i}{n}$.

The standard error of $\bar{y}$ is $s_{\bar{y}} = \sqrt{1 - \dfrac{n}{N}}\dfrac{s_y}{\sqrt{n}} = \sqrt{1-f}\dfrac{s_y}{\sqrt{n}}$ and so $s_{\bar{y}}^2 = (1-f)\dfrac{s_y^2}{n}$.

For a systematic sample, which is usually more convenient to select than a simple random sample, in principle there is no design-based biased estimate of the error.[9] It is common, however, and perfectly acceptable to treat a systematic sample like a simple random sample, provided the sample has no periodicity that coincides with the sampling interval or the sample was sorted randomly prior to selection. If the systematic sample is selected from a list that was previously sorted according to an auxiliary variable, such as size or location, and especially if the sample is small, the simple random sample formulae err on the side of caution, as they overestimate the errors – perhaps to a meaningful degree.

Stratified Samples ——

A simple stratified sample is merely a combination of simple random samples, one for each stratum. Instead of just one sample size n, in each of the H strata there is a sample of size n_h, selected from a population of size N_h. As Box 2 shows, the *weight* of each stratum, designated W_h – effectively its influence on statistics describing the entire population – is equal to the size of the population in each stratum divided by the total population, so $W_h = N_h/N$. From the sample, the estimated population mean is just the weighted average of the means of

---

[9] If, for example, every 10th case is selected after a random start, the systematic sample involves the selection of one out of 10 possible samples. With one selection it is not possible to estimate the error. Alternatively, think of the sample as the selection of one observation from many strata, each with 10 observations. With one selection per stratum, there is again no way to compute the error. A possible solution is to select, say, four systematic samples with a four times larger interval between selections, then estimate the errors from the difference between the four systematic samples.

each of the strata, while the estimated standard error of the mean is obtained by adding the error variances in all the strata, each weighted by W_h^2.

The sampling fractions in the different strata need not be equal. If the primary research goal is to compare groups in the different strata – the most common example is geographical areas – the same-size sample should be selected in each stratum, *regardless of its population*. If the goal is to obtain the most precise estimates of characteristics of the entire population, then the size of the sample in each stratum should be proportional to its population. If the standard deviation of the variable of concern varies substantially across strata – a classic example is the difference in income or wealth between geographical areas – the most precise estimate of the population mean is obtained by making the size of the sample in each stratum, n_h, proportional to the *product* of the size of the stratum population and the standard deviation of the variable of interest, $N_h\sigma_h$. This is called *Neyman* allocation, after statistician Jerzy Neyman (1934).

If there are also considerable differences in the cost of observations in the different strata the most precise population estimate, based on *optimal allocation*, is obtained by adding a term for the cost to the formula above, so that the size of the sample in stratum h is proportional to $N_h\sigma_h\sqrt{c_h}$, where c_h is the cost per case in stratum h. So the optimal sample has a higher proportion of observations in the strata where the cost of each observation is lower. In employing this strategy for face-to-face surveys, fewer selections are made in areas where the cost of travel is high.

Box 2

Stratified Samples

There are H strata whose total population is N.

In stratum h, n_h elements are selected at random from a population of size N_h:
    the sampling fraction f_h is n_h/N_h
    the mean of y is $\bar{y}_h$ and its standard deviation is s_h^2

The weight of stratum h is $W_h = N_h/N$ and the sum of the weights $\sum_h^H W_h = 1$.

The estimated mean is $\bar{y} = \sum_h^H \dfrac{N_h}{N} \bar{y}_h = \sum_h^H W_h \bar{y}_h$.

The error variance of $\bar{y}$ is $s_{\bar{y}}^2 = \sum_h^H \left(\dfrac{N_h}{N}\right)^2 (1-f_h)\dfrac{s_h^2}{n_h} = \sum_h^H W_h^2 (1-f_h)\dfrac{s_h^2}{n_h}$.

With cluster samples there are two sampling fractions, designated: f_a for the cluster or primary sampling units (PSUs), so in the formula in Box 3, $f_a = a/A$, where a clusters are selected at random from a total of A clusters in the population; and f_b for the elements within PSUs, where $f_b = b/B$, where each cluster has B elements, of which b are selected at random. The formulae in the box, which assume the clusters are equal in size, show how the error variance of the mean is obtained by adding two components, one for the variation between clusters and one for the variation within clusters. Selecting every cluster turns a cluster sample into a stratified sample; then $a = A$ in the formulae and the between-cluster variance term disappears. Alternatively, selecting every element in a cluster so that $b = B$, the within-cluster variance term disappears.

Because the elements in the same cluster are similar to some degree, each additional selection *from the same cluster* contributes less new information. So cluster samples yield estimates with less precision than a simple random sample of the same size; by how much less depends on the degree of homogeneity within clusters. The similarity of elements in the same cluster is measured by the ratio of the between-cluster variance to the total variance, called the *intraclass correlation*, signified by Greek letter rho, ρ. The value of ρ, and therefore the effect of clustering on the precision of estimates, is different for each variable.

Holding constant the total sample size and selecting fewer clusters and more observations within each cluster do lower costs but result in larger errors in estimates of characteristics of the population, unless ρ is negligible. In order to obtain the most precise estimates for the entire population at fixed cost, Kish (1965: 269) shows that the number of selections in each cluster should be proportional to $\sqrt{[C_a/c \times (1 - \rho)/\rho]}$, where C_a/c is the ratio of cost for each cluster to the cost of collecting data for each observation *within* a cluster, and ρ is the intraclass correlation. If the cost of adding clusters is high relative to the cost of additional selections within clusters, one should select fewer clusters and more selections in each cluster. As ρ approaches zero, so members of the same cluster are no more similar on average than members of different clusters, it is optimal to select fewer clusters and more observations within each one. As ρ approaches one, so observations in a cluster become more and more similar; after the first selection in a cluster, the additional selections in the same cluster tell us almost nothing more, so there should be very few selections per cluster (but the minimum is two).

Except where the size of clusters is determined intentionally, for example in school classes whose size is regulated, clusters are *un*equal in size. City blocks, neighbourhoods, communities, employers and other organizations are not the same size. With unequal size clusters the formulae in Box 3 no longer apply. Also, if there is variation in the size clusters, the size of the sample is no longer fixed and is only known after the sample is selected. Estimating the mean of a variable then involves what is known as a *ratio estimator*: because the estimate is equal to the sum of the values of the variable for all the observations, divided by the sample size, *both* of which have sampling variation. In general, ratio estimators are biased, but this problem is well understood statistically and can be corrected. Incidentally, if the clusters in a sample are ignored and the data treated as if they were from a simple random sample, the sampling errors will be underestimated, potentially by a large factor.

For cluster samples with only one selection per cluster, which is common in telephone- and address-based surveys of households, the within-cluster variation cannot be measured. The result is not a simple random sample of individuals because the probabilities of selection are unequal: in a one-person household, that person is selected with certainty; in a two-person household, each member has a 50 per cent probability of selection, and so on. To obtain unbiased estimates of population characteristics, each observation must be weighted by the household size: a respondent from a one-person household gets a weight of one; a respondent from a two-person household, who 'speaks' for those two persons, gets a weight of two, and so on. Effectively, this is a stratified sample, with stratification by size of household.

Box 3

Cluster Samples (assuming clusters of equal size)

From a total of A clusters, a are selected at random, so the sampling fraction for clusters (or PSUs) is $f_a = a/A$.

Each cluster has B elements, of which b are selected at random without replacement, so the sampling fraction for elements is $f_b = b/B$.

To estimate the mean, divide the sum of y for all the selected elements, where $y_{\alpha\beta}$ is the βth element in cluster α; β goes from 1 to b and α goes from 1 to a, by the number of selections, which is just ab.

The mean of y, an unbiased predictor of the population mean, is $\bar{y} = \dfrac{1}{ab}\sum_{\alpha}^{a}\sum_{\beta}^{b} y_{\alpha\beta}$

The variance of y *within* clusters and the variance *between* clusters, s_a^2 and s_b^2, is

$$s_a^2 = \frac{1}{a-1}\sum_{\alpha}^{a}(\bar{Y}_\alpha - \bar{Y})^2 \quad \text{and} \quad s_b^2 = \frac{1}{a(b-1)}\sum_{\alpha}^{a}\sum_{\beta}^{b}(y_{\alpha\beta} - \bar{Y}_\alpha)^2$$

and then the estimated variance of $\bar{y}_h$, which combines the within- and between-cluster variances, is

$$s_{\bar{y}}^2 = \left(1-\frac{a}{A}\right)\frac{s_a^2}{a} + \left(1-\frac{b}{B}\right)\frac{s_b^2}{ab} = (1-f_a)\frac{s_a^2}{a} + (1-f_b)\frac{s_b^2}{ab}$$

f_a and f_b are small enough to be ignored

$$s_{\bar{y}}^2 = \frac{s_b^2}{ab}\left(1 + b\frac{s_a^2}{s_b^2}\right)$$

It is useful to be able to compare the errors resulting from different sample designs. The natural metric is a simple random sample and so the *design effect* of any sample design, designated D_{eff}, is defined as the ratio of its error variance to the error variance of a simple random sample of the same size. A nice interpretation of D_{eff} is that it indicates how much larger a sample must be to provide the same precision as a simple random sample. For example, a cluster sample with $D_{eff} = 2$ must be twice as large as a simple random sample to achieve the same precision, while a stratified sample with $D_{eff} = 0.85$ need be only 85 per cent the size of a simple random sample to achieve the same precision.

A stratified sample can be more efficient than a simple random sample of the same size because of the statistical benefits of forcing the sample sizes in the strata to exactly reflect their populations and/or oversampling strata with higher variance. Due to the similarity of the elements within clusters increases sampling error, for a cluster sample D_{eff} is invariably greater than one and selecting more observations in each cluster results in larger design effect.

The use of D_{eff} as a criterion of sample efficiency has two limitations. First, it takes no account of the cost. Rather than comparing two sample designs to the same number of observations, it might make more sense to compare designs with the same cost – so, because of the cost savings that are often possible with a cluster sample, one might compare the precision of estimates from a simple random sample to those from a larger cluster sample costing the same amount. A second limitation is that the value of D_{eff} depends on which variable is being measured, so the design effects might be quite different for a measure of attitudes, a measure of the perceived quality of life and a measure of earnings – which would make the design less straightforward.

Multi-stage Samples and Error Estimation

Because there is no limit to the combination of simple random, stratified and cluster sampling in the different stages of a complex sample, no single formula can be used to estimate the errors from a complex sample. Estimating population parameters, such as mean, proportion or regression coefficient, is still simple because each element's probability of selection is just the product of the probabilities at each level, and the appropriate weights are just the inverses of the probabilities. But estimating sampling errors is a completely different matter because of the complex combination of stratification, finite population corrections, weights and clusters. Until the mid-2000s, error estimation relied on explicit features of the sample design, usually with a sample design called *paired selection* – the selection of two clusters in a stratum – described by Kish as 'probably the most important key to design in survey sampling ... [as it] ... facilitates multistage selection with PPS from unequal clusters' (1965: 223).

Paired selection uses the difference between the two PSUs in *each* stratum to esti-mate the error that arises from clustering. A statistical procedure called *balanced repeated replication* produces an estimate of the overall error that adds up variation between clusters in all the strata, following McCarthy (1969). Another strategy, called *the jackknife*, provides estimates of errors by analysing the change in the esti-mates of a parameter, when different fractions of the sample are removed in suc-cession. A less popular variant is to select a small number of *complete* independent samples, say 8 or 10, instead of one larger sample. Then errors can be estimated by looking at the differences in the parameters computed separately from each of the independent samples. Except for large surveys conducted and analysed by central statistical agencies, these methods have fallen into disuse.

While it has long been known that a mathematical procedure called lineariza-tion[10] could be used to estimate errors for complex samples, it was not until the mid-2000s that computers were sufficiently fast and analysts sufficiently interested for these methods to find their way into the main statistical packages.[11] While linearization is a general approach, it is complicated by the need for a different calculation to estimate the error for each different statistical parameter. Current implementations do provide proper estimates for the standard descriptive statis-tics as well as a wide variety of linear models. Of course, to obtain the estimates it is necessary to specify the weight, cluster and stratum of each observation and the population of each stratum, as well as the structure of the sample.

Bootstrapping, developed by Bradley Efron (the standard reference is Efron and Tibshirani, 1993) is an even more general approach. The idea is to think of the population as consisting of an infinite number of copies *of the sample*. Then, from this imagined population, a large number of 'bootstrap samples'[12] or 'replicates' are selected following exactly the same sampling scheme that was used for the observed sample. If the original sample was a stratified cluster sample, for example, each boot-strap sample must be a stratified cluster sample of exactly the same size. Because ran-domness enters into the selection of each separate bootstrap sample, each is unique and gives rise to a separate estimate of a population parameter. The confidence interval of *any* population parameter is computed from the distribution of its values over all the bootstrap samples. The 95 per cent confidence interval, then, is just the range that includes 95 per cent of the values of a parameter estimated from all the

---

[10]In a nutshell, linearization uses a Taylor series to approximate the standard error for a complex sample. The error is *exactly* equal to a Taylor *series* made up of an infinite number of terms, though the series has a finite sum because the terms become smaller at a rate exceeding the increase in number. In fact, each term is much, much smaller than the previous one, and a good approxima-tion of the error in a complex sample can be obtained by taking only the first 'linear' term of the series. This is why a Taylor series 'approximation' gives proper results.

[11]These are: in SPSS, the complex samples procedures; in SAS, a variety of special purpose proce-dures such as PROC SURVEYMEANS and PROC SURVEYREG; in Stata, the svy commands; and Thomas Lumley's *survey* package in R (see Lumley, 2010).

[12]The name 'bootstrap' comes from the idea of pulling yourself up by your bootstraps, because that imagined population is made up from the one sample.

different bootstrap samples. A tremendous advantage of bootstrap errors is that it is possible to estimate the sampling errors for, literally, any statistical parameter, for example coefficients from a complicated SEM.

A simplification is that new bootstrap samples need not be selected for each analysis. Instead it is possible to supply the researcher with many sets of weights, each of which defines one bootstrap sample.[13] If these weights are included in the dataset, the user does not need to know the cluster and stratum memberships of the observations, which can be used to preserve confidentiality. Another advantage of pre-specified weights is that for complex samples, generating bootstrap samples may be a complicated process that one would not want to repeat for each analysis. Statistics Canada has pioneered the use of this technique as a way to provide access to microdata without compromising the privacy of respondents. A drawback of using weights to conceal the groups of observations in sample clusters, typically geographical areas, is that researchers are unable to use the cluster information to determine the effects of neighbourhoods or other cluster criteria on the survey outcomes. Essentially the information embodied in the cluster identities correctly enters into the estimation of confidence intervals, but the analysis does yield any parameters describing the degree of clustering (which is a key result from – and why researchers use – multi-level models).

Because it is conservative to assume that the distribution of the bootstrap estimates is not normal, it is common to use very large numbers of bootstrap samples – 500 is common – to determine confidence intervals, looking at the exact distribution of values, perhaps smoothed. Even with a fast computer, applying a complex statistical procedure to a large sample 500 times can require hours or even days.

As long as the survey dataset identifies the cluster and stratum of each observation, linearization is a simpler and much faster way to obtain error estimates for complex samples. Bootstrapping is necessary if the sampling information is withheld in order to protect the confidentiality of respondents or if there is no linearized estimate for the required statistical model. To confirm the robustness of the analysis, a researcher who relies mainly on linearized estimates for the analysis of a complex sample may want to duplicate to some of the work using the bootstrap.

Implicit in this discussion of the classical framework for error estimation for complex samples is the assumption that the estimates of population characteristics should incorporate the features of the sample design, but the effects of the design should disappear into appropriate estimates of the model errors. The formulae in Boxes 2 and 3, and their more complicated extensions for unequal

---

[13]Each bootstrap sample is made up of some combination of the existing observations, with each observation being included in a particular bootstrap sample an integral number of times. Thus every one of the bootstrap samples can be thought of as giving each of the sample observations an integer weight, 0, 1, 2, … , equal to the number of times it was selected. Of course, if the observations have sampling weights, they must also be used in the estimate obtained for each bootstrap sample.

size clusters and multi-stage designs, provide no explicit measures of the effects of clustering and stratification on the precision of estimates. For example, consider a sample of students based on sampling schools and classes – both are clusters. From the design-based perspective, the problem is to account for the effect of the clustering on the errors *without* providing an estimate of the extent to which classes and schools vary from one another. To measure the class and school effects requires a different, model-based approach, where features of the sample design are represented by parameters in the model.

———— **Conclusion** ————————————————————————————

Much of this chapter and the next could be omitted if researchers could always select a simple random sample from a list of the population elements. Not only is this often impossible, even when a simple random sample can be selected there are often analytical advantages to stratification and clustering, alone or combined in a multi-stage design. No different from questionnaire design, this is why sample design is creative and why good designs are not simply dictated by technical considerations.

Whatever the type of sample, a separate question is whether to select an *epsem* sample that gives each element the same probability of selection and does not require weights in computations. Stratification and clustering allow for systematic differences in those probabilities. Indeed the objective of classical sampling theory is to produce estimates with the greatest precision, for a sample of fixed size or sometimes at fixed cost. If the goal is to measure a variable that is highly skewed, such as wealth, it is optimal to oversample the population at the top of the distribution. If the emphasis is on group comparisons, there is a strong argument for selecting approximately equal numbers from each group, regardless of their relative size. If the main purpose is to characterize the entire population or to compare the largest groups in the population, and especially when a survey has a number of different research objectives, an *epsem* design makes the most sense. Now we turn to these and other practical questions.

5

Applied Sample Design

The statistics of sampling are necessary but not sufficient to answer the basic questions about a sample design: Is a probability sample really necessary? What kind of sample and how large a sample are needed? And how does one compromise between more precise estimates of characteristics of the entire population versus subgroups? While these are fundamentally statistical questions, sample design is almost always constrained by cost and by the many different cultures of survey research that establish norms for credible research. Also, there is almost no upper limit on the size of the best sample. There is hardly any field of research where a substantially larger sample will not open up new questions about subgroups and the detailed shape of relationships between variables.

This chapter begins with a discussion of *non*-probability samples, here called 'purposive samples' in order to emphasize that any sample should be designed and not haphazard. Often and wrongly, purposive samples are characterized as the last resort of unfunded graduate students – not to mention the related and touching belief in the sanctity of surveys based on probability samples whose response rate is so low that the resemblance between the sample and population is more a matter of luck than science.

Then we address *the* two big questions, about the structure and size of probability samples. The challenge is to provide general advice based on transparent assumptions that, to a degree, speak to the diversity of research areas using surveys. The design of any sample is constrained by the available sampling frame, cost and limits on data collection. Most important, if there is no list of the individual members of the population, but only a list of household addresses or telephone numbers or the names of associations, schools or firms, the simplicity, flexibility and efficiency of a simple random sample are not available. The resulting cluster sample is more complex and less efficient than a simple random sample of the same size.

Then we consider 'two-stage' sampling, which is used to survey members of subgroups who can only be identified by first sampling and contacting a random sample from a larger list of the entire population, and then surveying 'rare' groups where there is no sampling frame at all. The chapter concludes with a discussion of non-response.

Purposive Samples

Devoting one page in their entire text to non-probability samples, Levy and Lemeshow

> consider only probability samples, since we feel very strongly that sample surveys should yield estimates that can be evaluated statistically with respect to their expected values and standard errors. (2008: 19)

Kish's quite different view is that:

> No clear rule exists for deciding exactly when probability sampling is necessary, and what price should be paid for it ... If a research project must be confined to a single city ... I would rather use my judgment to choose a 'typical' city than select one at random. Even for a sample of 10 cities, I would rather trust my knowledge of U.S. cities than a random selection. (1965: 29)

The question is whether every legitimate survey can and should be designed to produce unbiased estimates of population characteristics. If so, a probability sample is the gold standard, even if it is invariably tarnished by some degree of non-response.

Uses of Purposive Samples

Purposive selection makes sense when the sample is very small and the researcher can choose typical elements, weed out unusual elements that could be selected in a simple random sample, and informally assure that the range of elements is represented. This is a common strategy for sampling of communities, though it can be followed by the selection of a probability sample within the selected communities. A small, purposive sample is usually sufficient for pretests before a larger survey or to develop a survey questionnaire. A detailed discussion is left to the next chapter, but the key requirement is that a pretest sample should resemble the main survey population, not that it should be a probability sample yielding unbiased estimates of population characteristics.

Purposive samples are sometimes necessary because there is no feasible probability-based alternative. A nice example is the survey of protesters at the 2010 Toronto G20 meetings by Stalker and Wood (2013). At a very large demonstration covering many blocks of the city they selected a sample of locations, handed out paper and pencil questionnaires to every seventh person at the selected locations, and asked participants to complete the survey and return it, on the spot. The same logic applies to research on people at risk, including undocumented persons, people engaged in illegal activity and groups subject to harm; see the section on respondent-driven sampling below. Purposive samples are also used to survey rare populations for whom the cost of a probability sample is prohibitive.

Purposive samples are often used for social experiments. An example is a Canadian study of 'individual development accounts', which provided low-income people with an incentive to save for education and training by providing matching funds in a segregated savings account (Leckie et al., 2010). Participants were recruited through contacts in local social agencies, the media, posters and government offices, although 'word of mouth proved to be the most effective way to attract new participants' (p. 31). Recruits were randomly assigned to the treatment and control groups (half the respondents were surveyed and given advice but not enrolled in the savings scheme). The validity of this research does not rest on the assumption that the sample is representative of the people who would be eligible for such a programme, but on the weaker and more plausible assumption that the *difference* between the treatment and control groups is the same for the purposive sample as in the population.[1]

The risk is that willingness to join the study is positively related to a person's ability to make effective use of the programme being tested, potentially leading to overestimates of the programme's effect. If the intended programme is voluntary, however, the actual participants are likely to resemble the experimental participants, so there would be no bias.

The Framingham Heart Study, so far the basis for more than 2000 peer-reviewed articles, began in 1948 with a random sample of about 5200 women and men, two-thirds of the adult population between the ages of 30 and 62 of just one town in Massachusetts. The ongoing study now includes the children and grandchildren of the original survey respondents. Here is the argument about the causes of cardiovascular disease (CVD):

> Although the Framingham cohort is primarily Caucasian, the importance of the major CVD risk factors identified in this group have been shown in other studies to apply almost universally among racial and ethnic groups, even though the patterns of distribution may vary from group to group.[2]

In other words, while there may be systematic group differences in the incidence of CVD, the effects of smoking, diet and other personal characteristics on CVD do not vary.

---

[1] A common problem in social experiments, however, is differential attrition over the period of the study because the treatment group is offered a significant benefit while the control group is normally offered a small incentive to continue answering surveys. The problem is not that control group members are more likely to drop out, but that the dropouts will differ systematically from those who continue, thus compromising the comparison between the treatment and control groups. To some extent it is possible to use measures from the initial survey to adjust for attrition.

[2] http://www.framinghamheartstudy.org/about/history.html.

Nevertheless, the Framingham researchers eventually saw a 'need to establish a new study reflecting a more diverse community of Framingham', and in 1994 they added a sample of about 500 persons of African-American, Hispanic, Asian, Indian, Pacific Islander and Native Americans from Framingham and surrounding towns; another 400 non-whites were added in 2005. For a probabilistic phenomenon such as CVD, however, these samples are too small to measure differences between the different non-white groups,[3] implying that the main distinction is between whites and non-whites. But there is no reason to think that differences between the different non-white groups are small compared to the white/non-white difference.

Another example, on a huge scale, is the *Ontario Health Study*, initiated in 2010 with the aim of recruiting 2 million people out of a provincial population of about 13.4 million for a 'long-term study that will help us understand the causes, prevention and treatment of diseases such as cancer, heart disease, asthma, and diabetes'.[4] Participants were recruited by advertisements on public transit, in print media and on the Internet. Again the validity of the study rests on the assumption that fundamentally similar processes affect the health of different segments of the population and that the sample is sufficiently varied to measure variation due to socio-economic position and other important structural differences, even if the study volunteers are unusually interested in their own health. Also, a comparison of the health records of the sample to non-sample members provides a basis for statistical adjustment.

The question of whether a probability sample with high non-response is invariably superior to a purposive sample arises with 'opt-in' Internet panels, where the respondents are recruited by advertisements on the Internet and with other non-probability methods and paid to answer surveys on a regular basis. Unlike small-scale purposive surveys, the opt-in panels are intended to be low-cost substitutes for probability samples of the population. Yeager et al. (2011) compared a probability-based (RDD) telephone survey, an Internet survey with respondents recruited with a combination of probability-based telephone survey and randomly selected addresses, and seven different 'opt-in' Internet 'panels'. Although all the respondents were paid for their participation, the response rates were low: 35.6 per cent for the telephone survey; 15.3 per cent for the probability-based Internet survey conducted by Knowledge Networks; and between 2 and 51 per cent for the seven opt-in Internet surveys. The authors concluded that the probability-based telephone *and Internet* surveys offered somewhat better precision than non-probability Internet surveys. Demonstrating the unpredictable quality of these panels, the opt-in survey with the highest response rate, 51 per cent, had the largest bias, while the one with the lowest response rate, 2 per cent, had the smallest bias.

---

[3] A scientist colleague pointed out that this depends on what is being measured and how much additional information is gathered. Samples this size are not unusual for genome-related health surveys.

[4] See https://ontariohealthstudy.ca/en/AboutTheStudy.

The fundamental problem with large-scale purposive surveys designed as a substitute for probability samples is not that they must be biased, but that the degree to which they represent the population depends on a chain of selection processes about which little is known.

Design of Purposive Samples

Three principles should guide the design of a purposive sample. First, even if similarity cannot be defined or measured precisely, a purposive sample should resemble the population of interest. Research on the measurement of material deprivation, for example, should employ a sample of low-income people, and a survey about political attitudes should study typical, often marginally informed voters, not political science professors and students or party activists. When a purposive sample is used to study attitudes, the greatest risk is inadvertently focusing on unusually knowledgeable and articulate respondents, which is much more likely to result in bias than demographic differences between the sample and designated population.

Second, and no different than for probability samples, stratification improves – and clustering threatens – the ability to generalize from a sample. Purposive surveys of a single group pose the greatest risk and the solution is to diversify the sample, for example by surveying students at three or four schools instead of just one, or selecting several neighbourhoods for a quick door-to-door survey. Even a small purposive sample can be structured to reflect the diversity of the population, for example by taking small groups from economically diverse locations in a community.

Third, it is useful to obtain measures to allow comparisons between a purposive sample and the population. While usually the focus is on demographic variables such as age and gender, likely these are less important than variables directly related to the survey topic. For example, a purposive survey dealing with fitness could include some measures available from a population health survey. A corollary of the idea that purposive samples should be designed and not haphazard is that their analysis should incorporate structural features of the design, particularly any clusters, a point made forcefully by Sterba (2009: 716ff.).

Quota samples are sometimes used as a less expensive alternative to probability samples. A quota sample employs stratification to ensure conformity between a purposive sample and the population. The 'quotas' are just required numbers of observations in the different strata, usually based on the population distribution. Typically there are quotas for geographical areas and for respondents' visible characteristics, usually gender and age. Within a stratum, interviewers have considerable discretion in selecting respondents and they are under time and financial pressure to do so quickly. Lohr (2010) notes that quota sampling was implicated in mistaken predictions of the 1992 British general election. Quotas avoid gross demographic differences between the sample and population, but leave the possibility of systematic bias on aspects of personality and lifestyle that determine whether a person comes to the attention of an interviewer and is willing to be interviewed.

━━━How Large a Sample? ━━━━━━━━━━━━━━━━━━━━━━━━━━━━━━━━━━━━━

Perhaps the most common question about sampling is 'How large a sample do I need?' When there is a defined quantitative objective, for example if the objective is to measure the rate of unemployment in an area to a specified precision using a sample of addresses, this is a statistical question with an exact answer that can be computed using one of a family of algorithms known as *power analysis*. Power analysis is routinely used to determine sample sizes for clinical tests and experiments and it can be applied to an enormously wide range of problems. The definitive guide is by Cohen (1988) and there are good software implementations.[5]

In order to conduct a power analysis it is necessary to: (1) choose a *single* variable to serve as the criterion; (2) decide the type and level of statistical test to be applied, or specify the precision of the desired estimate in terms of the size of a confidence interval; and (3) specify the 'power' of the test, which is the probability that the test is significant or the confidence interval is the desired size – usually 80 or 90 per cent. The analytical outcome for the power analysis may be the value of the mean of a variable or a proportion, the correlation between two variables, a comparison of the means or proportions of two groups, or multiple group comparisons.

Conventional statistical tests measure the probability that a particular value (for example, a difference between means, correlation or regression coefficient) will be obtained from the sample, when its 'true' value in the population is zero. Power analysis deals with the distributions of sample outcomes when the population value *is not zero*, but is of a pre-specified magnitude, called the effect size.[6]

Survey projects often do not fit naturally into the mould of power analysis because the research does not have a single definitive outcome; rather there are multiple of analytical goals and, even taking them one at a time, the desired analytical results cannot be exactly quantified. Also there are often many subgroups of interest, and a larger sample is designed to allow analysis of smaller subgroups. Power analysis can still be useful, however, because it challenges the researcher to specify his research goals in quantitative terms.

Consider a simple example. Suppose that a survey is designed to compare two groups and the researcher specifies that 90 per cent of the time (this is the power of the test) a 10 per cent difference between the groups should be significant at the 0.05 level, using a one-tailed test because previous research strongly suggests the direction of the difference between groups. Assuming simple random samples of both groups, a power computation gives the required size as 447 observations in each group. Now say that the two groups are unequal in size and that one accounts for 20 per cent of the population and the other for 80 per cent of the

---

[5]In R, the pwr package implements Cohen's approach; Stata offers the built-in sampsi calculations and a variety of user-contributed procedures; and SPSS offers the SamplePower package.

[6]Power analysis is based on the non-central t and F distributions, which are generalizations of the common t and F distributions.

population, and assume that the two groups cannot be selected separately because group membership can be determined only from the survey. Then the required samples in the two groups are 279 and 1116, for a total of 1395. A larger sample is needed because the smaller subgroup is responsible for most of the uncertainty in the difference of means. A one-tailed 0.05 test is not very stringent and if, instead, a two-tail test at the 0.01 confidence level is used then the required numbers increase further to 465 and 1900, a total of 2365. The result of a power analysis depends critically on input parameters that represent judgements based on previous work in a field. If these are conservative, because the researcher wants to avoid the risk that the sample will be too small, the calculated sample size may be very large indeed.

The example above suggests that an appropriate size for a general purpose survey that would allow fairly precise comparisons between four or five subgroups is about 2000; comparisons between two or three groups would require a sample around 1000; and a survey designed only to characterize the entire sample could do with a sample of about 400.

Another way to think about sample size in general is using confidence intervals (CIs) of percentages. For a simple random sample of 100, the CI of a percentage around 50 per cent is ±10 per cent, so if the estimate from the sample is that 50 per cent of the population have some characteristic, 95 per cent of the time the population value lies between 40 and 60 per cent. This is a very wide interval. Increase the sample to 200 and it drops to ±7 per cent; and for a sample of 400 it is ±5 per cent, which seems more acceptable. Considering the error in terms of standard deviations gives similar answers. With a sample of 100, the CI of a mean is $\pm\,^1/_5$ of a standard deviation, which is not very precise. A sample of 400 decreases the interval to $\pm\,^1/_{10}$ of a standard deviation, which is much better. Though derived quite informally these numbers are quite similar to the results of the power analysis.

So, for surveys focusing on characteristics of the total population, where analysis is mainly simple descriptive statistics – say community views of a proposed housing development – 400 observations is sufficient for a basic but respectable survey. To compare subgroups there should be about 400 observations in the *smallest* subgroup. In Canada, with 10 provinces, detailed analysis of provincial differences would require no less than 4000 observations, and considerably more if there is also a need for more precise estimates in the larger provinces. If, in order to lower costs, we are content with samples of 200 in the five smallest provinces, the required sample size drops to 3000.

Thinking about sample sizes in this way may seem too generic and imprecise, but it is no different from the way that these decisions are often made in social science. Because it is always easy to see the research possibilities of a very large sample, the available funding is often the primary determinant of the sample size. There are diminishing returns to sample size – due to the ubiquitous $\sqrt{n}$ that figures in every error calculation – and if the goal is to explore a new area of research or a new population, a great deal can be learned with a sample from a few hundred to a thousand. In many areas samples of 2000–5000 provide for state-of-the-art research, but the sky is the limit – think of the new British longitudinal survey called *Understanding Society*, with a sample of 40,000 households, with data gathered from no less than 100,000 individuals!

What Kind of Sample?

The design of simpler samples hinges on just a few basic factors, shown schematically in Figure 2. The initial question is whether a list of the target population is available. With such a list it is possible to select a simple random sample, whose virtues include simplicity of computation and the democratic quality of treating each observation equally. The situation is quite similar when there is a surrogate for a list of elements, such as a list of household telephone numbers or addresses, which are clusters, *and there is one selection per cluster*. Selecting one respondent in each household results in unequal probabilities of selection and lowers the precision of estimates, compared to a simple random sample of the same size.

If two or more separate lists cover different parts of the population it is only necessary to select a separate sample from each one. While the lists constitute strata, if the sampling fractions are the same it can be treated like a simple random sample. With two or more *overlapping* lists, for example one for landlines and one for mobile telephones, elements appearing on more than one list have a greater probability of selection, so it is necessary to ask respondents if they could have been sampled from the other lists – this information should be used to weight the data.

Often a list of the population includes one or more measures that allow the population to be divided into strata, with a separate sample selected in each one. With proportional allocation, so that the probability of selection is the same in each stratum, the sample and the population correspond exactly in terms of the stratifying variable(s). If there is reason to expect response rates to vary by stratum, the initial samples in the strata can be adjusted so that the realized samples are proportional to the strata sizes. Stratification with proportional allocation usually adds nothing to the cost and is good practice, though there is little gain in precision compared to a simple random sample that ignores the strata, unless the sample is quite small. Selecting a systematic sample from a list sorted by the stratifying variable (but *not* actually creating strata) accomplishes the same thing.

With a list of the population, the bigger question is whether to stratify *and also vary the sampling fractions* across strata, thus giving some respondents a higher (and some a lower) probability of selection. Disproportionate allocation is often used to increase the number of observations in small strata, so they can be measured with more precision. It is also used to increase the precision of estimates in strata with more internal variation or increase the numbers of observations in strata where the cost per observation is lower, in order to increase the precision of estimates of the total.

Decision Tree for Sample Structure

Is there a complete list of population elements?

YES   Are there one or more auxiliary variables describing the elements on a basis relevant to the survey measures of interest?

      YES   Is there an interest in comparing groups defined by the auxiliary variable(s)?

           YES, it is the primary research interest   →**Divide the list according to the groups; in each group select a simple random sample of the same size**

           YES, to same degree it is a research interest   →**Divide the list according to the groups; in each group select a simple random sample that over-represents the smaller groups to some degree**

           NO   →**Select a simple random sample**

      NO   →**Select a simple random sample**

NO, there is only a list of clusters, such as geographical areas, household addresses or businesses

      Is the size of the clusters known and if it is do the cluster vary considerably in size?

      YES to both questions   →**Divide the clusters into strata based on their size; within each stratum select a simple random sample of clusters, where the stratum sampling fraction is proportional to the average within-stratum size; within each selected cluster select a random sample of the same size**

           or

           →**Select the clusters with probability proportional to their size; within each selected cluster select a random sample of the same size**

      NO to either question   →**Select a simple random sample of clusters; within each selected cluster select a simple random sample of the elements with the same sampling fraction for every cluster (but, if there is wide variation in cluster size, seek expert advice)**

Figure 2   Decision Tree for Sample Structure

A fourth reason for disproportionate allocation is because of a specific research interest. In surveying workers, for example, there might be an interest in comparing age groups, job categories, departments or locations. In surveying patients, one might want to compare groups defined by the type or seriousness of their medical condition, or whether they have a chronic condition, giving greater weight to patients with more serious conditions.

If the primary goal is to compare strata, the same size sample should be selected in each stratum, regardless of its population. But this can result in very unequal weights and markedly reduce the precision of estimates of total population characteristics. In Canada, for example, it is common to make comparisons among the 10 provinces, where the largest and smallest provinces account for 39 and 0.4 per cent of the total population respectively. In selecting samples of equal size from those two provinces, the ratio of the smallest to the largest weights is about 100:1. An alternative is to combine the smallest provinces in a single stratum, but a nicer compromise is to allocate most of the sample among provinces in proportion to their populations, and then increase the smallest samples to some minimum, say between 200 and 400.

Stratification with unequal probabilities carries two risks. First, it lowers the precision of estimates for the entire population, since the unequal weights needed to give unbiased estimates decrease the precision of estimates. The second problem might be characterized by the phrase 'putting all of your eggs in the same basket'. A sample designed to address a particular research problem can limit the exploration of new ideas arising from initial analysis. For example, the ability to explore differences between Canadian provinces of very unequal size, purchased with larger sampling fractions in the smaller provinces, limits the ability to examine regional differences *within* the two largest provinces (these regions are much bigger than entire smaller provinces). This is why the samples for large, multi-purpose survey projects, which are designed explicitly to share a costly resource, usually do not employ disproportionate allocation.

Although a simple random sample based on a list of population elements provides more precision and simpler statistics, it can be useful to create clusters intentionally. Consider a study of the perceptions of the safety of neighbourhoods in a large city. Because the typical subjective perception of a person's neighbourhood covers just a few square blocks, a simple random sample of addresses would not provide a good basis for estimating between- and within-neighbourhood variation. By spreading the selections evenly through the entire city, there would be very few groups of two or more respondents in the same neighbourhood. A better solution is to select clusters of respondents in neighbourhoods. Many other apparently individual-level phenomena are nested in some kind of physical and/or social hierarchy, and understanding this empirically requires that the hierarchy be incorporated in the sample design.

The precision of population estimates from a cluster sample depends on the relative variation between and within clusters, measured by the intraclass correlation ρ. If ρ is high, after the first few observations within a selected cluster, additional selections add very little information, so it makes sense to select many clusters and a small number of observations in each. The formula for the optimum is in the last chapter. Cost is a factor because of the additional expense of selecting each cluster, beyond the cost of collecting data for selected respondents in a cluster. The additional expense covers the time required to make an initial contact and explain the research to a household member or contact person in a firm or association. If the clusters are neighbourhoods and the survey uses face-to-face interviews, the per-cluster cost involves travelling to the neighbourhood repeatedly, since some households will have no one home and/or a respondent will ask the interviewer to return. If the per-cluster cost is low, the most precise design is to make just two selections per cluster. In household surveys, because of the travel cost, the optimal number of selections per area is closer to 10.

With cluster samples, a second major concern is variation in the size of clusters. If they are similar in size, it is sufficient to select a simple random sample of clusters, perhaps with stratification. With a simple random sample of clusters of *unequal* size, selecting the same *number* of elements from each cluster requires that the observations be weighted in proportion to the size of the clusters, and the resulting unequal weights dramatically reduce the precision of population estimates. No weighting is required if the same *proportion* of elements is selected in each cluster, but this may be unworkable if some clusters are very large and the estimates lose precision because the number of selected clusters is reduced by the need for so many selections in a large cluster.

If there is considerable variation in the size of clusters, the sample design should reduce the variation in the *number* of observations selected in a cluster *and* keep the probabilities of selection quite similar. This is accomplished by stratifying the clusters by size and selecting a simple random sample of clusters in each stratum. Then, in order to reduce the variation in the overall probabilities of selection, a higher proportion of *clusters* should be selected in the strata with larger clusters, and within a cluster about the same *number* of selections should be made, regardless of the cluster size. This works well when the overall sample size is large enough to allow, say, at least 10 selections per stratum. The same result can be achieved without stratification by selecting clusters with a probability proportional to some measure of their size, and making the same number of selections in each cluster. This is a better strategy if the number of selected clusters is small. In the difficult and rare case where the size of clusters is not known beforehand and exhibits wide variation, seek expert advice.

For multi-stage samples, it is difficult to go beyond quite general considerations. Stratification has no downside and can improve precision, but not by much with proportional allocation. There is no argument against stratifying to make the data collection more convenient and often this is done on the basis of geography in order to help organize fieldwork. Otherwise, a decision to stratify should be driven by research concerns, either to provide sufficient observations to analyse smaller sectors of the population or to facilitate comparisons between groups.

Additional levels of clustering are more likely to be driven by structural constraints. Samples of addresses often involve two or more levels of clustering: first larger geographical areas are selected (at the national level, say all communities of a certain size and a sample of smaller communities and rural areas), then larger areas within communities (often census tracts), then smaller areas (often enumeration areas or the equivalent). Another example is the selection of school classes, which cannot be selected directly, but only by first selecting schools. Within schools it may be desirable to treat the school grades as strata, so the classes are a stratified cluster sample. To make this allocation on purely statistical criteria requires a good guess about the variation between schools, between grades within schools, between classes within grades and between students within classes. This is a tall order and often the design of a sample like this is driven by cost considerations or data collection constraints.

A strong case for stratification can be made for surveys designed to study variables whose distribution is very unequal, for example income and wealth. The distribution of wealth is so highly skewed that the top percentiles account for much of the population total. With a simple random sample, there is wide variation in the number of observations from the top of the distribution, resulting in much greater sampling error.[7] This problem can be addressed by stratifying the population according to the skewed variable and selecting observations from the highest strata with greater probability – recall Neyman allocation, which has the sampling fraction proportional to the product of each stratum's population and the standard deviation of the variable of interest. If the variable of interest cannot be measured prior to the survey, an auxiliary variable must be used for stratification, such as characteristic of neighbourhoods available from a census (say the mean household income) or from housing records (taking assessed value).

An example is Statistics Canada's 2005 Survey of Financial Security, which was designed to provide 'a comprehensive picture of the net worth of Canadians'. The two parts of the sample were:

> The main sample, drawn from an area frame, consisted of approximately 7,500 dwellings. This area sample was a stratified, multi-stage sample … The second portion of the sample, approximately 1,500 households, was drawn from geographic areas in which a large proportion of households had what was defined as 'high-income'. This sample was included to improve the representation in the sample of high-income families, as a disproportionate share of net worth is held by such higher-income family units. For purposes of this sample the income cutoff was total family income of at least $200,000 or investment income of at least $50,000.

[7]Recall that the central limit theorem dictates that the mean of a sample of any size is unbiased and that the distribution of the mean tends towards the normal as the sample size increases. The greater the degree of skewness of a variable, however, the more slowly the distribution converges to the normal. When just a few observations, say 5 or 10 out of a sample of a few thousand, are so large that they affect the mean, sampling variation in the number of very high observations markedly increases sampling error and can affect the shape of the sampling distribution. The sampling distribution of the means of a very skewed distribution is itself skewed (and so not normal) until the sample becomes very large.

Another common use of this sampling strategy is to survey businesses, which can be stratified on the basis of size, perhaps measured by number of employees, amount of production, revenue or assets.

Two-Stage Samples

It is common to want to survey population subgroups, for example the parents of pre-school children, recent immigrants or members of an ethnic or racialized group, who account for a small percentage of the total population. Except for extraordinarily large samples or a census, often the group is too small a proportion of a representative sample to study in detail. The problem is not the absolute size of the group – in large populations a 'small' group still includes tens of thousands of individuals – but that no sampling frame directly identifies its members.

The traditional strategy for surveying a subgroup is called *double sampling*, or *two-stage sampling* or *two-phase sampling*. The idea is first to select a representative sample of the population, then at the beginning of the questionnaire ask if the respondent (or perhaps anyone in the respondent's household) is a member of the desired group; then the full interview is conducted only for that group. The short initial segment of the interview, which is called a screening interview or 'screener', could ask, for example, whether a person smokes, has a small child, is contemplating retirement, is a member of a particular ethno-racial group, or intends to vote. If the initial sample is a probability sample of the population, then the *second-stage sample* is still a probability sample of the designated group. Kish (1965: 440ff.) provides a good introduction to the topic.

The principal drawback of two-stage sampling is that the first stage of selection can be very costly. For surveys using interviewers, much of the cost of each interview is devoted to getting the respondent to answer the first question, including the time required to contact the respondent at her address or by phone, sometimes repeated calls after an initial contact, and the effort required to explain the request and convince the respondent to participate; and much of this effort is devoted to unsuccessful contacts and to contacted respondents who do not agree to participate. If just a small percentage of respondents are in the group of interest, most of the effort and cost of the survey involves those very short interviews with people who are not in the group of interest.

The cost can be lowered by stratifying the population using auxiliary variables, then selecting more of the sample from strata with high concentrations of the desired group. For example, the members of an ethnic group might be disproportionately selected from areas of a city where they are concentrated, as indicated by a census. The gain depends on the degree to which the group is concentrated, the availability of auxiliary variables measuring the concentration, and the ability to target surveys in the concentrated area. Often a census can be used for stratification, because members of an ethnic group, people at similar stages of the life cycle and people with similar income tend to live in somewhat homogeneous areas.

The downside of lowering the cost of double sampling by stratifying on the basis of concentration of the group of interest is that members of a group who live in a more concentrated area are often dissimilar from those living outside the area. Immigrants who live outside any local enclave, for example, are likely to have a better command of the country's majority language, less interest in their community, and more friends and maybe a partner from outside the community. The unequal probabilities of selection for respondents from areas of different concentration necessitate the use of weights in data analysis, resulting in a decrease in the precision of estimates and so cancelling out some of the gains from the stratification[8]. With a good estimate of the distribution of the population it is possible to allocate a sample between low- and high-concentration areas to maximize the precision of population estimates (for two strata, see Kalton and Anderson, 1986).

A nice use of this strategy is to select second-stage respondents from a very large earlier survey. For example, Statistics Canada has conducted large-scale 'post-censal' surveys of persons with disabilities and of Aboriginal persons, with samples selected on the basis of responses to the national census.[9] Also Statistics Canada recruits respondents for other surveys from people who were sampled for their very large and mandatory monthly Labour Force Survey.

Sampling Rare Groups

When the group to be surveyed is *very* small, statisticians refer to *sampling rare populations*, for example people with an uncommon medical condition, unemployed recent immigrants and stigmatized and at-risk groups, such as persons who are undocumented or drug dependent. For rare groups, one way to increase the efficiency of probability sampling is known as *multiplicity sampling*, invented by Monroe Sirken (1970; also see Sudman et al., 1988). This is a generalization of a common method of gathering proxy information in household surveys, for example when an 'informant' in a household is asked to report the labour force status of the other household members. Multiplicity sampling extends this idea by asking respondents to report on members of other households, for example siblings, parents, children or close friends. To estimate population characteristics from these reports it is necessary to account for the unequal probabilities of selection. An only

---

[8]This is the view from the 'design-based' perspective. With data from a stratified two-stage sample, a good case can be made for 'model-based' analysis, where the data are *not* weighted – thus improving the precision of estimates – and estimates are made using measures of the concentration of the group in the sampled area as covariates. Where this cannot help is in making comparisons between members of a group living in high- and low-concentration areas, but the sampling scheme results in the latter group being small in number.

[9]These are, respectively, the Participation and Activity Limitation Survey (conducted in 2001 and 2006, and predecessor surveys in 1986 and 1991) and the Aboriginal Peoples Surveys of 1991, 2001 and 2006. The 2011 long-form Census was cancelled by the government and was replaced with a voluntary survey which achieved a response rate of about 67 per cent.

child, for example, cannot report or be reported on by siblings. A more serious problem arises from respondent errors in reporting the number of individuals to which they are linked (which provides the denominator in estimating the prevalence of a rare trait) or when the respondent does not know or is unwilling to report characteristics of the persons to whom he or she is linked (an error in the numerator). Obviously there can be privacy concerns as well. Christman (2009) provides a nice summary of more recent developments.

When there are time or budget constraints, it may not be feasible to select a probability sample of the entire population or even a probability sample of an easy-to-reach segment of the population, for example immigrants living in an enclave or men living in a 'gay village'. Another strategy is a relative of multiplicity sampling called *snowball sampling*, known much earlier although the definitive formulation is by Goodman (1961). Rather than using an initial sample to count or obtain proxy information about other respondents, the idea is to begin with *any* initial sample of the group of interest. It could be obtained by probability-based double sampling or it could be a purposive sample recruited by friends and contacts, or advertisements. Data are collected from members of this initial sample are those initial respondents are asked to provide the names of other group members, from whom a second round of data is collection, and so on.

Thus the size of the sample increases – or 'snowballs' – with each additional stage of sampling. If the respondents of interest are a closed community, however, eventually new respondents will only give the names of previously selected people and the sample converges to *the entire population* of interest. One risk is that if the target population is made up of distinct subgroups – say, members of an ethnic group are divided according their place of birth or period of immigration – and the initial sample does not contain at least one member of each group, then a group will be missed entirely.

A variant of snowball sampling is called *random walk sampling*. The idea is to follow just one link from each previous respondent, chosen at random from his or her links to other members of the group. Sampling of this kind is known as *link-tracing* designs and also as chain sampling, chain-referral sampling and referral sampling (Thompson and Frank, 2000).

Link-tracing samples provide a means to reach really rare, hidden and stigmatized populations, though only if their members are sufficiently connected to avoid the sample petering out and if the members are prepared to provide the information necessary to contact new respondents. When the population is at risk, this can be difficult and success can depend on the skills of the researcher and her ability to gain the trust of the intended survey respondents.

Heckathorn (1997; 2002) developed a clever way to address this problem, which he called *respondent-driven sampling*. The idea is to ask members of an initial sample, called 'seeds', who are interviewed, to personally recruit other rare group members for an interview, selecting randomly from all the people that they know are members of the group. In turn, the second-stage respondents are asked to recruit more members. Financial incentives make this attractive, and confidentiality is preserved because the researcher herself is not the one who initially approaches the second- and later-stage respondents. Estimates of the size of the rare group are based on the number of group members that the respondents report, avoiding duplication by giving respondents unique identification numbers. Most prominently, respondent-driven sampling has been applied to the study of AIDS, including surveys of gay men, injection drug users and sex trade workers (Malekinejad et al., 2008).

There is debate about whether this method can provide unbiased estimates of the size of rare groups and their characteristics. Proponents argue that the nature of the networks of rare groups (essentially that one connected group includes almost everyone) and the randomness in successive rounds of selection make the final outcome insensitive to the fact that the seeds were not selected randomly (Volz and Heckathorn, 2008). Critics argue that the estimators are biased because even after many rounds of recruitment the composition of the sample remains dependent on the non-random initial selection and that estimates are affected by biases in recruitment at each stage (Gile and Handcock, 2010). While this dispute continues, respondent-driven sampling is the only extant systematic strategy for surveying these groups. Also, it is very difficult to gather empirical external to assess claims about the quality of respondent-drive samples.

Unit Non-response

It is impossible to underestimate the potential impact of non-response of the quality of survey data. Groves et al. (2002) provide a good introduction to this huge subject (and see Chapters 7 and 8, below). Almost any discussion of unit non-response begins with Little and Rubin's (1987) threefold classification, based on earlier work by Rubin (1976). In this literature the term 'missingness' is used to refer to the property of being missing.

In the first category, observations are *missing completely at random* (MCAR), which means that whether an observation is missing is unrelated to *any* of the characteristics measured in a survey. This could result from an accident, such as the loss of completed questionnaires, or it could be by design, for example when different subsets of questions are asked to random fractions of respondents, in order to increase the content of a survey. With MCAR the only concern is that the number of observations is reduced by non-response. It is difficult to imagine any real survey in which non-response is MCAR.

In the second category, observations are *missing at random* (MAR). This means that missingness is systematically related to one or more variables measured in the survey, but it is *not* related to the *response variable* or to any other variable that is not measured in the survey. If income is the response variable, for example, it could be that gender, education and age affect missingness, but *within categories of gender, age and education*, lower- or higher-income persons are no more or less likely to respond to a survey. It does not matter that, say, older, more educated men have higher incomes.

When non-respondents are MAR it is possible to make unbiased estimates of the response variable using auxiliary information about the distribution of the predictors of response in the population, obtained from a census, survey or administrative records. A *weighting adjustment* is used to compensate for the difference between the sample and population distributions of predictors of response. Classes of respondents who are more likely to respond are given lower weights to reduce their impact on the estimate of income, and vice versa. This is called *post-stratification* because it involves grouping the observations and developing weights that match the sample to the population *after* the survey was conducted. Post-stratification and weighting are *model-based* techniques because they make use of auxiliary information that is not obtained from the survey, though the weight must also account for stratification and clustering *in the sample design*.

The third category of missingness includes every other case where non-response *is* related to the response variable or to variables that are *not* measured in a survey. For example, for different reasons both people who are very wealthy and people who are very poor and have no wealth might be less likely to answer a survey measuring wealth. Then even if the values of the variables associated with missingness are known and measured *for the population*, they cannot be used to adjust the survey data. When observations are *missing not at random* (MNAR), statistical models can still be used to correct for non-response, but it is a much less certain proposition. As a threat to the analyst's ability to obtain unbiased estimates of population characteristics, MNAR is far worse than MAR.

To distinguish MCAR from MAR it is only necessary to compare the sample and population, and typically there *is* evidence of gender, age and education differentials in response rates. In any event, MCAR is usually implausible. Distinguishing between MAR and MNAR is much more difficult, because it rests on evidence that weighting adjustments *fail* to produce unbiased estimates of the response variable, whose population distribution is known from another source. For example, the predicted consumption of alcohol might be compared to alcohol sales figures. In actual surveys, the claim that data are MAR is hard to support. For example, net of demographic differences in response, non-response is likely related to a person's opinion of the value of surveys and to their interest in the survey topic, neither of which is usually measured in a survey – and the criterion for MNAR is the existence of variables that predict response, that are not measured in a survey.

A nice example is provided by surveys of charitable giving, since it is possible to compare survey statistics to tax records and to the financial records of charities (Bekkers and Wiepking, 2011). Surveys overestimate giving, first because donors tend to be older and older respondents are more likely to complete interviews. Because the age distribution of the population is usually known from other sources, this can be accounted for with weights; similarly, it is possible to compensate for non-response related to gender, education, location, etc. Even accounting for these demographic and socio-economic factors, however, donors are more civic-minded than non-donors and so more likely to agree to an unpaid interview for a research study. Abraham et al. make exactly this point regarding survey measurements of levels of volunteering:

> Because there are significant differences in volunteering between respondents and nonrespondents even after controlling for a rich set of demographic characteristics, standard weighting adjustments cannot be relied upon to fix the problem with estimates of volunteering. (2009: 1162)

So, the best surveys with the most sophisticated statistical adjustment still overestimate charitable giving, volunteering and other forms of social participation. An exacerbating factor, independent of the non-response bias, is measurement error that arises from respondents' tendency to overestimate giving, because it is socially desirable.[10]

A key technical question that is the subject of a large literature is how to use auxiliary information to compute weights to match a survey sample to known characteristics of the population. With just one variable this is easy: if there are equal numbers of women and men in the population, but 60 per cent of the respondents are women, it is only necessary to give weights of 50/60 to women and 50/40 to men. And the same strategy would work for, say, 5 categories of age or the 10 categories of gender × age, both of which are known from other larger surveys.

But suppose that information on the intersection of gender and age is not known for the population, but only the independent distributions of gender and age are available. It is possible to remove the bias arising from a number of variables simultaneously – knowing only their 'marginal' distributions for the population, but without their cross-classification, with a method called 'raking', developed by Deming and Stephan (1940). Going one step further, a technique known as *iterative proportional fitting,* also due to Deming and Stephan but with important statistical result extensions by Fienberg (see Bishop et al., 1975), produces weights that reflect any combination of known relationships between two or more variables.[11]

In general, using more variables to better predict survey response results in weights that more effectively reduce bias, but they may also increase error at the same time. Say that a survey and a source of auxiliary information both provide counts of the number of individuals in categories of gender (two groups) by age (five), by education (five) and by household size (six). While a census can provide very precise estimates of the population in the $2 \times 5 \times 5 \times 6 = 300$ categories, even a very large survey would have very small numbers in some of these cells, and the number in each cell would be subject to random variation. So the weights – just the ratio of the population count to the survey count in each of the 300 cells – would exhibit considerable

---

[10]There is no consensus about how to measure social desirability in a survey, or even whether it is possible.

[11]It does this by using the relationship observed in the sample but adjusted to the marginal distributions measured in the population. Fienberg proved that the iteration method suggested by Deming and Stephan would converge.

sampling variation; if by chance there was a zero cell in the survey, the weight would be infinite. To deal with this problem the alternatives are: to combine small cells before computing the weights; to employ raking, described above; and to develop a regression model of response to produce smoothed weights. A good recent summary is Brick and Montaquila (2009).

Conclusion ———

Although sampling involves statistical criteria in a way that questionnaire design does not, every survey researcher needs an understanding of the general principles. Quite like questionnaire design, often what seems like a unique problem in sample design has already come to light and been solved. Also, there are many neat, non-mathematical tricks in the lore of sample design.

While the approximate size of a sample is often determined by the available funds and by disciplinary standards, the relative importance of estimates for the entire population and for subgroups is often a major consideration. If the subgroups are of approximately equal size – usually for men and women, and often for age groups, but depending on how age is categorized – a larger overall sample evenly increases the size of all the subgroups. Dividing the sample by regions, or education or racialization, the groups of interest can vary dramatically in size. When it is possible to stratify and control the subgroup sizes, over-representing the small subgroups can substantially decrease the precision of population estimates. Also, structuring the sample more precisely to compare some subgroups can sacrifice comparisons between other groups. Disproportional allocation should only be used if it serves a clear analytical purpose.

More generally, simplicity is a virtue in sample design. Designs with a high degree of variation in the probabilities of selection are especially risky because they result in large design effects.

Complexity is unavoidable when it is necessary to select a cluster sample, because there is no list of the population elements. To survey students in schools, for example, it is rarely possible and economically feasible to select individuals; so schools and school classes must be selected and the result is a cluster sample. This is the point at which the expertise of a sampling statistician is needed, for apparently simple choices can dramatically affect the precision of the resulting survey data. The nice part is that multi-level models can turn this analytical complication into interesting substantive findings that are invisible to the classical design-based approach to complex samples.

6
Survey Pretesting

Varying from just a handful of cases to samples in the hundreds or thousands, survey pretests and pilot surveys are designed to detect and remedy problematic questions before data collection. Large pretests and pilot surveys are just surveys with a methodological purpose, subject to conventional data analysis. Due to considerations of the cost and time, but also because they are thought to be sufficient, small and inexpensive pretests are the norm. Pretesting is not primarily exploratory, the idea is to improve existing questions, rather than to develop new measures of a concept or decide between alternative questions.

Survey pretests also have the mundane but important purpose of quality assurance. Even a short questionnaire offers many opportunities for error, both in the original draft and in its conversion to a printed form, or marked-up code for a computer-assisted telephone or personal interview (CATI and CAPI, respectively) or Internet survey. After many drafts, survey designers have the same trouble recognizing their own errors as any other writers.

The underlying problem in questionnaire design addressed by pretesting is that survey *respondents* are often less interested in and knowledgeable about the survey topic than researchers, and many have less education and weaker cognitive skills. Researchers – but usually not their respondents – can understand the questions that they write in relation to their conceptual framework and data analysis experience. For Cannell and his colleagues, 'The interview is a meeting between the world of the researcher and the world of the lay person. The questionnaire serves as a translation of the researcher's goals into the language of the respondent' (1989: 2).

The chapter begins with conventional pretests and then considers ways in which they can be enhanced at relatively small additional cost. This is followed by a discussion of 'cognitive pretesting', which is the empirical side of the CASM movement. The chapter concludes with an assessment of the effectiveness of pretesting. The focus is on surveys employing interviewers, with a short section on self-administered surveys.

This discussion applies equally to pretests and small-scale 'pilot surveys'. Conventionally, a 'pilot survey' is a rehearsal of the final survey, often with the same kind of sample and data collection procedures, so there is more emphasis on survey administration and less on testing questions. For large surveys it is common to conduct a pretest and then a pilot survey with a larger sample.

Conventional Pretesting ————

Surveys with a few hundred to a few thousand respondents are usually pretested with 20 to 50 respondents similar in composition to the eventual sample, but not a probability sample with a high response rate. Because pretests are often completed in a day or two, even with exactly the same kind of sample as the main survey population, the pretest interviews over-represent respondents who are more easily contacted, more favourable to surveys and more interested in a particular topic. Except that it is common to employ more experienced interviewers,[1] pretest interviews are conducted in the same manner as ordinary interviews. Often researchers are able to listen to the interviews, either live or from recordings. The interviewers are debriefed in a group, to obtain their general impressions and review the items one at a time. Researchers then modify items that interviewers or researchers find awkward, result in frequent requests for clarification or have high non-response.

While they are a staple of the survey industry, little attention is devoted to conventional pretesting in the methodological literature (but see Cannell et al., 1989: 3–4 and Sheatsley, 1983: 225–227) and there is no consensus on important details, such as the sample size and composition. Some survey specialists are sceptical of the whole enterprise. Reviewing new methods for survey pretesting, Presser and his colleagues conclude:

> This faith in conventional pretesting is probably based on the common experience that a small number of conventional interviews often reveal numerous problems, such as questions that contain unwarranted assumptions, awkward wordings, or missing response categories. However, there is no scientific evidence to justify the confidence that this kind of pretesting identifies major problems in a questionnaire. (2004: 110)

Conventional pretests are limited by their small sample sizes. If an item that 15 per cent of respondents cannot answer is considered problematic, with 25 pretest interviews there is a 25 per cent chance that fewer than four respondents will be unable to answer it. A sample of 25, however, will identify really problematic items that, say, 20 per cent of respondents cannot answer. There is also a significant

---

[1]The argument is that more skilled interviewers are better able to detect problems in a questionnaire, but this risks overlooking problems that less experienced interviewers will encounter when they conduct the main survey interviews.

risk of identifying as problematic items that are not. If almost any survey item has 5 per cent non-response, with 25 pretest respondents about one-eighth of the time three or more respondents will not answer the question. For a survey with 100 'good' items, about a dozen would be misidentified as problematic.

Interviewers, and researchers if they listen to the interviews or review recordings, can flag questions that respondents answer properly, but only with the assistance of the interviewer. Also, listening to complete interviews it is possible to identify questions that are problematic for respondents who have no difficulties with the rest of the questionnaire. In conventional pretests, often researchers implicitly rely on the interpretative strategies used in qualitative research. The researcher may take notice even when only one respondent hesitates or asks for clarification or when one interviewer describes a question as difficult to read or confusing. Such intuition, however, is an imperfect means of distinguishing between an actual problem and the occasional difficulty that arises with almost any survey question.

Conventional pretests are also highly cost effective and quick. Much of the effort and time for a pretest is needed anyway, in order to prepare for data collection. Even if the results are not very precise, the return is high relative to the cost.

There are three general strategies for improving on conventional pretesting using resources on the same scale: expert review of the questionnaire *before* pretesting; broader, more systematic data collection, beyond the usual combination of the survey results and informal debriefing of interviewers; and adding questions to the pretest survey in order to help understand how respondents answer.

One shortcoming of small-scale pretests is that they cannot effectively check the instructions that route respondents between questions, based on information from the sampling frame (such as year of study in student surveys), previous answers (only those employed are asked about their work), or random numbers (used in experiments). Unless the logic is very simple, a small pretest does not have enough observations to test all the logical paths. Direct verification of this logic is imperative.[2] A second limitation is that once a problem has been identified, without a second pretest there is no guarantee that the revision will cure the problem.

———— Prior Review of the Questionnaire ————

Expert review involves a detailed assessment of every question in a survey by experts who *were not previously* involved in the questionnaire design, and they may also meet to reconcile their opinions. To obtain an indication of the reviewers' consistency, there should be at least three reviewers and they should make independent assessments, prior to any meeting.

---

[2]For a nice review of pretesting the logic of computer-assisted interviewing systems see Tarnai and Moore (2004). In principle, this is no different from debugging a computer program.

An alternative is to apply a detailed checklist of potential problems to each question. The typology developed by Lessler and Forsyth (1996) is guided explicitly by the cognitive model of survey response. Willis and Lessler's (1999a; 1999b) *Questionnaire Appraisal System* is entirely pragmatic. They identify seven types of problems, which involve: reading the question; instructions to the respondent; clarity; assumptions made by the question; knowledge and memory issues; whether the question is sensitive or prone to bias; and the response categories. Each category has a number of separate ratings, for a total of 27 ratings of each question. Question 'clarity', for example, includes ratings of whether a question: is 'lengthy, awkward, ungrammatical, involves complicated syntax'; includes terms that are 'undefined, unclear, or complex'; provides 'multiple ways to interpret the question or to decide what is to be included or excluded'; or has a temporal reference period that is 'missing, not well specified, or in conflict' (1999a: 2–3).

Instead of focusing on individual problems in a question, Saris et al. (2004b; also see Saris and Gallhofer, 2007a; 2007b: 173ff.) use a regression model based on MTMM meta-analyses to predict the reliability and validity of a survey question.[3] The predictors entered in the model are just the attributes of a question, including the survey topic, the nature of the concept being measured, the question format and response categories, the length and complexity of the item, the mode of data collection and the position of the item in the questionnaire. The researcher then decides whether to revise items whose predicted reliability or validity is low.

Graesser et al.'s 'Question Understanding Aid' (2006; also see Graesser et al., 1996) provides a completely automatic assessment of the linguistic structure of a question as well as the individual words. From the question text, just entered on a website, the program 'returns a list of potential problems with question comprehension, including unfamiliar technical terms, vague or imprecise relative terms, vague or ambiguous noun phrases, complex syntax, and working memory overload' (2006: 3).

—— More Systematic Measurement of Survey Responses ——

The results of a conventional pretest consist of the survey responses and the observations of interviewers and sometimes of researchers who listened to interviews. Even when a respondent changes an initial answer, perhaps after asking a question or because of an interviewer prompt, it is normal to record only the respondent's final answer. Interviewers are expected to notice and report on these queries and changes, but their ability to observe the respondent is compromised by the demands of conducting the interview. Also, observation shows that it is common for interviewers to make small changes to smooth out a questionnaire, and

[3]The *Survey Quality Predictor* program is available for free download from http://www.sqp.nl/media/sqp-1.0/.

they may be unaware of or forget these corrective actions. *Researchers* who listen to interviews can focus on these subtleties, but they may have trouble separating commonplace noise – minor errors in reading the question and chatter when questions are answered – from actual problems.

Bischoping (1989) demonstrates that there are often problems in consistently patching together the impressions of the group of interviewers who have each conducted a small number of pretest interviews. Problems slip through because the process depends on interviewers' memories and because the group dynamics of the discussion affect the reporting. Fowler (1989) found that better feedback is obtained from pretest interviewers if they identify difficulties with each question on a form *prior to a group discussion*, and it can be useful to repeat that exercise after the discussion.

One solution is to systematically code the pretest survey responses, either as the interview proceeds or from a recording. Cannell and Robinson (1971) first used *behaviour coding* in the late 1960s (also see Fowler and Cannell, 1996, and Van der Zouwen and Smit, 2004: 110). The response to each question is called a *question–answer (Q–A) sequence* of 'utterances' by the interviewer and respondent, and potentially by others who are present. The individual utterances are then classified according to some scheme, although there is no accepted convention. Ongena and Dijkstra compare no fewer than 48 coding schemes for survey interviews, which include a total of '134 different categories for interviewer behavior, 78 different categories for respondent behavior, and 14 different categories for behavior of third parties' (2006: 421). The codes cover the initial reading of the question, requests for clarification, answers that are correct initially, mistaken answers, unscripted efforts by the interviewer to assist the respondent that could introduce bias, and changes to initial answers – as well as noise and pleasantries used to facilitate the interaction. Especially for more complex schemes, coding the sequence involves some degree of error (2006: 428ff.).

Because behaviour coding records utterances of both the interviewer and respondent it can be used to train or evaluate interviewers. For efficient question pretesting, especially in what is often a limited time available to modify a questionnaire, the key is to differentiate what Schaeffer and Maynard (2002) term *paradigmatic sequences*, consisting only of an accurately read question followed by the respondent's choice of an appropriate response (maybe ignoring some 'noise') from problematic sequences. While overlooking the rich detail in the Q–A sequence, this distinction can be made consistently and recorded in 'real time', as the interview proceeds.

Van der Zouwen and Smit (2004) employ a threefold classification of individual survey questions into: 'paradigmatic sequences', where nothing goes wrong; 'problematic sequences', in which a correct answer is provided only after some additional interaction between the interviewer and respondent and/or the correction of an initial response; and all other 'inadequate' responses. Using this scheme, the difficulty is in differentiating normal helpful interviewer behaviour from situations where the interviewer compensates for a problematic question. Contrary to the conventional pretesting paradigm, which uses the skills of experienced interviewers in a detailed debriefing, for pretests with behaviour coding there is an argument for employing interviewers who are typical of those who will work on the main survey.[4]

Follow-up 'Probes' ——

Especially when supplemented by behaviour coding, a conventional pretest can detect questions about which respondents express their confusion or misunderstanding. But sometimes respondents can confidently answer a question that they understand, but not in the way that the researcher intended. This can be detected by direct questioning in the form of 'follow-up probes', which are just additional questions placed after the question being tested that ask the respondent to elaborate an answer, indicate how he or she understood the question, or describe how he or she answered. Usually probes immediately follow a question, but they may be placed later in the interview, perhaps after repeating the original question. The latter strategy prevents the probes from affecting the answers to other questions in the survey, but adds more to the length of the questionnaire, and may produce different responses than if probes immediately follow each question.

The use of probes dates to the first years of survey research (Cantril and Fried, 1944) and they were used extensively by Belson (1981) to demonstrate the wide variation in respondents' interpretations of factual questions about watching television and other ordinary activities. Oksenberg et al. (1989) provide examples of probes dealing with the respondents' comprehension, memory and choice of response categories, as well as general questions ('Could you tell me more about that?'). An advantage of specific follow-up probes is that they require the researcher to frame questions about what might be problematic in an item. In order not to unduly lengthen or change the style of the questionnaire, probes can only be added for selected questions.

Cognitive Interviewing ——

Cognitive interviewing proceeds on the assumption that understanding how questions are answered requires additional information directly from respondents, not just their spontaneous reactions to difficulties they encounter. Naturally, CASM advocates think of this evidence in terms of the model's four steps. First

---

[4]Another unobtrusive method is to measure how long respondents take to answer each question, known as the *response latency,* based on evidence that more problematic questions are answered more slowly. A good introduction is the special issue of the journal *Political Psychology,* edited by John Bassili (2000; see also Bassili and Fletcher, 1991; Bassili and Scott, 1996). The latency values can be employed diagnostically in pretesting a questionnaire – questions that take longer are more problematic – or they can be used to characterize the survey respondents.

developed in the mid-1980s, 'cognitive interviewing' is defined quite generally by Beatty and Willis as:

> Administering draft survey questions while collecting additional verbal information about the survey responses, which is used to evaluate the quality of the response or to help determine whether the question is generating the information that its author intends. (2007: 288)

In practice, cognitive interviewing describes a variety of ways to inquire into the process of answering questions, including asking follow-up questions that are not 'cognitive' in any specific sense. Roger Tourangeau's reflection on the cognitive movement, in which he was very prominent, is that

> the most dramatic impact, and practical achievement of the CASM movement, has been the radical change in how survey questions are pretested ... in the space of a year or two all the government statistical agencies set up cognitive laboratories. (Sirken et al., 1999: 98)

Because gathering more extensive information about responses adds substantially to the length of a survey, cognitive methods are usually used to pretest a small number of questions, not an entire questionnaire. Ordinarily, cognitive interviews take place in a lab using a non-probability sample of paid respondents.[5] The disciplinary context is that, of the academic disciplines most associated with surveys, psychology is much friendlier to laboratory study and less concerned about sample representativeness than sociology. Also, compared to the sociological tradition of muddling along, psychologists have a greater interest for model-grounded methodology.

Cognitive interviewing methods follow the work of psychologists K. Anders Ericsson and Herbert Simon, whose seminal 1980 article,[6] 'Verbal reports as data', was explicitly intended to reclaim a role for introspective personal 'reports', at a time when behaviourism was the orthodox and dominant paradigm in psychology:

> One of the most direct and widely used methods to gain information about subjects' internal states is to instruct them to think aloud or talk aloud ... a direct trace is obtained of the heeded information, and hence, an indirect one of the internal stages of the cognitive process.

> [a second method] ... retrospective verbalization, probes the subject for information after the completion of the task-induced processes. (p. 220)

Beginning with Elizabeth Loftus in 1984, survey researchers concentrated on the first strategy, called *think aloud* interviewing, or just 'think alouds', where the respondent is asked to describe what goes through her mind when answering a question.

---

[5]But see DeMaio and Rothgeb (1996) for a discussion of cognitive interviewing 'in the field'.

[6]See their more complete formulations in Ericsson and Simon (1993).

In mainstream cognitive psychology, 'think alouds' have mainly been applied to simple problem solving, where the task and how to formulate an answer are unambiguous, and the focus is on judgement, the third step in the cognitive model.[7] Testing survey questions, however, cognitive researchers have focused on the first two steps of the cognitive model, question comprehension and retrieval from memory,[8] and the fourth step, response; problems in survey questions are less likely to involve the third step, formulating a response. Problems with questions about the use of health care, for example, involve what qualify as an event (have you 'seen a doctor' if you were treated by a nurse?) and when they occurred.

The somewhat unstructured monologues recorded from 'think aloud' interviews present 'a sometimes complicated and meandering stream of verbal information' (Willis, 2005: 156). To be useful, these 'verbal protocols' must be coded. This is like behaviour coding of conventional pretests, but with much more variation. Bickart and Felcher (1996) provide a nice discussion and develop a coding scheme of their own.

Willis (2004) observes that when Ericsson and Simon developed cognitive interviewing they sought to minimize the impact of the researcher on the verbal data they gathered, so they suggested that the respondent face away from the researcher in the interview. Survey researchers, on the other hand, emphasize the social character of the interaction between the respondents and interviewers. Especially when combined with unscripted probes, this introduces variation in response due to the interviewer. With just a small sample of respondents and a few interviewers it may not be easy to separate interviewer effects from the variation between respondents.

While one drawback of 'think alouds' is that respondents vary in their ability to describe their reasoning, a more serious problem is that it may not be possible to map their account of answering onto the four steps identified by the cognitive model. Respondents may omit mention of problematic elements of a question and their answers may reflect elements of memory of which they are not aware as they answer (Banaji et al., 1996).

Willis's impression (2005: 47ff.; also see his detailed comparison on p. 53ff.) is that the use of 'think alouds' has declined in favour of *concurrent verbal probing*. This is different from the theoretically agnostic follow-up probes, described above, because cognitive theory implies that the *probes* should explicitly measure the steps

---

[7]Willis (2004: 28–29) notes that while survey researchers have applied the technique quite liberally, Ericsson and Simon's view is that only for certain tasks and in certain circumstances are respondents able to report their cognitive processes accurately without the additional task of reporting actually distorting the process itself.

[8]In terms of Ericsson and Simon's formulation, this is problematic because they argue that individuals are reporting on their own mental processes, without affecting them, only regarding information in 'working memory'. Retrieval of information from long-term memory involves quite different processes than manipulation of the small number of elements (typically three or four) available in short-term memory.

in the cognitive model of survey response, including comprehension, retrieval and so on. The probing questions can involve any combination of: predetermined ('scripted') questions asked of each respondent in order to address explicit concerns of the designer; scripted responses employed for particular respondent behaviours, such as hesitation; and spontaneous questions of the interviewer, potentially reacting to the respondent (Beatty and Willis, 2007: 299ff.). Especially with small samples, variation in the questions asked by different interviewers makes it difficult to reliably separate defects in questionnaire wording from variation between interviewers and respondents. For cognitive interviews, large survey organizations often employ people with academic training in cognitive psychology as well as providing specialized training.[9]

While conventional pretesting usually employs a probability sample, even if it is drawn from a restricted area and the hurried schedule results in a low response rate, cognitive pretesting typically does not begin with a probability sample. For example:

> The pretesting methodology was typical of NCHS [the US National Center for Health Statistics] cognitive interviewing projects ... Interviews were conducted with a total of 18 participants. Twelve of these participations were recruited from newspaper advertisements which offered $30 cash to participate ... [the] additional six were recruited from a local senior citizens' center, because staff had a particular interest in the experiences of older people. (Beatty, 2004: 247)

Why would researchers designing very large surveys with painstaking attention to sampling rely on cognitive interviews with small convenience samples? Because they assume that cognitive processes are basically similar across the population. Taking this a step further, flaws in questions are determinate and represent conceptual errors, so a problem can be identified if it arises in just one interview.

Rather than an alternative to conventional pretesting, where the pretest is the step between the initial questionnaire and data collection, cognitive interviewing can be treated as a questionnaire development *process*, described as follows by DeMaio and Rothgeb:

> Cognitive interviews are fairly unstructured in their probing content and are conducted with small numbers of respondents. They are also flexible. Researchers can do a round of interviews, review the questionnaire, and quickly do another round of interviews. Because of the small scale and unstructured nature of the research, however, the results are not generalizable to a larger population. (1996: 194)

---

[9]In addition to 'think alouds' and probes immediately following a question, cognitive techniques include: retrospective probes, where probes are placed at the end of an interview, not immediately after each question; vignettes, in which the respondent is presented with a description of a person and asked what would be an appropriate answer to a question for that person (see Martin, 2004); asking the respondent to paraphrase the question after it is asked; and asking the respondent how much confidence he or she has in the answer.

They note that the cognitive interviews should be followed by a larger scale 'field test' with a sample resembling the main survey population. Still another perspective is to think of cognitive pretesting as a method to 'provide questionnaire designers with insights about the consequences of various questionnaire design decisions. These findings may not always point to a clearly superior version of a question' (Beatty and Willis, 2007: 304).

Colm O'Muircheartaigh has a more critical view of the puzzling turn of national statistical agencies and large academic survey organizations, whose business is to conduct very large survey projects, to small scale qualitative cognitive pretesting in labs:

> First, the term cognitive has comforting connotations of hard information. Second, the term laboratory carries with it the symbolism of science and scientific investigation, and borrows from the natural sciences a professionalization (or certification) of elite expertise; this makes it a suitable (and defensible) vehicle for methodological work in larger accountable organizations. (1999: 57)

Pretesting Self-administered Surveys

There are a number of alternatives for pretesting self-administered surveys. When it is feasible to conduct a large pretest at low cost, which is common for Internet surveys, it is possible to rely on conventional data analysis to identify questions with high non-response or weak relationships with other variables, suggesting measurement error. A second alternative, whatever the size of the sample, is to add supplementary probing questions after suspect items.

The third possibility is just to use the techniques for interview surveys by asking respondents to complete questionnaires – either with paper and pencil or on a computer – in the presence of an interviewer. This requires bringing respondents to a common location and probably providing payment. Respondents may be asked to indicate problems as they arise or they can 'think aloud' as they write in answers or use a computer. An alternative is to assemble a group of respondents, ask them to complete the survey on their own, and then conduct a group debriefing, going over the questions in detail.

Is Pretesting Consistent and Effective?

Following their extensive review of survey pretesting, Presser et al. conclude:

> not a great deal is known about many aspects of pretesting, including the extent to which pretests serve their intended purpose and lead to improved questionnaires. (2004: 109)

And, after 25 years of cognitive pretesting and its widespread adoption by the pre-eminent governmental and academic survey organizations, Groves et al. find that

> there is a critical need for empirical studies of the reliability of findings from cognitive interviews, their value in improving data quality and the signifi-cance of the many variations in the way cognitive interviews are done ... As yet, though the evidence is limited about the extent to which cognitive testing generally improves survey data. (2009: 264–265)

This seems too pessimistic, even if there has been very little systematic evaluation of pretesting methods, probably because survey organizations treat pretesting as an initial element in the organizational process of data collection, rather than as a step in survey design.

It is appropriate to ask whether the various methods of pretesting are reliable and valid, but the more difficult *and different* question is whether pretesting improves questionnaires. They are distinct from the first, because discovering a defect in a question is different from remedying it, not to mention demonstrating with a second pretest that the revision was successful. Even with extensive development efforts, there are questions that respondents cannot answer because they make unrealistic assumptions about what respondents know, understand, remember or can solve.

Presser and Blair (1994) compared conventional pretests, expert review, behav-iour coding and cognitive interviews, applying each method at least twice to a 130-question survey. Expert review identified 70 per cent more problems than any of the other methods. Also, there was quite extreme variation in the outcomes using the *same* methods. One of the two conventional pretests reported 27 prob-lems, and the other 154, despite an identical reporting strategy that involved 'sep-arate debriefings conducted by two different senior staff members. Interviewers reported on their overall experience and went through the questionnaire item by item' (p. 78). The numbers of problems identified in behaviour coding of these two apparently very different conventional pretests were very similar, however, at 89 and 102. The three cognitive interviewers reported 54, 92 and 138 problems, while the two expert panels reported 140 and 182 problems.

Presser and Blair also compared which questions were identified as problem-atic (and for what reason) by the different methods.[10] The conventional pre-test and behaviour coding of those interviews found more problems related to interviewers, while the problems identified in the cognitive interviews were almost exclusively semantic. The two expert reviews, the two behaviour

---

[10]Unfortunately, except for counts of the total numbers of problems, there were no within-method comparisons, except for behaviour coding. Instead, the researchers compared summaries of all the expert reviews, the two conventional pretests and interviews by the three cognitive interviewers: 'Relying on the summary reports (which incorporated authors' judgments) ... [researchers were] sometimes confronted with conflicting opinions or meager evidence' (Presser and Blair, 1996: 82–83).

coding exercises, two of the three cognitive interviews, and one of the two conventional pretests tended to identify the same problems, although there was more agreement between pretests using the same method than pretests using different ones.[11] One of the conventional pretests and one cognitive interviewer were 'outliers', where the reported problems were much different from all the others.

While no other comparison of pretesting methods includes conventional pretesting, there are some more limited comparisons. Willis et al. (2000) compared a total of 83 cognitive interviews by two organizations. The application of cognitive interviewing involved asking respondents to 'think aloud' when answering and interviewers also followed up with scripted and spontaneous probes. Second, behaviour coding was applied to recorded face-to-face and telephone interviews. And, third, there were separate question-by-question reviews by no fewer than 21 experts.

On average, the expert reviews, behaviour coding of telephone interviews and behaviour coding of face-to-face interviews identified problems with 27.0, 26.1 and 20.7 per cent of the questions, respectively. There was a great deal of variation between the experts – the standard deviation in the percentage of items with problems was 20.5 per cent. The cognitive interviews conducted by two different survey organizations, however, identified only about half as many problems as the experts, 11.9 and 12.3 per cent of questions. In terms of the questions determined to be problematic, the strongest agreement was between the two cognitive tests and between the behaviour coding for the face-to-face and telephone interviews; the experts agreed least with the two other methods.

Rothgeb et al. (2001) compared expert review, checklist-based appraisal of questions and cognitive interviews (nine interviews by each of three organizations) for 83 questions. The experts and the cognitive interviews both found problems in about half the items and, improbably, the checklist identified almost every question as problematic. Across questions, the correlation (Spearman's r) between the summary scores for expert review and cognitive interviews was discouragingly low, just 0.27. The three organizations that carried out the pretesting identified about the same numbers of problems, but the agreement on which questions were problematic was also quite low (the pairwise Spearman's r values were around 0.36).

Even rarer than systematic comparisons of pretesting methods is evidence of whether pretesting improves a survey questionnaire. As part of the study described above, Forsyth et al. (2004) used item non-response rates, behaviour coding and

---

[11]With, Yule's Q, used by Presser and Blair (1994: 92) to measure agreement in the identification of the same problems among pretesting methods, it is possible to have very high measured agreement between methods that identify dramatically different *numbers* of problems. For example, $Q = 0.71$ for the two conventional pretests, one of which identifies 27 problems and the other 154. While it is possible that the 27 problems were almost all among the 154, the converse cannot hold. The extreme disparity between these two pretests suggests something went seriously wrong in one or both of them, and the disparity in the numbers of problems identified by the three cognitive interviewers poses the same problem.

interviewer coding to measure the effectiveness of pretesting-based revisions of 12 highly problematic items. A larger survey demonstrated that pretesting did identify problematic items, *but the revisions failed.* Compared to the originals, items revised on the basis of the pretesting had somewhat lower non-response, about the same level of problems identified by behaviour coding, fewer respondent problems, but *more* problems with interviewers reading the questions.

An earlier study is more positive. Oksenberg et al. (1989: 59) examined the effect of revisions to questions with at least 15 per cent problem answers, based on behaviour coding and special probes. The revisions markedly decreased the proportion of respondents who interrupted a question as it was being read, asked for clarification or gave a qualified or inadequate answer, but they did not affect the number of 'don't know' answers.

To put it mildly, there is no strong evidence that the different pretesting methods identify the same problems in a survey. Even when the same method is used more than once, the degree of consistency varies considerably. A sympathetic reading of the sparse evidence would say that the various procedures succeed in identifying many problems in surveys, but that these errors are not determinate, like mechanical devices that fail. Rather, short of extreme carelessness or accident, researchers design questions that most respondents can understand and answer, but they are not perfect. Since imperfections are a matter of degree, the various pretesting methods have the ability to identify true problems only with some uncertainty. A surer way to improve pretesting is to use somewhat larger pretest samples, rather than applying still more refined procedures to a few pretest respondents.

Perhaps the survey items that are the focus of the published research on pretesting are unusually difficult to improve. This methodological research is conducted by large, competent survey organizations and focuses on factual questions from existing surveys, many of which have been previously pretested in some manner. In these situations pretesting appears to confer minor benefits at best. Survey pretesting is more likely to benefit smaller survey organizations and individuals and groups who conduct surveys on their own, and also research on new and more difficult topics.

———— Conclusion ——

What constitutes a sensible pretest depends on a researcher's confidence in the quality of a draft questionnaire and the size and importance of the survey. Extensive and time-consuming pretesting is the norm for national censuses and official surveys, but surveys that consist mainly of previously pretested items and are conducted by experienced survey organizations need only small conventional pretests – administering the survey in the normal way to about 25 respondents, followed by an interviewer debriefing.

At some additional cost, two strategies considerably improve conventional pretests. First, behaviour coding of conventional pretest interviews increases the reliability of the pretest findings by extracting more information from the responses and putting it together systematically. Oksenberg et al. (1989: 33) demonstrate that detailed coding of the interaction is unnecessary and that simple coding, done by a coder (*not* the interviewer) as the interview proceeds, is adequate to the task. Second, the addition of follow-up probes addressing explicitly identified concerns about a question can effectively resolve puzzles in design.

Expert review is inexpensive and quick, but is characterized by high variability and the tendency to discover non-existent problems. It is better to incorporate the advice of experts directly into the questionnaire design process rather than treating expert review as a separate stage. If experts are treated as an external panel, it makes sense to concentrate on problems identified in the independent ratings of a majority. There should be enough experts – at least four – to identify an outlier. Of course, none of this argues against obtaining the advice of individual experts, especially if the research team does not include a survey expert.

The jury is out on automated identification of problems in survey questions, based on semantic analysis (Graesser et al.) or the characteristics of items (Saris et al.), such as the question topic, length, response options and so on. Because its analysis is really automated – all that is necessary is to paste the text – Graesser's method is easier to use. So far, evidence for the efficacy of these methods comes largely from their developers.

Cognitive pretesting usually involves interviews conducted in a 'lab' setting, and for only part of a questionnaire. There is a consensus that using probes after a question, essentially a cognitively guided version of follow-up probes, is more effective than 'think aloud' interviews. But cognitive testing ordinarily involves very small numbers of interviews and somewhat haphazard attention to the resemblance between the pretest respondents and the survey population. Implicitly, the argument is that this is sufficient to ferret out conceptual problems in a deterministic way.

In line with conventional pretesting and a more statistical view that takes account of variation, even if it is between somewhat atypical pretest respondents, Blair et al. (2006) argue that increasing the number of cognitive interviews to about 40, and ensuring that respondents approximately represent the full range of cognitive ability, significantly increase the power of this method. Beatty and Willis (2007: 296) agree.

Because cognitive interviewing is not completely standardized it is advisable to employ a sufficient number of interviewers, at least four, to get some idea of between-interviewer variability and to identify any outlier. In other words, cognitive interviews are most reliable when there is more standardization and they look more like an elaboration of conventional pretesting.

It is impossible to argue against larger pretests. While it is usually not feasible to reach the threshold of about 300 pretest interviews – which allows rudimentary statistical analysis – a sample of 200 or 100, or even 40 or 50, is significantly better than the norm of about 25 observations. For both conventional and cognitive pretests, it is valuable for researchers to listen to interviews, live or recorded. A second pretest of a survey, modified on the basis of the first pretest, can also be valuable.

The artful interpretation of small pretests does not make their statistical limitations go away. Conventional pretests are quite effective in detecting problematic questions that pose problems for, say, 15 per cent of respondents. But they do not provide sufficient data to choose between good and optimal versions of a question, which is why critical national statistics have such large pretests. For the same reason, small pretests do not provide acceptable estimates of the reliability of multi-item scales.

What does the small and somewhat confusing body of research on pretesting tell us about surveys? Most important perhaps, it implies that researchers who are knowledgeable about the subject matter and skilled in survey writing can write pretty good questions. Pretesting helps incrementally and it is an indispensable part of the survey craft. And an unheralded advantage of any pretest is that it establishes a separate stage between writing the questionnaire and the initiation of data collection. This can help researchers cast a more critical eye over their work and provide an opportunity for input from survey staff. Perhaps the usefulness of small-scale pretesting has more to do with its effect on the organization of a survey project than with concrete improvements to the questions.

7
Survey Data Collection

Modes of survey data collection just refer to the different forms of communication used to contact and solicit respondents, ask questions and record the answers. The mode affects a respondent's willingness to answer a survey and his or her ability and motivation to understand and answer answers. *Interviewer effects* on survey response arise from subtle differences in the way that interviewers and record responses as well as respondents' perceptions of interviewers.

The chapter begins with a description of the four principal modes of data collection – personal and telephone interviews and 'paper and pencil' and Internet self-administered surveys – and then looks at the effect of survey mode on response rates and data quality and the impact of interviewers. The second part of the chapter examines the factors affecting the survey response rate and the impact of response rates on estimates of population characteristics.

To a greater degree than sample and questionnaire design, survey data collection is shaped by its local context, and its success depends critically on respondents' understanding of and sympathy with the survey enterprise. For example, telephone surveys are a cost-effective alternative to face-to-face household surveys, but only if: nearly everyone can be reached by telephone; it is possible to draw a sample of numbers; and most people will answer the survey calls and agree to be interviewed.

At this time, any discussion of data collection takes place in the shadow of a widely perceived crisis in the ability to gather data adequately representing a 'general' population. Recently, Groves (2011) characterized the present period of survey research, beginning in 1990, largely in terms of declining response rates coupled with and in many respects caused by advances in technology. While data collection is hugely varied – a function of the survey sponsor, research topic, data collection agency and the length and demands of the survey – declining response rates are a general, formidable and worsening problem. Rationalizing the decline in response rates, there has been a revision of the traditional view that a high response rate is a necessary criterion of a good survey. Instead the emphasis has shifted to measuring the impact of non-response on estimates of population characteristics. These issues are also taken up in the next chapter on the future of surveys.

———— Modes of Data Collection ————————————————

Traditionally, a mode of data collection combined a method of contacting respondents with a method of asking questions and recording responses. For example, respondents would be contacted and interviewed by telephone or they would be contacted by email and respond on the Internet. But other combinations are possible and have become increasingly common. Respondents may be contacted by telephone and asked to complete an Internet questionnaire or face-to-face interview, or they may be contacted in more than one way and be able to complete a survey in more than one mode.

Face-to-Face Surveys

Because this was the only way to select a probability sample and administer questionnaires with an adequate response rate, surveys began with face-to-face interviews. They continue to be used when there is no other way to select a representative sample and when other methods do not result in an acceptable response rate, including mandated government surveys, surveys over about 20 minutes in length and surveys in locales or regions where a substantial part of the population cannot be surveyed by telephone. Because of their much higher cost, face-to-face surveys are used when no other mode will provide the required data.

As laptops became more capable and less expensive, face-to-face interviewing moved from paper and pencil questionnaires to computers, using portable versions of the software first developed for centralized telephone surveys. Computer-assisted personal interviewing (CAPI) both eliminates the cost, delay and errors introduced by a separate data entry step and prevents errors in navigation between questions. Computerization also allows complex sequences of questions tailored to the characteristics of respondents, facilitates experiments in question wording and order, and can be used to provide the interviewer with additional information as the survey proceeds, such as the answers to questions commonly raised by respondents and advice on dealing with unusual responses.

The drawback of face-to-face surveys is their cost. Locating and interviewing a respondent can require several trips, because no one is home or the selected respondent is not present or will not do an interview at the time. Controlling costs requires limiting the number of calls to each address, because the likelihood of obtaining an interview declines with the number of unsuccessful previous calls. Almost always cost considerations require the selection of clusters of addresses, typically 10 to 15, in small geographical areas, and it is also common to exclude remote or sparsely populated areas altogether. This clustering decreases the precision of estimates because neighbours tend to resemble one another in socio-demographic characteristics and in other ways.

Face-to-face surveys can easily incorporate alternative modes of response. Small printed cards called 'show cards' may be used to present the response options for a complicated question or respondents may be asked to sort cards or carry out other tasks with materials provided by the interviewer. For sensitive questions, respondents can be given a printed form to complete in private and return to the interviewer in a sealed envelope, or respondents' may be asked to use the interviewer's computer themselves, for privacy or to answer questions with a visual component. The latter is known as computer-assisted self-interview, or CASI, and A-CASI is the same, except the respondent listens to questions with headphones (the A is for 'audio'). Adding another mode of data collection to a face-to-face survey does not make it a 'mixed-mode' survey, because each question is answered using one mode.

In longitudinal surveys a common strategy is to use an initial face-to-face interview to obtain a higher response rate and conduct a longer initial interview and, perhaps most important, develop rapport with a respondent whose long-term commitment to the survey is critical. In later waves, data collection may be switched to a telephone or perhaps an Internet survey, but continue with face-to-face interviews for respondents who cannot or will not use another mode. An initial face-to-face interview is also a good time to ask a respondent for permission to access health, taxation and other administrative records and to obtain the names and coordinates of contacts who could locate the respondent if she moves.

Telephone Surveys

Telephone and face-to-face surveys are similar in that an interviewer is able to select a respondent within a household and ask questions and record the answers, but telephone sample coverage is generally not as good. Almost everyone has an address, but even where telephones are almost universal, some people have no telephone, never answer calls, or reject any survey request over the telephone. Compared to a face-to-face survey, the anonymity of the telephone makes it difficult for an interviewer to tailor the invitation to the characteristics of a potential respondent and also makes it easier for the respondent to refuse.

Typically, each telephone interview is one-third to one-fifth the cost of a comparable face-to-face interview. Not only are travel costs eliminated, but the centralization of telephone surveys provides efficiencies in the organization and supervision of interviewing. Because telephone numbers are generally not clustered geographically,[1] a telephone sample has lower sampling error than the

---

[1] Even with traditional switching systems, the addresses reached by telephone numbers that differ by only one digit are not sufficiently close to result in significant clustering, and the adoption of electronic telephone switching removes any need to associate telephone numbers with geographical areas.

same-size face-to-face survey. For variables with a significant degree of neigh-bourhood variation a telephone survey might have the precision of a face-to-face survey with 20 to 40 per cent more observations.

Self-administered Surveys

To conduct a self-administered survey of the general population requires a sam-pling frame listing individuals by name. It cannot be assumed that instructions about how to select a household member at random, which are enclosed with a survey with only a household address, will be followed correctly by whoever opens the envelope. This is no problem if the questions pertain to the entire household and can be answered by any competent household member, but then it is dif-ficult to obtain an adequate response rate if a mailed survey has only an address. Self-administered surveys are often used to survey organizations and businesses, by postal mail or over the Internet, and in a few countries the availability of a population register makes it possible to conduct mail surveys with a probability sample of the population.

The cost of a mailed survey is somewhat lower than a comparable telephone survey, depending on the efforts made to contact selected respondents. After the start-up cost, mail surveys have no economies of scale because the survey costs are mainly printing, postage and the computer entry of completed questionnaires. Internet surveys involve a substantial start-up cost, especially for visual design, programming and testing with the more advanced proprietary software used by major survey organizations, but except for any incentives their cost is essentially unrelated to the sample size . For researchers willing to format their own Internet questionnaires and live with the limitations of the software of commercial online providers, Internet surveys are very low in cost.

Because self-administered surveys allow respondents to answer at their own pace, they can include more complex questions than surveys employing inter-viewers. Especially compared to telephone interviews, respondents' answers are less affected by their ability to remember the details of a complicated question or keep in mind a number of possible answers. Self-administered questionnaires can make use of the visual design of questions, including illustrations, but the layout can also introduce bias. Compared to surveys conducted by an interviewer, order effects are diminished when the respondent is able to see a number of questions on the same printed page or screen and also because the respondent can double back and change the answers to earlier questions. In self-administered question-naires, the answers to adjacent questions are likely to be more consistent and less prone to order effects.

While a self-administered questionnaire allows the respondent the time to answer questions carefully, without an interviewer there is no social pressure to discourage carelessness and encourage the respondent to answer every question. The distracting environment of multi-tasking computers could also lead to less accurate response.

Interactive voice response (IVR) surveys are a hybrid between telephone and self-administered surveys. Contact is made by telephone, with automated dialling or the respondent calling in, and respondents answer by using the telephone keypad or by voice. There are no interviewer effects, since every respondent hears the same pre-recorded voice and the responses are recorded automatically. While IVR response rates tend to be low and the survey must be very short, the cost is also very low. IVR is increasingly used for quick polls during an election campaign.

Multi-mode Surveys

Since the mid-2000s survey researchers have increasingly used multi-mode surveys, in order to lower costs, but more to address declining response rates in household telephone surveys. Many combinations of the modes of recruitment and data collection are possible (de Leeuw, 2005: 237ff.). For example, with a sample of addresses, respondents may be contacted in person, by telephone if a number can be linked to the address, by postal mail and potentially by email. The survey can be administered by an interviewer, in person or by telephone, or the respondent can complete a mailed or Internet questionnaire.

Savings are possible if lower cost, self-administered questionnaires can substitute for interviews or if telephone interviews take the place of face-to-face interviews. The idea is to combine the better coverage of address samples with the lower cost of self-administered questionnaires, reserving interviews for respondents who will not otherwise respond. These cost differences may be sufficient to pay for moderate incentives to respondents who use a lower cost mode. For an interesting discussion of the European Social Survey (ESS) changing from face-to-face interviews to mixed-mode form, see Martin (2011: 6ff.).

Net of the characteristics of respondents, the mode of data collection itself can give rise to differences in response. Because the choice of mode is likely related to respondent characteristics, this could result in bias in the estimates of population characteristics and between-group differences. This is the subject of much current research (for example, see de Leeuw et al., 2010 and Vannieuwenhuyze et al., 2010). The issue is complicated because characteristics of the respondent, *not* all of which are measured in a survey, are likely to affect the *mode* chosen by the respondent *and his or her survey responses*, so it may not be possible to fully remove the mode-related bias.

Except where there are known and large mode effects, for example surveys on alcohol consumption, the consensus is that the benefits of lower cost and higher response outweigh the risks of undiscovered mode-related bias. Also, single-mode surveys are not free of mode bias – it is just that any such bias cannot be measured. Mode effects in 'ordinary' questions are typically quite small, and no larger than other unavoidable errors that, for example, arise from the choice of nearly synonymous words in writing a question, the order of response options and the respondents' occasional and unsystematic misunderstandings.

Survey Mode and Response Rates

The two most comprehensive comparisons find that face-to-face surveys have higher response rates[2] than telephone surveys, by a small margin. De Leeuw (1992: 26) reports a 75 per cent mean response rate for face-to-face surveys, versus 71 per cent for telephone surveys and Goyder (1987: 56) obtains similar results, after accounting for the number of contacts with a respondent, the use of incentives and the survey topic and sponsor. Especially in light of the very large cost difference, this evidence lent support to the shift from face-to-face to telephone surveys from about the mid-1970s.

These findings, however, long predate the decline in landline coverage in a number of countries, the difficulties in sampling and completing interviews with mobile phones and the widespread adoption of 'call screening', not to mention the overall decline in response rates. For the USA, Holbrook et al. report that 'a diverse group of the nation's most expensive, long-term, large-scale, federally funded survey studies of national samples involving long questionnaires have retained the face-to-face method while most other survey research moved to the telephone' (2003: 81).

In recent meta-analyses, Lozar Manfreda et al. (2008) and Shih and Fan (2008) found average response rates of about 45 per cent for mail surveys and 35 per cent for Internet surveys. While the 10 per cent average difference is quite large, this does not mean that a mail survey will invariably result in a higher response rate, because the standard deviation in the response rates of the surveys using each mode is about 20 per cent. In choosing the survey mode, cost is likely to be a big factor. For a small sample, the effort required to program an Internet survey might be similar to the resources needed to design, print and mail a survey and enter the returned forms. For a larger sample, however, the printing, postage and data entry costs of a mailed survey make the Internet survey much less expensive.

Because survey response can only be compared for samples of the same type, there are not many comparisons between self-administered and interview

---

[2]In principle, the response rate is just the number of completed questionnaires divided by the number of selected respondents. But there is some uncertainty in both the numerator and denominator. For the numerator, we must decide what constitutes a completed questionnaire. Some respondents quit before the end or complete the questionnaire but leave many questions unanswered. For the denominator, we must determine whether selected respondents who we never contacted are *eligible* respondents. A conservative estimate of the denominator is just the average eligibility for respondents *who were successfully contacted*. Alternatively, an estimate can be obtained by regressing the probability of eligibility on auxiliary variables, such as location, that are available for all selected respondents and on measures of the difficulty of contacting respondents, such as the required number of calls. To encourage uniform and fair assessments, as well as create a level playing field for researchers and survey organizations that would prefer to report higher response rates, there is wide acceptance of the expert guidelines of the American Association for Public Opinion Research (2011). It defines six alternative response rates, based on whether partially completed surveys are counted and the assumptions made about the eligibility of selections who were not contacted.

surveys. Fricker et al. (2005) and Chang and Krosnick (2009) obtain a higher response rate for a telephone survey than an Internet survey, but their comparisons are based on a sample initially contacted by telephone, so the telephone respondents are immediately asked to continue with a telephone survey while the Internet group is asked to log on at some later time. Contacted on the telephone, more respondents will proceed with an interview immediately, or maybe arrange a time to call back, than will agree to and then fulfil their commitment to answer an Internet survey.

It follows that offering respondents a choice of mode *when they are first contacted* does not improve response rates, again because of the failure to follow through on promises to complete a self-administered survey. If the alternative modes are offered *in sequence*, however, some respondents who refuse to answer an interview will complete a self-administered survey (de Leeuw, 2005: 240), which produces some improvement in the response.

There is considerable international variation in response rates. For 21 countries, Stoop et al. (2010: 93) report that response rates for the 2006 ESS, a biennial face-to-face survey, varied between 46 and 73 per cent. Within nations, however, there are also differences between modes. While the ESS response rate for the Netherlands is 59.8 per cent, a bit below average, the elaborate *Internet* LISS panel study, based on a probability sample drawn from the Netherlands national register, has a response rate around 80 per cent.[3] This reversal of the usually higher response rate of face-to-face surveys must in part be due to the LISS panel's use of incentives and its providing a free computer with Internet access to households without one. The average cost of ESS face-to-face interviews is €120, which would provide for a healthy incentive if it was possible to switch to a self-administered survey.

Survey Mode and Data Quality ———

As the total survey error perspective emphasizes, like each of the other steps in the survey process, the mode of data collection contributes to measurement error. The two common forms of mode-related bias, *acquiescence* and *social desirability*, were discussed in Chapter 2, in relation to question design.

[3]See the ESS at http://www.europeansocialsurvey.org and the LISS project at http://www.lissdata.nl. Another large international survey project, the International Social Survey Program (ISSP), allows the researchers in each country to decide the mode of data collection and does not provide response rate comparisons. Surveys for the 'EU statistics on income and living conditions' (EU-SILC) are conducted by the different EU nations' central statistical agencies, also using a variety of modes, including multiple modes in some nations, to study income, poverty, social exclusion and living conditions. Response rates in 2009 varied from 52 to 96 per cent in the 32 participant countries (Eurostat, 2011: 27).

More concern has been directed to the effect of survey mode on random error, non-response and response patterns indicative of satisficing and inattention. A number of differences have been observed, for example:

- because they cannot see the interviewer or read questions themselves, telephone survey respondents have the most difficulty understanding and answering complex questions;
- self-administered surveys allow respondents to set their own pace and also it is easier to reread a difficult question than to ask an interviewer to repeat it;
- compared to the telephone, face-to-face interviewers communicate more effectively and are better able to sense and try to clarify respondent confusion;
- face-to-face interviews and self-administered surveys permit the use of visual material on a show card, printed page or monitor;
- interviews generally, and especially telephone interviews, put more burden on the respondent's ability to remember and consider the details in a question and to consider all the response categories; and
- only interview surveys allow respondents to ask for help, though there is evidence that they do not often do so. (Conrad and Schober, 2005: 221)

The environment and technology of telephone interviews and Internet surveys seem to encourage less thoughtful responses than face-to-face interviews or paper and pencil surveys. Answering a survey on the telephone at home or a mobile phone, the respondent is in a potentially distracting environment where it is easy to surreptitiously multi-task. Modern computer environments, where the Internet survey is just in one 'window', might also encourage quicker, less thoughtful responses.

The possibility that the survey mode affects a respondent's motivation and the quality of her or his responses is captured by the idea of survey *satisficing*, put forward by Jon Krosnick (1991; also see Krosnick and Alwin, 1987). First identified and given the name by Herbert Simon in 1957, satisficing describes decision making that aims for a good and acceptable outcome, rather than the optimal outcome.[4] Applying the concept to survey respondents, Krosnick distinguishes 'weak' and 'strong' satisficing, respectively, as:

> being less thorough in comprehension, retrieval, judgement, and response selection … [being] less thoughtful about a question's meaning, they may search their memories less thoroughly, they may integrate retrieved information more carelessly, and they may select a response choice more haphazardly;

> omitting the retrieval and judgement steps from the response process altogether. That is, respondents may interpret each question only superficially and select what they believe will *appear* to be a reasonable answer to each question. (1991: 215)

---

[4]Satisficing makes sense in many aspects of everyday life, and it plays a role in more important personal decisions when it is hard to judge outcomes exactly or where the cost of securing an optimal outcome is greater than the expected gain over a pretty good outcome. For example, job seekers may curtail their search for a better job when they find an acceptable one, because finding a better alternative takes time and after an initial substantial search is likely to result in only small gains.

Satisficing results in increased item non-response and in the proportion of neutral and middle answers, as well as patterns of *non-differentiation*, whereby a respondent gives the same answer to a series of consecutive questions, regardless of their content.

Ideally, mode effects would be measured by comparing survey responses to factual external information. Even in the rare circumstance when this is possible, however, validation studies are expensive and difficult, and often they involve special populations from which it is difficult to generalize. For attitudes and many other common survey measures, of course, there is no such external reference and so mode effects are measured with experiments were respondents are assigned to a survey mode at random. In principle, any survey with mixed-mode data collection provides a basis for comparing modes, but such comparisons are often compromised by incompletely measured differences between respondents using the different modes. Mode effects are especially difficult to measure when respondents are first asked to answer in the lowest cost, self-administered mode, and then switched to more costly modes if they do not respond.

Empirical Comparisons

Accompanying and rationalizing the growth of telephone surveys in countries with good landline coverage in the 1970s, a large body of research compared face-to-face and telephone surveys. At the time response rates were quite high for both modes, typically around 70 per cent. In the most extensive comparison, which was conducted by Groves and Kahn (1979), there was no evidence of systematic differences, with two exceptions:

- For questions that used seven *labelled* categories, telephone respondents were more likely than face-to-face respondents to choose the middle category and the extreme positive category, and less likely to choose the extreme negative category; using seven points labelled only at the ends and in the middle, however, there was virtually no difference between modes (p. 148).
- For open questions that allowed multiple responses, telephone respondents gave fewer answers and the telephone and face-to-face response distributions differed (p. 149).

Ye et al. (2011) find similar 'extremity bias' in telephone surveys, compared to both self-administered questionnaires and face-to-face interviews, but only for positive answers. What they call 'The MUM effect [that is, 'keeping mum']' applies to situations in which the message is undesirable for the receiver. This is quite distinct from the concept of social-desirability bias, which refers to respondents' reluctance to reveal embarrassing information about themselves' (p. 351).

Summarizing a number of studies, de Leeuw (1992: 28) finds that, to a small degree, telephone surveys exhibit more item non-response and they are more likely to elicit similar responses to a series of consecutive questions (indicating satisficing) and fewer responses to open questions. She finds no difference in social desirability in surveys conducted in the 1980s, but slightly more social desirability in telephone surveys prior to 1980. Comparing face-to-face and telephone interviews in US surveys from 1976, 1982 and 2000, Holbrook et al. found that telephone survey respondents were more likely 'to satisfice (as evidenced by no-opinion responding, nondifferentiation, and acquiescence), to be less cooperative and engaged in the interview … [and] to present themselves in socially desirable ways' (2003: 79).

Also comparing face-to-face to telephone interviews in an experiment, Jäckle et al. (2010) found that telephone interviews elicited more socially desirable responses for 16 out of 28 variables tested, including moderate, statistically significant effects (around 5 per cent in magnitude) on reported interest in politics and political efficacy, religiosity and attendance at religious services, household income and large effects (around 15 per cent) on the total time spent watching television and watching television news, and attitudes towards immigration. They also showed that for typical ordinal measures of attitudes and behaviour, the estimated magnitude of the mode effect depends strongly on the statistical model employed (p. 7ff.).

The extent of mode effects is related to the question topic. In a large Canadian health survey, Béland and St-Pierre found no difference between face-to-face and telephone interviews for 'the vast majority of health indicators … such as tobacco use (all ages), chronic conditions, activity limitations, fruit and vegetable consumption' (2008: 6). There was evidence of social desirability bias, however, in telephone responses to questions about height, weight, physical activity, contact with physicians and unmet health care needs.

There is also evidence of international differences. Comparing face-to-face and CATI interviews, Martin finds that

> in the ESS CATI experiment … telephone respondents were more likely than face-to-face respondents to use extreme points on response scales, while face-to-face respondents were more likely to agree with the premise of questions (acquiescence effects) and to use scale mid-points. Importantly, the results were not uniform in all participating countries. (2011: 11)

Comparisons between interviews and self-administered surveys demonstrate one advantage and one disadvantage of each. First, there is extensive evidence that self-administered surveys, whether mail or Internet, result in more truthful answers to sensitive questions than face-to-face and telephone surveys (de Leeuw, 1992: 30; Aquilino, 1994; Tourangeau and Smith, 1996; Tourangeau and Yan, 2007: 863; Krauter et al., 2008). On the other hand, self-administered surveys by mail and especially Internet surveys show evidence of more satisficing in the form of item non-response, random error and non-discrimination (Fricker et al., 2005; Heerwegh and Loosveldt, 2008). Chang and Krosnick (2009: 641) report that a telephone survey 'manifested more random measurement error, more survey satisficing, and more social desirability response bias' than their comparable Internet survey.

In terms of data quality, the clear winners are face-to-face interviews over telephone interviews, and paper and pencil self-administered surveys over Internet surveys. For most surveys, which employ a single mode of data collection, the evidence of mode effects can only be cautionary. Except for sensitive topics which demand self-administered surveys, the choice of survey mode is almost always determined by the ability to sample the population of interest, budgetary considerations and sometimes the length of the survey questionnaire.

In multi-mode surveys, mode effects may give rise to methodological artefacts because of the correlation between mode and respondent characteristics. This is also a concern for comparative surveys where modes vary across nations and for surveys employing multiple modes in succession in order to increase response rates or reduce costs.

The correlation between survey mode and respondent characteristics also affects the analysis of mixed-mode data. Unless respondents are assigned to modes randomly, which is rare unless the surveys are designed explicitly for methodological research, it is a good idea to include questions that predict the mode preferred by a respondent. If possible, a better strategy is to embed an experiment that randomly allocates a subsample of respondents to the different modes.

A special case is longitudinal surveys that switch from interviews in the first wave(s) to less expensive self-administered modes. Then it is often possible to draw on previous research and effectively account for the impact of changing modes. If the resources are available, the gold standard is to gather data with both methods in the wave when the transition takes place, with at least part of the sample assigned to modes randomly. A similar strategy is commonly employed when official surveys change the wording of critical questions.

Minimizing mode effects in multi-mode surveys can come into conflict with maximizing the quality of questions in each mode. For example, a technique known as unfolding can be used in interviews to increase the precision of response. The respondent is first asked whether he or she agrees or disagrees with a statement, and then a second question asks whether he or she (dis)agrees or *strongly* (dis)agrees. This makes up for the inability of the interview respondent to see all the alternatives easily on paper or a screen, but could account for at least a small difference between modes. Similarly, since the visual design of a question can affect response, it can also give rise to a mode effect if some observations are collected by interview.

There is no perfect solution to the problem of designing questionnaires for use in more than one mode, but Dillman (2007: 232ff.) makes a convincing case for *unimode construction*, which he defines as 'writing and presenting ... questions to respondents in a way that assures receipt by respondents of a common mental stimulus, regardless of the survey mode'. The question is to what degree it is possible to present respondents with 'a common mental stimulus' in light of the cognitive differences between modes, as well as differences in the setting. De Leeuw is more tentative:

> Hardly any theoretical or empirical knowledge is available on how to design optimal questionnaires for mixed-mode data collection (e.g., unimode and generalized mode design). Empirical research is needed to estimate what constitutes the same stimulus across different modes, and especially how new media and new graphical tools will influence this. (2005: 249–250)

Likewise, there is a need for the further development of analysis of multi-mode surveys. Overwhelmingly, the existing literature is concerned with the use of multi-mode surveys to increase, or least arrest the decline in, response rates, rather than with the design of multi-mode questionnaires or analysis of the resulting data.

Interviewer Effects

Interviewers do what letters, emails and invitations on websites cannot: they actively convince respondents to participate, often arranging for a return call or visit; they select respondents within a household; and they answer questions during an interview. There is also variation between interviewers in the ability to secure cooperation, read questions and record answers accurately, and in how they answer queries from respondents. Training and supervision designed to standardize interviewers' behaviour cannot completely eliminate the differences arising from interviewers' personalities, skills and experience and it cannot control the effects of *respondents'* perceptions of the voice and appearance of interviewers.

Since surveys are intended to capture variation in respondents' answers to identical questions, *any* effect of an interviewer on respondents' answers is a form of measurement error. Such error can be classified into two categories. First, in their role as intermediaries between a researcher's questions and respondents' answers that they record, interviewers contribute some *random* error, adding to errors arising from respondents' varying ability to understand and answer questions and the effort put into their answers. Interviewer random error arises from minor misreading of questions and unintended emphases and mistakes in recording responses; it is difficult to separate from the other error contributions, but it is not problematic. The second form of interviewer effect involves systematic differences between the groups of respondents allocated to each interviewer – in statistical terms these constitute clusters – that cannot be attributed to the attributes of the respondents in each cluster. 'Interviewer effects' refer to this second component only.

What should the interviewer do when a respondent clearly misunderstands a question or asks for clarification? If she steps in to correct the misunderstanding or answers a question, the result is a better answer. But another interviewer might respond differently and so the different styles of interviews can give rise to interviewer effects. This is why it is common for survey organizations to attempt to reduce interviewer variation by instructing the interviewer to do no more than reread the question when a respondent asks for clarification, even if this does not help the respondent give a better answer. So there is potentially a trade-off between interviewer- and respondent-related error.

Measuring Interviewer Effects

Like clusters of respondents that arise from the sample design, interviewers potentially increase the similarity of responses of the respondents in the same cluster. This is measured by the intraclass correlation due to interviewers, symbolized ρ_{int}. If each interviewer conducts an average of m interviews, the error variance is increased by a factor of $deff_{int} = 1 + \rho_{int}(m - 1)$, where $deff_{int}$ is called the design effect. So, if ρ_{int} is zero or if each interviewer does just one interview, there is no interviewer effect!

Say that $\rho_{int} = 0.02$ for some question and each interviewer conducts an average of 30 interviews. Then, from the formula above, $deff_{int}$ is 1.58, meaning that the allocation of groups of respondents to interviewers results in a 58 per cent increase in the error variance and a 26 per cent increase (since $\sqrt{1.58} = 1.26$) in the confidence interval of a mean or proportion. This is substantial, since it means that making up for the loss in precision due to the interviewer effect would require a 58 per cent increase in the sample size. Clearly the aim of training and supervising interviewers should be to minimize the variation in interviewers' behaviour that increases the value of ρ_{int}. The magnitude of the interviewer effects is different for each variable in a survey, and is potentially a function of the survey population, mode, survey topic and style of interviewers.

Following Kish (1962; also see Hartley and Rao, 1978), the intraclass correlation is equal to the proportion of the total variance in a variable that is due to variation between interviewers. If respondents were randomly assigned to interviewers, estimating ρ_{int} would require only a one-way analysis of variance (ANOVA). In face-to-face surveys where each geographical cluster is assigned to a single interviewer, the geographical and interviewer effects cannot be separated. Separating them requires an *interpenetrated* design, whereby the addresses in each cluster are divided randomly between at least two interviewers. This raises travel costs because it decreases the likelihood that each interviewer's travel to a cluster will result in an interview, though it is more feasible in cities where the population density is higher. With an interpenetrated design, interviewer effects *net of geographical clustering* can be estimated with a two-way ANOVA or, more elegantly, with a mixed model.

For centralized telephone surveys it is quite easy to allocate respondents to interviewers at random, though it is necessary to suspend the common practice of assigning the most skilled interviewers to 'convert' respondents who refuse an initial request and deal with respondents who repeatedly delay but never refuse to complete an interview outright.

Because of the effort required to estimate the interviewer effects, the number of reported studies is a small and not-likely representative sample of all surveys. For the 12 pre-1985 studies located by O'Muircheartaigh and Campanelli (1998: 68), the average of the value of ρ_{int} for face-to-face interviewers is about 0.01. So, if each interviewer averaged 40 interviews, $deff_{int}$ was about 1.4. They also contribute a nice analysis of the 1992 wave of the British Household Panel Survey, estimating ρ_{int} for no less then 802 variables. The median ρ_{int} is about 0.01, but there is substantial variation; ρ_{int} is significantly different from zero for 28 per cent of the attitude questions and 26 per cent of the factual questions.[5] The value of ρ_{int} was unrelated to whether the question was from the 'cover sheet' (completed by the interviewer and recording household composition and similar measures), or whether questions related to the individual respondent or the respondent's household. Moreover, 17 per cent of the items that respondents answered privately on a printed form also had ρ_{int} values significantly greater than zero. These results are consistent with results reported by Schnell and Kreuter (2005).[6]

Interviewer effects are smaller in telephone than face-to-face surveys, although the two largest comparisons, both American, are quite dated. In analysing 1980 election polls, Tucker (1983) found an average value for ρ_{int} of 0.04. Groves and Magilavy (1986) report that the average value of ρ_{int} was 0.009 for nine surveys conducted between 1978 and 1982, with slightly higher values of ρ_{int} for factual items, 0.0098, than for attitudinal items, 0.0085. More recently, Lipps (2007) found negligible interviewer effects in a Swiss telephone survey.

A fine summary of research by Davis et al. (2010) provides unequivocal evidence that visible and audible characteristics for the interviewer, most notably gender and racialization, affect the answers to questions *related to those statuses*. For example, both women and men are more likely to endorse women's rights if the interviewer is female. The argument can be made that the interviewer and respondent should be matched on the assumption, for example, that women respondents are most likely to give unbiased responses to women interviewers and the same is true for men. In reviewing the empirical evidence, however, Schaeffer et al. (2010: 443) find no support for this conjecture. Matching interviewers and respondents is difficult in household surveys because the characteristics of the respondent are not known before contact with the household. An easier strategy is to control for characteristics of the interviewer in data analysis, provided they are sufficiently diverse (a problem if the interviewers are predominantly women).

Minimizing and Accounting for Interviewer Effects

If interviewer effects potentially result in bias, how can they be minimized? The conventional strategy is greater 'standardization', insisting that questions be read exactly as written, limiting responses to respondent queries to rereading the question, and asking respondents to answer in terms of what 'the question means to

---

[5]But, as usual, a non-significant result is not evidence that the value is zero.

[6]Analysing a recent German survey, Schnell and Kreuter obtain a mean design effect of 1.39 for geographical clusters and find that 77 per cent of the between clusters is due to interviewers and 23 per cent to the sampling point (pp. 400–401). The magnitude of the effects is slightly higher for sensitive items, non-factual items and open questions, but is unrelated to the difficulty of items (2005: 402).

you'. In a recent review, however, Schaeffer et al. (2010) conclude that standardization is unlikely to significantly decrease interviewer effects. This makes sense because the observed design effects are computed from surveys conducted by large and professional organizations whose interviewers were already highly trained.

A number of aspects of the working conditions of interviewers militate against the likelihood that standardization will decrease interviewer effects. Often interviewers work part-time and are poorly paid. The resulting high turnover means that investment in more intensive training largely evaporates. Second, a heavy emphasis on standardization makes the job less pleasant, which may lower the quality of work, decrease productivity and increase turnover. Third, for most survey organizations an interviewer's most important skill is convincing respondents to be interviewed, which requires an outgoing but not overbearing personality that might not fit with a highly regimented approach to conducting interviews.

The literature on survey research displays disturbingly little interest in the quality of the workplace and its effect on the quality of survey data. Stoop et al. comment:

> Considering the importance of the role of the interviewer, it is key that their payment reflects the efforts required. Levels of interviewer pay and the pay structure are highly likely to affect interviewers' willingness to try and enhance their response rates … Payment systems, assignment sizes, training programmes and other practical issues are specific to each fieldwork organization. Differences between countries are to be expected. No empirical studies are available on the effect of such differences. (2010: 23)

Excessive standardization of interviews may actually lower the quality of responses, because the rigidity alienates respondents and the interviewers do not help the respondents give better answers. Thus decreasing the measurement error due to interviewer effects may increase the random measurement error, because it restricts the ability of interviewers to help respondents give better answers.

A number of methodologists (Beatty, 1995; Schober and Conrad, 1997; Conrad and Schober, 2000; 2005; Maynard and Schaeffer, 2002) advocate greater efforts to clarify the meaning of questions, including improving the explanations embedded in questions, actively clarifying questions raised by respondents, and intervening when there are hints of a problem – such as non-verbal communication in a face-to-face interview, pauses in responding and qualified answers. Biemer and Lyberg (2003: 150ff.) argue that more interactive and conversational interviewing by more knowledgeable and better-trained interviewers will lower measurement error, without increasing interviewer effects. High interviewer turnover makes this difficult and so their strategy assumes a more stable workforce, almost exclusively found in central statistical agencies, which offer higher rates of pay and better working conditions than most academic, and especially commercial, survey organizations.

Ideally, interviewing should combine flexibility and standardization, so that for each question interviewers know how much they should assist, and they have scripted answers to the most common respondent queries. With CATI or CAPI, these answers can be on the interviewer's screen. Interviewing techniques are moving in this direction at the same time as the distinction between self-administered and interviewer surveys is decreasing. Schober and Conrad envisage:

> A next generation of interviewing systems ... likely to make use of 'paradata' (process measures) from respondents during the interaction, as a way of diagnosing when help might be needed so that the system can intervene appropriately ... One could imagine making use of respondents' typing errors, changed answers, response times, speech disfluencies, or facial expressions to assess their confidence in their answers or their likelihood of having misunderstood. (2008: 6)

Complexity and ambivalence are at the heart of survey interviewing. On the one hand, the idea is to take advantage of the flexibility and intelligence of conversation, so that interviewers select respondents within a household, improve answers by answering respondents' questions, and motivate the respondent. On the other hand, the interviewer's role and the respondent's task completely lack the spontaneity and egalitarianism of conversation.

Since the measurement error resulting from the use of interviewers is proportional to the number of interviews conducted by each interviewer, in order to reduce interviewer effects it is only necessary to lower the average workload. But this results in serious financial and logistic problems. Even if a survey organization is conducting many surveys at one time, so that interviewers can switch between studies, an interviewer who conducts only a small number of interviews with a particular questionnaire makes more errors. So a smaller interviewer effect comes at the cost of greater random error. Also this raises the cost of training, since more interviewers must be trained for each project.

It is unrealistic to expect that interviewer effects can be reduced to zero. Even with careful training, to a small degree, responses may be affected by minor differences in intonation and judgement calls about answering respondent queries, not to mention *respondents'* perceptions of the interviewer. It is cautious and sensible, and the cost is very small, to test for and if necessary statistically control for interviewer effects. To make this possible survey datasets should identify the interviews conducted by each interviewer and provide the interviewers' basic characteristics, including their gender, racialization, any accent, age and experience in the job.

In face-to-face surveys, the assignment of one interviewer to each cluster makes it difficult to separate neighbourhood from interviewer effects, but accounting for the sampling-point clusters still results in correct errors. Dividing geographical clusters between two interviewers in order to obtain a robust measure of interviewer effects is justified only if there is a specific methodological interest or a research focus on neighbourhood effects.

———————————————— **Improving Survey Response** ————

This section takes its name from a recent book by Stoop et al. (2010), titled *Improving Survey Response: Lessons Learned from the European Social Survey.* 'Improving' is apt because there is no silver bullet, only strategies to improve response rates that involve tradeoffs between the cost, representativeness of the achieved sample and the content of surveys. Testifying to the difficulty of the problem, the efforts of a major industry with a financial stake in high response rates have not prevented a steady erosion of response rates in many countries. Where the decline in response rate has been arrested, usually it is because of increased effort to obtain interviews, especially extensive efforts to reach every selected respondent and to change the minds of respondents who refuse initially.

Before considering the research on factors affecting survey response, it is appropriate to review the ideas about why people respond to surveys. Typically, a survey begins with an anonymous request to commit a small amount of time, seldom more than 25 minutes, to complete an interview or mail or Internet survey. Face-to-face interviews are usually not much longer, but they can last an hour or more. If no compensation is offered, the request to answer a survey is comparable to doing a favour for a neighbour or co-worker who is only an acquaintance, making a small donation to charity, or walking a couple of blocks to a voting station. For some respondents, answering a survey is a form of self-expression and perhaps self-affirmation.

For most respondents, none of this is much changed by a small incentive, which acts like an honorarium acknowledging the respondent's contribution, rather than payment for her time. The respondent is more likely to expect an incentive if the survey has an explicitly commercial purpose. Participation in a survey may also involve a straightforward economic transaction; for example it is common practice to pay physicians generously to complete surveys. Longitudinal surveys are a special case because they entail a greater and continuing commitment and because of the expectation that respondents will identify themselves and provide information required to find them if they move. Usually this includes the respondents' name, address and telephone numbers and the names and coordinates of (usually two) people who could find the respondent if direct contact is lost.

Theories of Survey Response

In 1978, Donald Dillman put forward the idea that survey participation involves social exchange, which he differentiates from economic exchange, as follows:

> social exchange is a broader concept. Future obligations are created that are diffuse and unspecified. The nature of the return cannot be bargained over as in economic exchange, but must be left to the discretion of the one who owes it ... Fundamentally, then, whether a given behavior occurs is a function of the ratio of ... costs and ... rewards. (2007: 14)

In return for the time and effort involved in answering the survey, Dillman argues, the respondent is rewarded with the interviewer's 'positive regard', the interviewer's thanks, a sense of accomplishment because he or she responded to a request for help and advice, the chance to 'support group values', and so on (pp. 15–16). He believes that 'providing a tangible incentive, even a token one, is effective because it evokes a sense of reciprocal obligation which can easily be discharged by returning the completed questionnaire' (p. 16). In order to engage this reciprocity, Dillman advocates providing a token incentive *prior* to obtaining a respondent's agreement to participate.

A complete contrast is the application of Ajzen and Fishbein's theory of reasoned action (1980) to survey response by Hox et al. (1995: 5ff.). Instead of invoking a general social principle, they think of survey participation in terms of individual differences. The likelihood of answering a survey is affected, first, by a person's general attitude towards survey research, which affects their attitude towards the topic and the time and effort to complete a specific survey; and, second, by the person's 'normative' beliefs about their friends' willingness to respond to surveys, which affect the person's own views of whether they would respond to surveys on different topics. In testing the model in an introductory psychology class, measures of attitudes and norms were disappointingly weak predictors of survey response (p. 8). Also, the theory has a certain tautological character when it predicts that people who approve of a survey are more likely to respond.

At this time, the closest to a conventional explanation of survey response is Groves et al.'s (2000) 'leverage-saliency theory'. The idea is that individuals vary in the importance they ascribe to the different attributes of a survey, including the survey topic, any incentive and the credibility and worth of the survey sponsor. In deciding whether to answer a survey, the respondent combines her assessments of its attributes, weighting each attribute according to its salience.[7] Someone who is concerned about public policy, for example, might be convinced by an appeal emphasizing the impact of the findings, while being unaffected by a monetary incentive; while someone with no interest in the survey topic might be attracted by the incentive. Groves et al. (2000: 305ff.) demonstrate that respondents who are not interested in the survey topic are most affected by incentives, while Groves and other colleagues (2004) observe a similar, though weak, effect.[8]

---

[7]More precisely, the predictor of response is the sum, over all the attributes of a survey, of the *product* of the importance of each attribute and the evaluation of that attribute.

[8]In a comprehensive review of the effect of incentives on telephone survey response, Cantor et al. (2008) find no pattern of variation in the effect of incentives on demographic groups, except that 'respondents with intrinsically low-response propensity are more affected by an incentive' (p. 497). While they interpret this as inconsistent with the prediction of leverage-saliency theory, the theory predicts that incentives raise the response rates of individuals who are not otherwise motivated to cooperate, not that particular socio-demographic groups are differentially sensitive to incentives.

Exchange and leverage-saliency theory are rational choice theories, as is Singer's (2011) very similar 'benefit–cost' theory, whereby respondents agree to be interviewed if the benefit outweighs the costs. Dillman cautions that social exchange is inexact and, compared to Groves et al., he gives more emphasis to the benefit of a respondent's opportunity to express his or her mind and gain the attention and respect of the interviewer.

According to leverage-saliency theory, respondents decide whether to answer a survey by weighing the pros and cons; indeed they use an illustration of a balance scale. Lin and Schaeffer (1995) observe that this model implies that individuals are located along a 'continuum of resistance', ranging from 'high-propensity' respondents who are most easily contacted and persuaded, to the 'lowest-propensity' respondents who are hard to find, not interested in the topic and indifferent to an incentive. The response propensity can be estimated empirically from the number of calls required to reach a respondent and how readily he or she consented to an interview. It is possible to use propensity scores to weight the data, giving higher weights to respondents with low propensity, because they 'represent' respondents who mostly refused to answer the survey. We return to this point in the last section of this chapter.

Neither exchange theory nor leverage-saliency theory effectively addresses the decline in survey response rates. In focusing on a transaction between the respondent and the survey sponsor, exchange theory does not connect survey participation to characteristics of the individual or society. While leverage-saliency theory links respondents' values to survey participation, it is hard to argue that, say, declining response rates reflect a decreased interest in public policy. To a significant degree, the decline in survey response must reflect changing attitudes towards surveys themselves and towards the institutions – governmental, academic and commercial – that sponsor and conduct them.

Field Strategies for Increasing Survey Response

In empirical research on survey response spanning more than 40 years, from a number of countries and using different modes with widely varying topics, there is a high degree of consensus on the factors affecting survey response. These can be divided into three classes: attributes of an entire survey; data collection procedures; and the characteristics of individual respondents. This section focuses on aspects of survey data collection practices that the researcher does control: efforts to contact and convince a respondent to participate; the pitch made to respondents; and incentives.

The 'fixed' attributes of a survey that affect the response rate include the identity of the survey sponsor and data collection agency, the survey mode, the topic of the survey and the target population. Surveys conducted for government agencies have higher response rates than academic surveys, which have higher response rates than commercial surveys; and there are corresponding differences in the response rates of surveys conducted *by* government agencies and academic and commercial organizations. Also, longer surveys and surveys on more difficult topics have lower response rates. On these points, see meta-analyses by Heberlein and Baumgartner (1978), Goyder (1987) and Hox and de Leeuw (1994). These findings are of no practical help in increasing survey response rates because, for a given survey, they are not subject to change. Similarly, the demographic, socio-economic and attitudinal characteristics of respondents affecting the response rate are dictated by the composition of the sample. Nice reviews can be found in Groves and Couper (1998), Stoop (2005: 64ff.) and Stoop et al. (2010: 24ff.).

Persistence The most important predictor of response that is under the control of the data collector is simply persistence, which involves no more than repeated and effective attempts to contact respondents. For telephone surveys it is common to specify a minimum number of calls to each selected number, to space the calls over a long period (typically at least three weeks), and to vary the time of day and day of the week when calls are made. The idea is to contact respondents who are not often at home, who do shift work or have unusual hours for another reason, or who go on vacation. With each unanswered call the probability of ever obtaining a response declines and analysis of the success of reaching respondents with different numbers of calls indicates when it makes sense to give up. This also holds for face-to-face surveys, though cost considerations loom much larger.

For interviewer surveys it is important to systematically follow up successful contacts that do not result in an interview, including respondents who repeatedly say they are busy. Persistence also involves attempting to 'convert' refusals into completed interviews, unless the initial refusal was adamant or the jurisdiction does not allow a subsequent call. Depending on the circumstances, 'converted refusals' typically account for 15–30 per cent of completed interviews. Refusal conversion is highly cost effective; not only is there information about how to contact the person. A relatively high proportion of calls are successful.

Similar considerations hold for self-administered surveys. For mailed surveys, where the cost of each contact attempt is significant, the normal routine is to send an initial questionnaire, followed by a brief reminder – often just a postcard, followed by a second copy of the questionnaire, followed by a second reminder. Accounting for the vagaries of mail distribution, these might be sent at 10-day intervals. A typical distribution of the percentage of the total returns after the four contacts might be 40 per cent after the first message and questionnaire, then 25, 20 and 15 per cent for the three subsequent mailings.

For Internet surveys the cost of additional email solicitations is very low or negligible and the response to each is nearly immediate. After each email request there is a sharp peak of responses in the first day or two, followed by a steep decline, so that there are very few additional respondents after the fourth or fifth day. There is significant additional response until at least five or six messages.

When the contact information is available, another strategy is to employ a second mode of contact, such as making telephone calls to non-respondents of face-to-face, mail or Internet surveys or sending postal mail reminders to telephone or Internet survey non-respondents. The novelty of a reminder sent in a different mode and perhaps the implicit message that the response is important add to its value. Special delivery mail or other means of embellishing an invitation can increase the response rate. In some countries initial recruitment by telephone is effective for face-to-face interviews and results in significant cost savings because the interviewer can make an appointment (Stoop et al., 2010: 131ff.).

For telephone surveys, a common strategy is to send an 'advance letter' describing the survey and saying the household will receive a call. De Leeuw et al. (2007) found an increase of 5–10 per cent in response rates, which is substantial and cost effective, but no such effect was found by Singer et al. (2000) or Holbrook et al. (2008).

The Pitch   While care should be taken in composing the appeal to respondents, what can sensibly and honestly be said about a given survey is quite limited and, without significant information about the respondents, mail and Internet survey invitations cannot be 'tailored' to individuals. Writing these invitations is a form of advertising on which many textbooks provide advice. In a nutshell, the appeal should be brief (three or four short paragraphs), engaging and direct, invoke a good cause, attest to the confidentiality of responses, and where appropriate note the approval or authorization of significant others or organizations. For advice on 'cover letters', as well as reminders for subsequent contacts see Dillman (2007: 149ff.).

Surveys with interviews are different because there is potentially some exchange between the interviewer and selected respondent and there is substantial variation in interviewers' abilities to recruit respondents (Blom et al., 2011). Effective interviewers steer the conversation in the direction that responds to subtle clues from the respondent and they know to break off the conversation and promise to call back when a respondent is on the verge of refusal (Groves and Couper, 1996; Snijkers et al., 1999; Schaeffer et al., 2010: 445ff.).

Incentives   There is no reason to dispute the conclusions of Church's 1993 meta-analysis of studies of controlled experiments which found that: cash incentives, and to a smaller degree gifts and lottery tickets, provided *before* a survey rather than after, increased mail survey response rates; that the effect of incentives increased with their size; and that promised incentives paid only after a survey was completed had small or negligible effects. On average, providing a cash incentive prior to the survey increased the response rate by 19 per cent, but the increase was only 4.5 per cent when the incentive was paid only after the survey was completed. The median cash incentive of the surveys analysed by Church was just $0.86 – even at the time a very small amount. Non-monetary incentives were much less effective. They increased the response rate by 8 per cent if offered in advance, by just 1 per cent afterwards.

Singer et al. (1999) addressed the same questions about telephone and face-to-face surveys, again with a meta-analysis of experimental comparisons. While the surveys they considered were more recent than those examined by Church (51 per cent were in the 1990s) and the mean payment was much higher (US$11.39), the results were similar. Prepaid cash incentives increased response rates to a greater extent than incentives paid after completing the survey, and gifts had smaller effects than cash. Incentives paid after the survey still increased response rates significantly, but the overall effect of incentives was weaker than Church reported.[9] Perhaps an interviewer's promise of an incentive is more credible than a written promise to pay. They found positive effects of incentives for both cross-sectional and panel surveys and for high-burden (longer or more difficult) and low-burden surveys. Singer et al. (2000) found that a US$10 incentive increased telephone survey response rates by over 10 per cent and that being paid to complete a survey did not decrease a respondent's willingness to answer a subsequent survey with no incentive. Promising payment after the interview had no beneficial effect at all.

In a more recent meta-analysis for RDD telephone surveys, most of which were conducted after 2000, Cantor et al. (2008) found that a prepaid US$1 or $2 incentive increased the response rate for a screening interview (where a household member is contacted and a respondent selected within the household) by about 5 per cent, and a $5 incentive increased it by about 8 per cent. An incentive promised after the interview also increased response rates, but only if the amount was at least $15.

Unfortunately, almost all the reported research on incentives is American. Stoop et al. (2010: 102) note that the different national components of the ESS each adopt their own policy on incentives and that the response rate was 3 per cent *lower* in countries which provided incentives than those that did not. Hopefully, this is because researchers are more likely to offer incentives in countries where response rates are lower.

Incentives pay for themselves when the value of the additional responses is greater than their cost. But, typically, most respondents would do a survey without an incentive, even if the incentive induces more response. Ideally one would pay only respondents who would not respond otherwise, but rewarding uncooperative behaviour in this way might not be ethical and risks poisoning the well for future surveys.

──── Response Rates, Bias and Error at the Margin ──────────────────

While the response rate is widely considered the best indicator of survey quality, the harder question is whether there are any differences between surveys with, say,

---

[9]Singer et al. (2000: 225) describe the effects as 'relatively modest once other variables have been controlled'. Because the effects are reported only as standardized regression coefficients, so it is not possible to describe them in terms of percentages. They also find that incentives have a smaller effect on surveys that have a high response rate without an incentive – an effect that might disappear if they predicted the logits rather than the absolute response rates.

45 and 50 per cent response rates, when the 5 per cent increment is obtained with incentives, more effective refusal conversion, or making extraordinary numbers of calls to reduce non-contact.

The preponderance of evidence is that a small increase in the response rate does little to change population estimates (Curtin et al., 2000; 2005; Groves, 2006; Keeter et al., 2000). While this is a sensible test if the goal is only to estimate population characteristics, it is a weak statistical criterion, because that 5 per cent of difficult-to-reach respondents are a small proportion of all respondents and their presence would measurably change the population figures only if they were radically different from the other respondents. In any event, the evidence is that hard-to-reach and reluctant respondents are *not* very different from the easier-to-reach respondents, and that both may be different from the remaining respondents.

The diminishing returns of efforts to increase the response rates by a few per cent suggests that *for a given survey* the target population consists of two classes. One class includes potential respondents, differentiated according to how easily they can be reached and convinced to participate, while the second consists of persons who will never participate. That second class includes people who were never contacted despite repeated attempts and people who were contacted but refused to do the survey – who immediately refused categorically or who give a 'soft' refusal at first, but did not respond to subsequent appeals.

Fricker and Tourangeau (2010) suggest that hard-to-get respondents contribute disproportionately to measurement error because their lack of interest is compounded by an inability or unwillingness to respond *well*. Their analysis of the (US) Current Population Survey and the American Time Use Surveys revealed the predicted negative relationship between response propensity and data quality, but it was very weak and other research also finds little or no relationship (for example, Yan et al., 2004).

Using the third wave of the ESS panel surveys for Belgium, the Netherlands, Norway and Sweden, Kaminska et al. (2010) look at the relationship between propensity to respond and data quality. They find that respondents with lower cognitive skills are more likely to satisfice, measured by item non-response, straight-line response (giving the same answer to a whole series of questions), choosing the middle response, and giving inconsistent answers to substantively similar questions. Their measures of cognitive skills included education, interviewer evaluations of respondents' understanding of the survey questions, and how often respondents asked for clarification. They find a negative relationship between response propensity and data quality, *but* controlling on cognitive skills makes the relationship disappear. Kaminska et al. argue for the need to actively recruit low-propensity respondents because they are disproportionately from groups with lower cognitive ability, which tend to be under-represented in surveys. The implication is that recruiting reluctant respondents guards against bias in comparisons of population subgroups, even if it does not affect estimates for the total population.

If the members of a survey sample can be characterized by a reasonably smooth distribution of the propensity to respond, it should be possible to compensate for non-response by weighting that gives more influence to *low*-propensity respondents. For respondents, the propensity can be measured by the effort required to obtain a response, indicated by the number of calls required to obtain an interview and distinguishing initial respondents from 'converted' refusals. But Stoop et al. (2010: 264ff.) find that propensity-based weighting produces almost no difference in variable distributions and from this conclude that respondents do not fall along a single 'continuum of resistance'. This is further support for the 'two-class' argument that differentiates potential respondents. The size of the second class is a function of the survey topic and length and the national setting, and it has increased over time.

Now, say that time, mode, cost or other constraints result in a response rate of 30 per cent for a population and on a topic where an exceptional and expensive survey could conceivably achieve a 70 per cent response rate. So, many potential respondents are not successfully surveyed. Although propensity-based weighting would still not tell us anything about the 30 per cent absolute non-respondents, it might produce better estimates for the 40 per cent of the population who are potential, but not actually surveyed, respondents. A nice example is provided by Biemer and Link (2008).

Beyond what is known from the sampling frame, it is difficult to find out much about non-respondents in telephone and self-administered surveys. In face-to-face surveys, however, it is possible to gather information about a dwelling and its neighbourhood and possibly fragmentary information about the selected respondent with a brief questionnaire ('If you won't do the survey, would you consider answering a few short questions?'). Nice examples of this kind of research implemented as part of the ESS are described by Stoop et al. (2010: 243ff.).

Statisticians have also considered the relationship between non-response and bias, which is different for each variable in a survey, as the formulation due to Bethlehem (1988; 2002: 276) shows. If ρ is the propensity (just the probability) that a person will answer a survey and Y is any variable measured in the survey, then the bias in $\bar{y}$, the estimated mean of Y, is $\text{cov}(\rho, Y)/\bar{\rho}$, where $\text{cov}(\rho, Y)$ is the covariance of ρ and Y, and $\bar{\rho}$ is the response rate. For a given survey, $\bar{\rho}$ is fixed, so the degree of bias depends on the relationship between the variable Y and the probability that a person will respond to the survey.[10] There is bias in estimates of charitable giving, recall, because the donors are more likely to answer a survey about donations! Similarly, more satisfied students and employees are more likely

---

[10]The formula allows us to remove the bias in estimates of $\bar{y}$ *if* $\text{cov}(\rho, Y)$ *is known*. But that covariance must be estimated from the respondents only, since Y is missing for the non-respondents. For respondents, ρ can be estimated (with some error) from the number of contracts required to obtain a completed survey and, for interview surveys, also whether the respondent refused before being successfully interviewed. If the survey has contacted almost all the selected respondents, then the value of ρ for non-respondents is close to or exactly zero and usually it is not possible to differentiate among them. The question is whether the value of $\text{cov}(\rho, Y)$ *in the realized sample* is a good estimate of the *population* value of $\text{cov}(\rho, Y)$.

to respond to surveys conducted by their school or employer, and surveys about attitudes towards surveys are highly prone to bias.[11]

Groves and Peytcheva (2008) were able to locate published reports of 59 studies with 959 estimates of non-response bias, and they conclude that

> the meta-analysis shows much variability in nonresponse bias within surveys, across estimates ... when influences on survey participation are themselves measured in the survey, they will show the largest nonresponse bias. To predict what survey estimates are most susceptible to nonresponse bias, we need to understand how each survey variable relates to causes of survey participation. (p. 183)

Overall, higher response rates result in lower bias, but some surveys with a low response rate have very little bias. This points to the need to determine whether the data collection process more effectively reaches individuals who are distinctive in terms of the particular survey measures. If there is such a relationship, there is a strong argument for weighting to compensate for bias, ideally using auxiliary measures from the sampling frame, but otherwise using response propensity estimates derived from the survey data.

A disturbing and important finding from Groves and Peytcheva's study is that when the overall mean of a variable is biased, subgroup differences, for example comparing women and men or age groups, also tend to be biased (2008: 182). If simple comparisons are biased, it is likely that model coefficients are also biased.

Conclusion ———

Survey data collection is the subject of a huge body of publication, far from completely summarized in this chapter. Research in this area largely involves weakly theorized comparisons of alternative strategies, driven by the hope of gathering better or more data without increased cost. Given a survey topic and population and the funds available, there is an impressive body of practical knowledge on how best to gather data and on the key tradeoffs, for example between response rate and survey length and between the surveying of more respondents (to lower sampling error) and a higher response rate (to decrease bias). There are practical answers questions such as how many attempts should be made to contact respondents and how the survey length affects the response rate. Even when the

---

[11]One strategy for studying the effect of attitudes towards surveys on survey response is to begin with a captive audience that can initially be surveyed in its entirety, for example students in a university class, and then regress whether members of that group complete a subsequent survey on their initial attitudes. But it is difficult to find a captive group that is representative of a typical non-institutional survey population and it is hazardous to generalize about population phenomena from captive groups, such as college students.

reported evidence is mixed, for example regarding whether 'advance letters' to selected respondents increase the response rate, often it is possible to predict the outcome for a particular topic and sample. The people who manage surveys have these answers at their fingertips.

Both for the operational decisions in conducting surveys and the academic understanding of the field, the methodological research has done more to assess the effects of alternative strategies on data quality than to identify superior methods, at least when the cost is fixed. Because of logistic and cost constraints, only rarely do 'big' questions – such as whether to conduct a telephone or face-to-face survey, or use a longitudinal survey or repeated cross-sectional surveys – identify realistic alternatives. At the same time, the well-developed knowledge of the impact of survey mode on data quality represents a major research achievement of increasing practical use as mixed-mode surveys proliferate. Similarly, while the reported magnitude of interviewer effects is highly variable and (except for sensitive questions) cannot be predicted accurately from the survey topic or sample, we know both how to analyze them and that the potential effects should not be ignored.

Advances in survey data collection have been driven by the increasing sophistication of communications and computing and by researchers' demands for higher-quality and more complex surveys. Not only experiments, but also the questions routinely used to ask about employment, education and other conventional demographic characteristics routinely employ complex 'skips' that demand computerized questionnaires. The second major source of innovation has been the changes in communications technology, especially how telephones are used, and increasingly negative public attitudes towards surveys in general and towards the organizations that sponsor them and collect data. Especially in the last decade, the struggle has been to prevent a decline in the capacity to gather data.

The entire enterprise of survey data collection has been shaped by the idea that survey participation involves a worthwhile and voluntary activity, and the task of data collection is to spread that message and accommodate the volunteers. Even when there are 'incentives', which are not the norm in academic, government or even commercial surveys, the idea is to offer respondents a token of a survey's worth rather than to buy their time. It is very difficult, however, to imagine the alternative of a market for survey participation of the general population. The inherent problem of voluntary participation, however, is that it is vulnerable to changes in the capabilities and credibility of communications technology and in respondents' willingness to answer.

8

The Future of Survey Research

In 1995, Floyd Fowler could reasonably argue that 'the design of survey questions is the most fertile current methodological area for improving survey research' (p. vii). No longer so. Whatever the limitations of sample and questionnaire design, respondents' ability to answer questions and analysis of surveys with measurement error and missing data, *the* methodological problem of this age is declining response rates. As the 1990 founding date of *The International Workshop on Household Survey Nonresponse* shows, concern about non-response is nothing new, but it has become far more serious since about 2000. The nature and magnitude of the problems are a function of the survey sponsor, topic and population, and there is international variation, but the decline is still widespread and increasing (de Leeuw and de Heer, 2002; Dixon and Tucker, 2010). Unlike problems in sample and questionnaire design, declining response rates is a social phenomenon, rather than a problem in statistics or psychology.

Previous chapters have dealt with data collection strategies to obtain better response and have touched on the statistical issues arising from non-response. This chapter focuses on the magnitude of the problem of non-response and what it means for the future of the survey enterprise. There is no scientific answer or even consensus to report.

Some Surveys

Using face-to-face interviews, in different countries the response rates of the European Social Survey range from 46 to 73 per cent and the Longitudinal Internet Studies for the Social Sciences (LISS) household panel survey in the Netherlands achieves about 80 per cent response. Around 2000, Kohler (2007) reported average response rates of about 60 per cent for a number of multinational European surveys. The US National Opinion Research Center obtained a response rate of 70 per cent for its 2010 General Social Survey, a decline of only 5 per cent since the mid-1970s.[1] So, with careful effort and substantial funding it is possible to achieve high response rates.

With a 60 per cent response rate and careful treatment of non-response, there is a good claim that a survey provides an acceptable representation of a population. Then the concern is less that estimates of characteristics of the entire population are biased, but that figures for low-response groups, perhaps young people in transition between school and steady employment, or new immigrants, overestimate the social stability and socio-economic conditions and so perhaps also the health and well-being of these groups. In addition to demographic differences, it is safe to assume that the survey response propensity is correlated with behaviour and attitudes whose distribution in the population is not known, so there is no basis for statistical adjustment.

In the USA in the 1970s, 30-minute telephone surveys conducted by academics typically achieved a 70 per cent response rate. Along with much lower costs, this led to the widespread adoption of telephone surveys in place of face-to-face surveys. Forty years later, a similar survey, but shortened to 20 minutes, might have a 40 per cent response rate, requiring many more telephone calls and better supervision of interviewing, at perhaps 50 per cent greater real cost. Even with a sample including mobile telephones, the response rate would be much lower for young people. This introduces bias into comparisons between age groups, because age is strongly correlated with both the level *and the predictors* of non-response.

Averaging the surveys in each of the 50 US states, the median response rate of the *Behavioral Risk Factor Surveillance System*, a very large-scale telephone survey on health conditions, is about 36 per cent, down from about 65 per cent in the late 1980s.[2] About 60 per cent of the survey respondents are women, 9 per cent above the population figure. The situation is somewhat better in Europe, where a 2007 telephone survey of 14 EU nations on crime victimization by Gallup Europe[3] had a median response rate of about 45 per cent, though sampling landlines only. It is sensible to weight data from these surveys to match the population distributions of gender, age and maybe education in order to reduce bias. But it is difficult to make a strong argument that weighting adjustments based on a few demographic variables eliminate all bias.

Many researchers and research consumers would now say that a well-designed survey with a 40 per cent response rate is acceptable, especially if measurably increasing the response rate could raise the per-case cost by 30–50 per cent. This depends on the research topic, however. For surveys on electoral politics or public policy,

---

[1]See http://www3.norc.org/NR/rdonlyres/21C53AAC-1267-43B6-A915-A38857DC9D63/1942/GSS_Codebook_AppendixA1.pdf, pp. 3105 and 3106 (accessed 23 April 2012).

[2]ftp://ftp.cdc.gov/pub/Data/Brfss/2010_Summary_Data_Quality_Report.pdf (accessed 23 April 2012).

[3]See http://www.europeansafetyobservatory.eu/downloads/WP_methodology.pdf, p. 6 (accessed 23 April 2012).

a good argument is that not everyone votes or has an opinion, and so bias in the direction of over-representing the most informed members of the population might be a good way to measure the balance of opinion. This bias is very problematic, however, for research on who is knowledgeable about and interested in policy, as well as who is active in politics and turns out to vote. For other survey topics, such as population health, one might be less sanguine about the bias potentially arising from the under-representation of the poor, sick and elderly and also perhaps under-representation of very healthy people who do not give it much thought.

Now consider the experiments conducted as part of the *Time-sharing Experiments for the Social Sciences*, which use the *Knowledge Networks* online panel of Americans that 'combine[s] traditional random-digit-dialing telephone surveying techniques with an address-based technique that allows the sample to be representative of cell-phone-only households as well as those with land-lines'.[4] For one such poll Chang and Krosnick (2009: 652) report a 25 per cent response rate and for another Yeager et al. (2011: 714) report a 15.3 per cent response rate. While the selection of the *initial sample* is based on probability methods, the response rate is affected by attrition at each step between the initial contact and participation in a particular online poll. Bias also results from the differential effects of financial incentives, following the leverage-saliency argument, and from 'panel conditioning', which involves systematic changes in response as the number of surveys completed by a person increases. Even if the *Knowledge Networks* sample approximately matches the population in terms of gender, age and other demographic variables, or weights are used to make up for any such differences, it is hard to argue that these surveys are unbiased, or even that they meet the supposedly less stringent criterion that group differences are unbiased.

For day-to-day political polls often reported in the media, the situation is far worse. In Ontario, Canada, in 2012, a telephone survey conducted over a three-day period gave the party in government the support of 42 per cent of adults, based on a telephone survey of 500. While advertised as 'accurate plus or minus 4.4 percentage points, 19 times out of 20', the figures only describe the probable result of conducting exactly the same poll again *with the same bias*.[5] With that three-day window, the response rate could be 15 per cent. Just eight days later, a one-day poll reported just 28 per cent support for the government on the basis of an 'interactive voice-response telephone poll of 1,065 people … considered accurate to within 3 percentage points, 19 times out of 20'.[6] The 14 per cent difference between the polls cannot possibly result from sampling error.

---

[4]See http://www.tessexperiments.org/introduction.html#data (accessed 13 March 2012).

[5]The poll was conducted by the firm Nanos Research, reported on 15 March in the *Toronto Globe and Mail*; the findings are at http://www.nanosresearch.com/library/polls/POLONT-W12-T528.pdf.

[6]The poll was conducted by Forum Research, reported in the *Toronto Star* on 15 March; see http://www.thestar.com/news/canada/politics/article/1146319--ontarians-oppose-olg-plan-for-more-casinos-poll-finds.

At about the same time, there was an outright debacle in poll predictions of the provincial election in the province of Alberta, Canada, where a victory by the extreme right predicted by polls up to two days before the election did not materialize. The difference of approximately 15 per cent between the predictions and the actual vote[7] is due to some combination of a last-minute change in party support, higher-than-expected voter turnout and bias in the polls' results. Most of the Alberta surveys employed interactive voice response, and no response rates were reported. Whether a poll begins with a probability sample becomes moot when a very low response rate disconnects the statistical logic that relates sample-based estimates to population values. The danger is that biased polls can affect the political process, in favour of the people who pay for them.[8]

Finally, consider some surveys conducted by Statistics Canada, historically one of the finest national statistical agencies. Its monthly Labour Force Survey (LFS) is the Canadian version of the mandatory survey used in many countries to estimate employment, unemployment and other labour force characteristics at national and regional levels. The LFS household-level response rate is 90 per cent, even though the data collection period is just one week. While Canadians are legally obligated to answer the LFS, it is not practical to pursue the non-respondents who can effectively refuse by repeated delays that 'run out the clock' on a survey with a short timeline.[9]

Statistics Canada's Survey of Household Spending (SHS) is used to measure changes in the cost of living, a fundamental economic yardstick. In 2009 the reported response rate for this voluntary CAPI survey was 64.5 per cent. But there was also 12.2 per cent undercoverage,[10] because the survey-based prediction of the size of the Canadian population fell short of the known population by that amount. Compounding the two figures, the overall response rate is 57 per cent and non-response bias is clearly a concern for the economic measures it generates.

For Statistics Canada's 2010 General Social Survey (GSS), in that year devoted to time use, the sample was selected from telephone landlines estimated by Statistics

---

[7]For a compendium of poll results, see http://www.electionalmanac.com/ea/alberta-election-polls/ (accessed 23 July 2012). Six of seven polls in the last week of the campaign gave the *Wildrose Party* a lead averaging 8 per cent, but the poll closest to the election gave the party a 2 per cent lead only. The election result was that *Wildrose* had 10 per cent less support than the winning *Progressive Conservative Party*; see http://www.theglobeandmail.com/news/politics/alberta-election-2012-riding-by-riding-results/article4102152/ (accessed 23 July 2012).

[8]No general principle governs the nature of the bias, but in this case and similar comparisons conducted in another Canadian province, there is strong evidence that the IVR poll favours the political right.

[9]See http://www.statcan.gc.ca/cgi-bin/imdb/p2SV.pl?Function=getSurvey&SDDS=3701&lang=en&db=imdb&adm=8&dis=2#b8 (accessed 15 March 2012).

[10]See Georgina House, Denis Malo, Marie-Hélène Miville, Sylvain Nadon and Johanne Tremblay (2011) 'Survey of Household Spending 2009: Data Quality Indicators', Canada, Ministry of Industry. Available at http://www.statcan.gc.ca/pub/62f0026m/62f0026m2011001-eng.pdf (accessed 12 September 2012).

Canada to cover 86 per cent of the population (about 2 per cent had no telephone at all and about 13 per cent had only a mobile phone). The response rate was just 45 per cent, 39 per cent accounting for undercoverage.[11] The website notes that 'Little or nothing is known about the non-responding cases.' The risk is that aspects of lifestyle related to time use affect the probability of answering. This particular survey has been repeated in about five-year intervals for many years, and the 1986 response rate was about 80 per cent. This decline in the response rate compromises the measurement of change. In comparison, Statistics Canada's Canadian Community Health Survey (CCHS), which combines face-to-face and telephone surveys, had a 72.3 per cent response rate in 2010,[12] down only somewhat from 85 per cent in 2000–2001.[13]

National statistical agencies are not immune from the factors affecting academic and private sector survey organizations. Statistics Canada's LFS, the most important ongoing national survey, is excellent, though it still needs some adjustment for non-response that might not have been necessary 20 years ago; the SHS and CCHS have significant non-response and require complex adjustment; and the GSS likely has substantial non-response bias and its exclusion of mobile phones is problematic.

It appears that the most acute declines in response rates involve telephone surveys in the USA and Canada and there is evidence that Australia and the UK are similar.[14] Europe is not exempt from this decline and in a number of European countries for which the response rates are higher, landlines cover less than half the population (De Keulenaer, 2008; also see Häder et al., 2012). Kuhne and Häder's (2012) report on a survey in Germany is illustrative. In order to maximize the response, fieldwork was spaced out over *seven months* beginning in October 2007 and up to 15 calls were made to each selected telephone number. For mobile phones, 15 per cent of the numbers resulted in a full or partial interview; 22 per cent resulted in refusal or the interview could not be completed for some other reason; and an astonishing 63 per cent of numbers were classified as 'voice mail – don't know if household' (p. 234). The small number of non-household numbers identified as outside the scope of the survey suggests that most of those voice mail numbers were non-answers by eligible respondents. For the landline numbers, the results were 23 per cent full

[11]See http://www.statcan.gc.ca/cgi-bin/imdb/p2SV.pl?Function=getSurvey&SDDS=4503&lang=en&db=imdb&adm=8&dis=2 (accessed 15 March 2012).

[12]See http://www23.statcan.gc.ca:81/imdb-bmdi/pub/document/3226_D7_T9_V8-eng.htm (accessed 23 April 2012). Although perhaps increasing the reported response rate, it is not clear whether mobile numbers are included in the sampling frame.

[13]See http://www23.statcan.gc.ca:81/imdb-bmdi/document/3226_D9_T9_V1-eng.pdf (accessed 16 July 2012).

[14]See the September 2011 report, 'Four Country Project Waves 2–8 Technical Report', *International Tobacco Control Policy Evaluation Survey*, at http://www.itcproject.org/documents/keyfindings/4cw28techreportmay2011_2_pdf (accessed 4 July 2012).

or partial interviews, 55 per cent refusals or non-interviews for another reason, and 22 per cent 'voice mail – don't know if household'.

The decline in response rates appears to have two components. First, there is evidence of a gradual decline in response rates for all surveys. This reflects concerns about privacy and security, changes in lifestyle that make people more difficult to reach, changing attitudes towards requests from strangers, loss of confidence in survey organizations and diminished belief in whether the survey sponsors will heed survey findings.

These changes affect telephone surveys, but an entirely different process is also at work. The behavioural aspects of the decline in telephone survey response rates are clear. People are less willing to answer calls from telephone numbers they do not recognize and from survey firms they do recognize; people who do answer are more likely to turn down requests for surveys; and both tendencies are more pronounced for mobile phones, which are often answered in situations where it is impossible or inconvenient to answer a survey. These changes in the use of telephones have been accelerated by the increasing use of automated calls for advertising and IVR surveys. And postal 'junk mail' and email spam produce exactly the same problems for mail surveys and Internet surveys employing email invitations.

Underlying the precipitous decline in telephone survey response rates is a fundamental devaluation of telephone calls. Increasingly telephone calls are not used for conversation but to make arrangements to meet in person and for various transactions of daily life. One result is the increasing proportion of text messages relative to telephone conversations. The changing use of the telephone is related to, at least, age, family structure, economic means, skills and friendliness to new technology. The result is bias in telephone survey estimates, which cannot be entirely corrected by weighting; and it cannot be assumed that the bias is uniform, so differences between groups may also be biased.

Neither of the prevailing theories of survey response is very helpful here. The overall decline in the response rate and special problems of telephone surveys cannot be explained by a change in the nature of the transactions between interviewers and respondents, which is the focus of exchange theory. An increasing proportion of calls are not answered, and so never reach the point where there is an exchange to be negotiated. The decline can be explained by the leverage-saliency theory, but only in the unhelpful way of saying that the negative aspects of survey participation are becoming stronger than the positive aspects.

The Response of Survey Users

Heavily invested in their research, and usually without a good, comparably priced alternative, survey researchers by and large have addressed declining response rates by proceeding as usual, compensating for non-response as best they can with weighting, imputation and occasionally more complex data analysis. Consider three examples, starting with an article on income and well-being by Kahneman and Deaton, whose brief description of the sample explains that:

> Of all calls that resulted in contacts with an eligible candidate, 31% of the candidates agreed to be interviewed; of these, 90% completed the entire interview. Despite the sampling limitations, available evidence suggests that the estimates of population parameters were not compromised; for example, the survey predicted recent election results within an acceptable margin of error. (2010: 16492)

The article does not report a conventional response rate, which must be considerably lower than the cited 31 per cent because some of the non-contacts must be households that include an eligible respondent. That the survey produces 'acceptable' predictions of 'recent election results' is less an indicator of sample representativeness than of bias in the direction of more politically engaged respondents. American election turnout often does not reach 50 per cent of registered voters, not every qualified voter is registered, and not every adult is a citizen entitled to vote.

Also in the USA, the Pew Research Center mounts an extraordinary programme of survey research on public policy. Between 1997 and 2012 the response rate for its 'standard five-day surveys' declined from 36 per cent to just 9 per cent (Pew Research Center, 2012: 1). The response rates for its 'high-effort' surveys, 61 per cent in 1997, fell to 27 per cent in 2012 counting only landlines, and to 22 per cent including the mobile phone numbers required to assure representativeness in 2012. The Center's 'high-effort' surveys involve 'an extended field period, monetary incentives for respondents, and letters to households that initially declined to be interviewed, as well as the deployment of interviewers with a proven record of persuading reluctant respondents to participate' (2012: 4).

For a variety of demographic measures, including age, racialization, education, marital status and home ownership, the Pew Research Center's responses from the 'standard' and 'high-effort' surveys are similar and close to the findings of government surveys with very high response rates. Also, for both the 'standard' and 'high-effort' surveys there is convincing evidence that the political attitudes and party support of survey respondents are close to the population values. But there is a striking difference for questions asking whether in the last year a person has: 'volunteered for an organization' – 55 per cent for the Center's surveys versus 27 per cent in a government survey; 'contacted a public official' – 30 versus 10 per cent; and 'talked with neighbors weekly', 58 versus 41 per cent. Considering the difference in cost and response rates, it may seem surprising that the Center's 'standard' and 'high-effort' surveys do not differ on these three measures. So the most easily interviewed respondents, who answered the standard survey in the course of a five-day field period, are quite similar to respondents who are harder to find and convince, but do answer. What is not known is how those respondents compare to determined non-respondents, who will neither answer the survey under any circumstances, nor provide supplementary information so that they can be compared to respondents.

The Pew surveys benefit from good fortune, not from any principle that makes the surveys with 10 per cent response rates free of bias, but this too depends on the research question. Their surveys are a good basis to study ideological and partisan conflict in the USA, but not the differences between politically engaged and unengaged Americans, because the unengaged are much less likely to respond.

Last, consider the *International Tobacco Control Policy Evaluation Project*.[15] With surveys in 20 nations by 2012, the project employs longitudinal surveys to measure the impact of measures to reduce smoking, such as package labelling, price and restrictions on smoking in public space. Response rates for the four initial surveys, conducted in 2002 in Australia, Canada, the UK and the USA, ranged from 26 to 50 per cent and the most recently reported rates for those countries are about 30 per cent[16], with attrition between survey waves made up by sample replenishment. Because the effects of policy changes on tobacco use are often quite large, the surveys can provide quite credible estimates of their magnitudes, even if attrition between survey waves compromises the longitudinal comparisons.

Despite the evidence of increasing non-response, politicians and policy makers are telling us that survey results are still credible, or maybe that they are more credible than any feasible alternative.

The Response of Survey Researchers

Survey methodologists and organizations have not been passive in the face of falling response rates. Journals are filled with reports on efforts to increase response rates; more money is being spent on efforts to obtain responses, including the increasing use of multi-mode surveys; and survey statisticians have directed their attention to survey non-response. There is international variation, and the survey topic, data collection agency and sponsor are factors, but increasingly it is clear that only face-to-face surveys result in response rates high enough to make credible claims that the survey respondents resemble the population in all respects.

The decline in survey response rates combines steady, across-the-board erosion affecting all modes of data collection and a precipitous decline in telephone surveys. To the extent that there is a crisis of declining response rates, it is about cost: face-to-face surveys are much more expensive than telephone surveys and the

[15]From www.itcproject.org/about (accessed 5 July 2012).

[16]These figures can be found, respectively, in the 2004 (p. 23) 'Wave 1 Technical Report' and the 2011 (pp. 27–28) 'Waves 2–8 Technical Report' of the *Four Country Report of the International Tobacco Control Policy Evaluation Survey*, at www.itcproject.org/key_findings/technical (both accessed 5 July 2012).

per-interview costs of all kinds of surveys are rising in an effort to prevent further decline. Internet surveys can provide very inexpensive and good-quality surveys, but only when sample members are known by name, have email addresses and use the Internet routinely. Extraordinary efforts to select Internet survey respondents with probability-based address and telephone samples and providing free computers and Internet access to people who do not have them result in more representative samples, but the response rates are too low to assure unbiased estimates of population characteristics, even with weighting.

In light of the high initial cost of a face-to-face survey, when there is a need to measure change over time, it is easy to see the advantages of a panel survey, due to the lower cost of contacting respondents after the first wave and the possibility of switching to lower-cost self-administered or telephone surveys in later survey waves. Even after paying an incentive this can be cost effective, and it provides the extraordinary advantages of longitudinal data for understanding change and estimating measurement error for individual questions.

For surveys of all kinds, there is a need for qualitatively better and different information on non-respondents. At present, much of the research on non-response begins with a conventional survey and involves comparisons between easy and difficult or very difficult respondents who do eventually consent to an interview. Many of the people who reject the usual invitation to answer a survey also reject further entreaties, leaving researchers with no choice but to assume that impossible-to-reach respondents are similar to difficult-to-reach respondents. If national statistical agencies can be convinced to cooperate, mandatory government surveys provide a means to address this problem, especially if they can be enhanced with a few *non*-demographic questions known to be related to survey response, for example questions about attitudes towards surveys, whether a person responds to voluntary surveys and measures of community participation and charitable giving. As well as researchers outside of government, this would aid government statistical agencies, which also conduct some *non*-mandatory surveys.

One way around the difficulties of surveys is to use other forms of data. Groves foresees a growing role for 'organic' data – the inconceivably large amount of tweets, purchases recorded by scanners, and electronic messages:

> The challenge to the survey profession is to discover how to combine designed data with organic data, to produce resources with the most efficient information-to-data ratio. This means we need to learn how surveys can be designed to incorporate transaction data continuously produced by the Internet and other systems in useful ways. Combining data sources to produce new information not contained in any single source is the future. (2011: 869)

This might answer some new research questions, but it is difficult to see how this could address the topics of most current surveys. Also, these 'organic data' are corporate and property and their distribution may compromise individual privacy.

A related strategy is to analyse government administrative records, especially on income and health. On their own, these records lack critical covariates such as a person's education, place of birth and occupation. Combined with survey data, however, records can provide information that individuals cannot accurately recall or do not remember at all. Using administrative data, however, requires the permission of respondents, the cooperation of government agencies and the means to provide researchers with access to data in a secure environment. So this is likely to remain a niche strategy, available only for government and government-supported surveys in a few countries.

Reversing the slow decline in response rates, which affects even the best face-to-face surveys, is a political and not a technical problem. Researchers and the people and institutions that depend on survey data need to convince the public that surveys accurately represent and benefit communities.

Since the 1930s, survey researchers have developed a marvellous and reliable method to answer practical and academic questions about how societies work. We have learned how to conduct really good surveys and we have developed a deeper understanding of the limitations of survey questionnaires and samples. Before concluding that declining response rates spell the end of surveys as we know them, or demanding a switch to much more expensive face-to-face surveys for which there might not be funds, remember that for many research questions there is no good alternative.

———

Final editing of this book took place in fall 2012, during the US presidential election. An extraordinary number of polls, each conducted over a very short period and sometimes in just one day, followed the campaign in minute detail. The individual polls were fodder for a new breed of 'aggregators', especially the celebrated Nate Silver, whose FIVETHIRTYEIGHT blog was carried by the *New York Times*. As the election results demonstrated, Silver's meta-analysis of the many polls, whose average response rates might have been just 10 per cent, was extraordinarily accurate. And this was no fluke, for Silver was repeating his bravura forecast of the 2008 election.

How is it possible that such hasty polls, with at best barely unacceptable and in some cases laughably low response rates, produced such accurate results? There are four reasons, I believe. First, the huge quantity of data drastically reduced classical sampling error and, especially as the election grew closer, measurement error also decreased, at least among the people who intended to vote. Second, the large number of data collection agencies made it possible to compensate for 'house' variation and to eliminate outliers, which in this case included the Gallup poll whose estimates of Republican support were unusually high during the campaign and, as the actual voting showed, overestimated the actual Republican vote. Third, the visibility of the campaign, in part based on reports of the polls, combined with the continuation of polls until just before the vote, reduced the risk of a last-minute shift in party allegiance that would be missed – one of the main causes of past debacles in election forecasting.

The fourth and most important reason for the polls' accuracy is that bias related to *un*measured characteristics of voters must be quite small. This is helped by the tendency for non-voters to avoid election polls and for prospective voters to answer them. But the critical point is that respondents and non-respondents must be very similar in their political views, as the Pew Research Center Polls showed. Of course, there were very large differences in party support related to gender, racialization, age and location and these also affect the response rate. Because the distributions of these characteristics of the population are well known, however, it is easy to weight the survey data to compensate for such differential non-response.

Perhaps Edward Deming was right in saying that we overestimate the need for precision in surveys.

References

Abraham, Katharine G., Sara Helms and Stanley Presser (2009) 'How social processes distort measurement: the impact of survey nonresponse on estimates of volunteer work in the United States', *American Journal of Sociology* 114(4): 1129–1165.

Achen, Christopher H. (1975) 'Mass political attitudes and survey response', *American Political Science Review* 69(4): 1218–1231.

Ajzen, Icek and Martin Fishbein (1980) *Understanding Attitudes and Predicting Social Behavior.* Englewood Cliffs, NJ: Prentice Hall.

Alves, Wayne M. and Peter H. Rossi (1978) 'Who should get what? Fairness judgments of the distribution of earnings', *American Journal of Sociology* 84(3): 541–564.

Alwin, Duane F. (1992) 'Information transmission in the survey interview: number of response categories and the reliability of attitude measurement', *Sociological Methodology* 22: 83–118.

Alwin, Duane F. (1997) 'Feeling thermometers versus 7-point scales', *Sociological Methods and Research* 25(3): 318–340.

Alwin, Duane F. (2007) *Margins of Error: A Study of Reliability in Survey Measurement.* Hoboken, NJ: Wiley.

Alwin, Duane F. and Jon A. Krosnick (1991) 'The reliability of survey attitude measurement: the influence of question and respondent attributes', *Sociological Methods and Research* 20(1): 139–181.

Anderson, Ronald, Judith Kasper and Martin Frankel (1979) *Total Survey Error: Applications to Improve Health Surveys.* San Francisco: Jossey-Bass.

Andrews, Frank M. (1984) 'Construct validity and error components', *Public Opinion Quarterly* 48: 409–442.

Aquilino, William F. (1994) 'Interview mode effects in surveys of drug and alcohol use: a field experiment', *Public Opinion Quarterly* 58(2): 210–240.

Atzmüller, Christiane and Peter M. Steiner (2010) 'Experimental vignette studies in survey research', *Methodology: European Journal of Research Methods for the Behavioral and Social Sciences* 6(3): 128–138.

Banaji, Mahzarin R., Irene V. Blair and Norbert Schwarz (1996) 'Implicit memory and survey measurement', in Norbert Schwarz and Seymour Sudman (eds) *Answering Questions: Methodology for Determining Cognitive and Communicative Processes in Survey Research.* San Francisco: Jossey-Bass. pp. 346–372.

Bartle, John (2000) 'Political awareness, opinion constraint and the stability of ideological positions', *Political Studies* 48(3): 467–484.

Bassili, John N. (2000) 'Editor's introduction: reflections on response latency measurement in telephone surveys', *Political Psychology* 21(1): 1–6.

Bassili, John N. and Joseph F. Fletcher (1991) 'Response-time measurement in survey research: a method for CATI and a new look at non-attitudes', *Public Opinion Quarterly* 55: 331–346.

Bassili, John N. and B. Stacey Scott (1996) 'Response latency as a signal to question problems in survey research', *Public Opinion Quarterly* 60(3): 390–399.

Beatty, Paul (1995) 'Understanding the standardized/non-standardized interviewing controversy', *Journal of Official Statistics* 11(2): 147–160.

Beatty, Paul (2004) 'The dynamics of cognitive interviewing', in Stanley Presser et al. (eds) *Methods for Testing and Evaluating Survey Questionnaires*. Hoboken, NJ: Wiley.

Beatty, Paul C. and Gordon B. Willis (2007) 'Research synthesis: the practice of cognitive interviewing', *Public Opinion Quarterly* 71(2): 287–311.

Bekkers, René and Pamela Wiepking (2011) 'Who gives? A literature review of predictors of charitable giving: I – religion, education, age, and socialization', *Voluntary Sector Review* 2(3): 367–389.

Béland, Yves and Martin St-Pierre (2008) 'Mode effects in the Canadian Community Health Survey: a comparison of CATI and CAPI', 2004 *Proceedings of the American Statistical Association Meeting*, Survey Research Methods. Toronto, Canada.

Belli, Robert F. (1998) 'The structure of autobiographical memory and the event history calendar: potential improvements in the quality of retrospective reports in surveys', *Memory* 6: 383–406.

Belli, Robert F., Michael W. Traugott, Margaret Young and Katherine A. McGonagle (1999) 'Reducing vote overreporting in surveys: social desirability, memory failure, and source monitoring', *Public Opinion Quarterly* 63(1): 90–108.

Belli, Robert F., Lynette M. Smith, Patricia M. Andreski and Sangeeta Agrawal (2007) 'Methodological comparisons between CATI event history calendar and standardized conventional questionnaire instruments', *Public Opinion Quarterly* 71(4): 603–622.

Belli, Robert F., Frank P. Stafford and Duane F. Alwin (eds) (2009) *Calendar and Time Diary Methods in Life Course Research*. Thousand Oaks, CA: Sage.

Belson, William (1981) *The Design and Understanding of Survey Questions*. London: Gower.

Berger, Yves G. and Yves Tillé (2009) 'Sampling with unequal probabilities', in Danny Pfeffermann and C.R. Rao (eds) *Sample Surveys: Design Methods and Applications. Handbook of Statistics*, Vol. 29A. Amsterdam: Elsevier. pp. 39–54.

Bergman, Manfred Max and Dominique Joye (2005) 'Comparing social stratification schemata: CAMSIS, CSP-CH, Goldthorpe, ISCO-88, Treiman and Wright', Cambridge Studies in Social Research, No. 10. Cambridge: SSRC Publications.

Berinsky, Adam J. (2006) 'American public opinion in the 1930s and 1940s: the analysis of quota-controlled sample survey data', *Public Opinion Quarterly* 70(4): 499–529.

Bethlehem, Jelke G. (1988) 'Reduction of nonresponse bias through regression estimation', *Journal of Official Statistics* 4(3): 251–260.

Bethlehem, Jelke G. (2002) 'Weighting nonresponse adjustments based on auxiliary information', in Robert M. Groves, Don A. Dillman, John L. Eltinge and Roderick J.A. Little (eds) *Survey Nonresponse*. New York: Wiley. pp. 275–287.

Bethlehem, Jelke G. (2009) 'The rise of survey sampling', Discussion Paper 09015. The Hague: Statistics Netherlands.

Bickart, Barbara and E. Maria Felcher (1996) 'Expanding and enhancing the use of verbal protocols in survey research', in Norbert Schwartz and Seymour Sudman (eds) *Answering Questions: Methodology for Determining Cognitive and Communicative Processes in Survey Research*. San Francisco: Jossey Bass. pp. 115–142.

Biemer, Paul P. (2010a) 'Overview of design issues: total survey error', in Peter V. Marsden and James D. Wright (eds) *Handbook of Survey Research*, 2nd edn. Bingley: Emerald. pp. 27–57.

Biemer, Paul P. (2010b) 'Total survey error: design, implementation, and evaluation,' *Public Opinion Quarterly* 74(5): 817–848.

Biemer, Paul P. and Michael W. Link (2008) 'Evaluating and modeling early cooperator effects in RDD surveys', in James Lepkowski et al. (eds) *Advances in Telephone Survey Methodology*. Hoboken, NJ: Wiley. pp. 587–617.

Biemer, Paul P. and Lars E. Lyberg (2003) *Introduction to Survey Quality*. New York: Wiley.

Billiet, Jaak B. and Eldad Davidov (2008) 'Testing the stability of an acquiescence style factor behind two interrelated substantive variables in a panel design', *Sociological Methods & Research* 36: 542–562.

Binder, David A. and Georgia R. Roberts (2003) 'Design-based and model-based methods for estimating model parameters', in Ray L. Chambers and C.J. Skinner (eds) *Analysis of Survey Data*. Chichester: Wiley. pp. 29–48.

Bischoping, Katherine (1989) 'An evaluation of interviewer debriefing in survey pretests', in Charles Cannell, Lois Oksenberg, Floyd J. Fowler, Graham Kalton and Katherine Bischoping (eds) *New Techniques for Pretesting Survey Questions*. Ann Arbor, MI: Survey Research Center. pp. 15–29.

Bishop, George F. and Andrew E. Smith (1997) 'Response-order effects in public opinion surveys: the plausibility of rival hypotheses', Paper presented at the Annual Conference of the American Association for Public Opinion Research, Norfolk, VA.

Bishop, George F. and Andrew E. Smith (2001) 'Response-order effects and the early Gallup split-ballots', *Public Opinion Quarterly* 65(4): 479–505.

Bishop, Yvonne M.M., Stephen E. Fienberg and Paul W. Holland (1975) *Discrete Multivariate Analysis*. Cambridge, MA: MIT Press.

Blair, Johnny, Frederick Conrad, Allison Castellano Ackermann and Greg Claxton (2006) 'The effect of sample size on cognitive interview findings', Paper presented at the Meeting of the American Association of Public Opinion Research, Montreal.

Blom, Annelies G., Edith D. de Leeuw and Joop J. Hox (2011) 'Interviewer effects on nonresponse in the European social survey', *Journal of Official Statistics* 27(2): 359–377.

Blumer, Herbert (1956) 'Sociological analysis and the "variable"', *American Sociological Review* 21(6): 683–690.

Boarini, Romina and Marco Mira d'Ercole (2006) 'Measures of material deprivation in OECD countries', *OECD Social, Employment and Migration Working Papers*.

Bohner, Gerd and Nina Dickel (2011) 'Attitudes and attitude change', *Annual Review of Psychology* 62: 391–417.

Bose, Christine E. and Peter H. Rossi (1983) 'Gender and jobs: prestige standings of occupations as affected by gender', *American Sociological Review* 48(3): 316–330.

Bradburn, Norman M. and Carrie Miles (1979) 'Vague quantifiers', *Public Opinion Quarterly* 43(1): 92–101.

Brewer, Ken and Timothy G. Gregoire (2009) 'Introduction to survey sampling', in Danny Pfeffermann and C.R. Rao (eds) *Sample Surveys: Design Methods and Applications. Handbook of Statistics*, Vol. 29A. Amsterdam: Elsevier. pp. 9–38.

Brick, J. Michael and Jill M. Montaquila (2009) 'Nonresponse and weighting', in Danny Pfeffermann and C.R. Rao (eds) *Sample Surveys: Design Methods and Applications. Handbook of Statistics*, Vol. 29A. Amsterdam: Elsevier. pp. 163–185.

Brown, Roger (1965) *Social Psychology*. New York: Free Press.

Browning, Martin, Thomas F. Crossley and Guglielmo Weber (2003) 'Asking consumption questions in general purpose surveys', *Economic Journal* 113 (November): F540–F567.

Brzozowski, Matthew and Thomas F. Crossley (2011) 'Viewpoint: measuring the well-being of the poor with income or consumption: a Canadian perspective', *Canadian Journal of Economics* 44(1): 89–106.

Bulmer, Martin, Levin Bales and Kathryn Sklar (1991) *The Social Survey in Historical Perspective 1880–1940*. Cambridge: Cambridge University Press.

Byrne, Barbara M. (2010) *Structural Equation Modelling with AMOS: Basic Concepts, Applications, and Programming*, 2nd edn. New York: Routledge.

Cahalan, Don (1989) 'The *Digest* poll rides again', *Public Opinion Quarterly* 53(1): 129–133.

Campbell, Donald and Donald Fiske (1959) 'Convergent and discriminant validation by the multitrait multimethod matrices', *Psychological Bulletin* 56(2): 81–105.

Cannell, Charles and Sally Robinson (1971) 'Analysis of individual questions', in John B. Lansing et al., *Working Papers on Survey Research in Poverty Areas*, Ann Arbor, MI: Institute for Social Research. pp. 236–291.

Cannell, Charles, Peter V. Miller and Lois Oksenberg (1981) 'Research on interviewing techniques', *Sociological Methodology* 12: 389–437.

Cannell, Charles, Lois Oksenberg, Floyd J. Fowler, Graham Kalton and Katherine Bischoping (1989) *New Techniques for Pretesting Survey Questions*. Ann Arbor, MI: Survey Research Center.

Cantor, David, Barbara C. O'Hare and Kathleen S. O'Connor (2008) 'The use of monetary incentives to reduce nonresponse in random digit dial telephone surveys', in James Lepkowski et al. (eds), *Advances in Telephone Survey Methodology*. New York: Wiley. pp. 471–498.

Cantril, Hadley (ed.) (1944) *Gauging Public Opinion*. Princeton, NJ: Princeton University Press.

Cantril, Hadley and Edrita Fried (1944) 'The meaning of questions', in Hadley Cantril (ed.) *Gauging Public Opinion*. Princeton, NJ: Princeton University Press. pp. 3–20.

Chang, Linchiat and Jon A. Krosnick (2009) 'National surveys via RDD telephone interviewing versus the internet: comparing sample representativeness and response quality', *Public Opinion Quarterly* 73(4): 641–678.

Christman, Mary C. (2009) 'Sampling of rare populations', in Danny Pfeffermann and C.R. Rao (eds) *Sample Surveys: Design Methods and Applications. Handbook of Statistics*, Vol. 29A. Amsterdam: Elsevier. pp. 109–124.

Church, Allan H. (1993) 'Estimating the effect of incentives on mail survey response rates: a meta-analysis', *Public Opinion Quarterly* 57(1): 62–79.

Cohen, Jacob (1988) *Statistical Power Analysis for the Behavioral Sciences*, 2nd edn. Hillsdale, NJ: Lawrence Erlbaum.

Committee on Analysis of Pre-Election Polls and Forecasts of the Social Science Research Council (1948) 'Report on the analysis of pre-election polls and forecasts', *Public Opinion Quarterly* 12(4): 585–599. (The full report is in Frederick Mosteller, with the collaboration of Leonard W. Doob and others (1949) *The Pre-election Polls of 1948: Report to the Committee on Analysis of Pre-Election Polls and Forecasts*. New York: Social Science Research Council.)

Connelly, Gordon M. (1945) 'The questions the polls ask: now let's look at the real problem: validity', *Opinion Quarterly* 9(1): 51–60.

Conrad, Frederick G. and Michael F. Schober (2000) 'Clarifying question meaning in a household telephone survey', *Public Opinion Quarterly* 64(1): 1–28.

Conrad, Frederick G. and Michael F. Schober (2005) 'Promoting uniform question understanding in today's and tomorrow's surveys', *Journal of Official Statistics* 21(2): 215–231.

Conrey, Frederica R. and Eliot R. Smith (2007) 'Attitude representation: attitudes as patterns in a distributed, connectionist representational system', *Social Cognition* 25(5): 718–735.

Conti, Gabriella and Stephen Pudney (2011) 'Survey design and the analysis of satisfaction', *Review of Economics and Statistics* 93(3): 1087–1093.

Converse, Jean M. (1984) 'Strong arguments and weak evidence: the open/closed questioning controversy of the 1940s', *Public Opinion Quarterly* 48(1b): 267–282.

Converse, Jean M. (1987) *Survey Research in the United States: Roots and Emergence, 1890–1960*. Berkeley, CA: University of California Press.

Converse, Jean M. and Stanley Presser (1986) *Survey Questions: Handcrafting the Standardized Questionnaire*. Beverly Hills, CA: Sage.

Converse, Philip E. (1964) 'The nature of belief systems in the mass public', in David E. Apter (ed.) *Ideology and Discontent*. New York: Free Press. pp. 206–261.

Coutts, Elisabeth and Ben Jann (2011) 'Sensitive questions in online surveys: experimental results for the randomized response technique (RRT) and the unmatched count technique (UCT)', *Sociological Methods & Research* 40: 169–193.

Cowan, Charles D., Linda R. Murphy and Judy Wiener (1978) 'Effects of supplemental questions on victimization estimates from the National Crime Survey', Proceedings of the American Statistical Association, Chicago.

Crossley, Archibald M. (1937) 'Straw polls in 1936', *Public Opinion Quarterly* 1(1): 24–35.

Crossley, Thomas F. and Steven Kennedy (2002) 'The reliability of self-assessed health status', *Journal of Health Economics* 21(4): 643–658.

Crowne, Douglas P. and David Marlowe (1960) 'A new scale of social desirability independent of psychopathology', *Journal of Consulting Psychology* 24(4): 349–354.

Curtin, Richard, Stanley Presser and Eleanor Singer (2000) 'The effects of response rate changes on the index of consumer sentiment', *Public Opinion Quarterly* 64(4): 413–428.

Curtin, Richard, Stanley Presser and Eleanor Singer (2005) 'Changes in telephone survey nonresponse over the past quarter century', *Public Opinion Quarterly* 69(1): 87–98.

Davis, Rachel E., Mick P. Couper, Nancy K. Janz, Cleopatra H. Caldwell and Ken Resnicow (2010) 'Interviewer effects in public health surveys', *Health Education Research* 25(1): 14–26.

De Keulenaer, Femke (2008) 'Europeans cut the phone cord: methodological consequences for the Flash Eurobarometer', Paper presented at the Conference on the 35th Anniversary of the Eurobarometer, Paris, available at http://ec.europa.eu/public_opinion/paris/pdf/35-years-eurobarometer_paris_de-keulenaer.pdf (accessed 19 July 2012).

de Leeuw, Edith D. (1992) *Data Quality in Mail, Telephone and Face to Face Surveys*. Amsterdam: TT-Publikaties. (Electronic edition (2002) available at http://edithl.home.xs4all.nl/pubs/disseddl.pdf (accessed 12 September 2012)).

de Leeuw, Edith D. (2005) 'To mix or not to mix data collection modes in surveys', *Journal of Official Statistics* 21(2): 233–255.

de Leeuw, Edith D. and Wim de Heer (2002) 'Trends in household survey nonresponse: a longitudinal and international comparison', in Robert M. Groves, Don A. Dillman, John L. Eltinge and Roderick J.A. Little (eds) *Survey Nonresponse*. New York: Wiley. pp. 41–54.

de Leeuw, Edith, Mario Callegaro, Joop Hox, Elly Korendijk and Gerty Lensvelt-Mulders (2007) 'The influence of advance letters on response in telephone surveys: a meta-analysis', *Public Opinion Quarterly* 71(3): 413–443.

de Leeuw, Edith, Joop Hox and Annette Scherpenzeel (2010) 'Mode effect or question wording? Measurement error in mixed mode surveys', Presented at the Annual Meeting of the American Association for Public Opinion Research (AAPOR), Chicago.

DeMaio, Theresa J. (1984) 'Social desirability and survey measurement: a review', in Charles F. Turner and Elizabeth Martin (eds) *Surveying Subjective Phenomena*, Vol. 2. New York: Russell Sage Foundation. pp. 257–282.

DeMaio, Theresa J. and Jennifer M. Rothgeb (1996) 'Cognitive interviewing techniques: in the lab and in the field', in Norbert Schwartz and Seymous

Sudman (eds) *Answering Questions: Methodology for Cognitive and Communicative Processes in Survey Research*. San Francisco: Jossey-Bass. pp. 177–196.

Deming, W. Edwards (1944) 'On errors in surveys', *American Sociological Review* 9(4): 359–369.

Deming, W. Edwards and Frederick F. Stephan (1940) 'On a least squares adjustment of a sampled frequency table when the expected marginal totals are known', *Annals of Mathematical Statistics* 11(4): 427–444.

DeVellis, Robert F. (2012) *Scale Development: Theory and Applications*, 3rd edn. Thousand Oaks, CA: Sage.

Dillman, Don A. (1978) *Mail and Telephone Surveys: The Total Design Method*. New York: Wiley.

Dillman, Don A. (2007) *Mail and Internet Surveys: The Tailored Design Method*, 2nd edn. Hoboken, NJ: Wiley.

Dixon, John and Clyde Tucker (2010) 'Survey nonresponse', in Peter V. Marsden and James D. Wrights (eds) *Handbook of Survey Research*, 2nd edn. Bingley: Emerald. pp. 593–630.

Eagly, Alice H. and Shelley S. Chaiken (2007) 'The advantages of an inclusive definition of attitude', *Social Cognition* 25(5): 582–602.

Efron, Bradley and Robert J. Tibshirani (1993) *An Introduction to the Bootstrap*. Boca Raton, FL: Chapman & Hall.

Eid, Michael, Fridtjof W. Nussbeck, Christian Geiser, David A. Cole, Mario Gollwitzer and Tanja Lischetzke (2008) 'Structural equation modeling of multitrait–multimethod data: different models for different types of methods', *Psychological Methods* 13(3): 230–253.

Ericsson, K. Anders and Herbert A. Simon (1980) 'Verbal reports as data', *Psychological Review* 87(3): 215–251.

Ericsson, K. Anders and Herbert A. Simon (1993) *Protocol Analysis: Verbal Reports as Data*, 2nd edn. Cambridge, MA: MIT Press.

Eurostat (2011) '2009 Comparative EU intermediate quality report', Directorate F: Social and information society statistics, Unit F-3: Living conditions and social protection, Doc. LC 61/11/EN, rev.1, available at http://epp. eurostat.ec.europa.eu/portal/page/portal/income_social_inclusion_living_ conditions/documents/tab9/LC61-11EN2009IntermediateEUQRver.3.pdf (accessed 7 November 2012).

Fazio, Russell H. (2007) 'Attitudes as object-evaluation associations of varying strength', *Social Cognition* 25(5): 603–637.

Fazio, Russell H., Jeaw-Mei Chen, Elizabeth C. McDonel and Steven J. Sherman (1982) 'Attitude accessibility, attitude-behavior consistency and the strength of object-evaluation association', *Journal of Experimental Social Psychology* 18(4): 339–357.

Fienberg, Stephen E. and Judith M. Tanur (1983) 'Reconsidering the fundamental contributions of Fisher and Neyman on experimentation and sampling', *International Statistical Review* 64(3): 237–253.

Forsyth, Barbara, Jennifer M. Rothgeb and Gordon B. Willis (2004) 'Does pretesting make a difference? An experimental pretest', in Stanley Presser et al. (eds) *Methods for Pretesting and Evaluating Survey Questionnaires*. Hoboken, NJ: Wiley. pp. 525–546.

Fowler, Floyd F., Jr (1989) 'Evaluation of special training and debriefing procedures for pretest interviews', in Charles Cannell, Lois Oksenberg, Floyd J. Fowler, Graham Kalton and Katherine Bischoping (eds) *New Techniques for Pretesting Survey Questions*. Ann Arbor, MI: Survey Research Center. pp. 63–71.

Fowler, Floyd F., Jr (1995) *Improving Survey Questions: Design and Evaluation*. Thousand Oaks, CA: Sage.

Fowler, Floyd F., Jr and Charles F. Cannell (1996) 'Using behavioral coding to identify cognitive problems with survey questions', in Seymour Sudman, Norman M. Bradburn and Norbert Schwarz (eds) *Thinking About Answers: The Application of Cognitive Processes to Survey Methodology*. San Francisco: Jossey-Bass. pp. 15–36.

Fox, James A. and Paul E. Tracy (1986) *Randomized Response: A Method for Sensitive Surveys*. Beverly Hills, CA: Sage.

Frankel, Lester R. and J. Stevens Stock (1942) 'On the sample survey of unemployment', *Journal of the American Statistical Association* 37(March): 77–80.

Frankel, Martin and Benjamin King (1996) 'A conversation with Leslie Kish', *Statistical Science* 11(1): 65–87.

Freedman, Debora, Arland Thornton, Donald Camburn, Duane Alwin and Linda Young-DeMarco (1988) 'The life history calendar: a technique for collecting retrospective data', *Sociological Methodology* 18: 37–68.

Fricker, Scott and Roger Tourangeau (2010) 'Examining the relationship between nonresponse propensity and data quality in two national household surveys', *Public Opinion Quarterly* 74(5): 934–955.

Fricker, Scott, Mirta Galesic, Roger Tourangeau and Ting Yan (2005) 'An experimental comparison of web and telephone surveys', *Public Opinion Quarterly* 69 (3): 370–392.

Friedman, William J. (1993) 'Memory for the time of past events', *Psychological Bulletin* 113(1): 44–66.

Ganzeboom, Harry B.G. and Donald J. Treiman (1996) 'Internationally comparable measures of occupational status for the 1988 International Standard Classification of Occupations', *Social Science Research* 25: 201–239.

Gaskell, George D., Daniel B. Wright and Colm A. O'Muircheartaigh (2000) 'Telescoping of landmark events: implications for survey research', *Public Opinion Quarterly* 64(1): 77–89.

Gile, Krista and Mark S. Handcock (2010) 'Respondent-driven sampling: an assessment of current methodology', *Sociological Methodology* 40: 285–327.

Goodman, Leo A. (1961) 'Snowball sampling', *Annals of Mathematical Statistics* 32(1): 148–170.

Goyder, John (1987) *The Silent Minority: Nonrespondents on Sample Surveys*. Boulder, CO: Westview.

Graesser, Arthur C., Sailaja Bommareddy, Shane Swammer and Johnathan M. Golding (1996) 'Integrating questionnaire design with a cognitive computational model of human question answering', in Norbert Schwarz and Seymour Sudman (eds) *Answering Questions: Methodology for Determining Cognitive and Communicative Processes in Survey Research*. San Francisco: Jossey-Bass. pp. 143–176.

Graesser, Arthur C., Z. Cai, Max M. Louwerse and F. Daniel (2006) 'Question Understanding Aid (QUAID): a web facility that pretests question comprehensibility', *Public Opinion Quarterly* 70(1): 3–22.

Grice, Paul (1975) 'Logic and conversation', in P. Cole and J. Morgan, *Syntax and Semantics, 3: Speech Acts*. New York: Academic Press.

Groves, Robert M. (2006) 'Nonresponse rates and nonresponse bias in household surveys', *Public Opinion Quarterly* 70(5): 646–675.

Groves, Robert M. (2011) 'Three eras of survey research', *Public Opinion Quarterly* 75(5): 861–871.

Groves, Robert M. and Mick Couper (1996) 'Contact-level influences on cooperation in face-to-face interviews', *Journal of Official Statistics* 12(1): 63–83.

Groves, Robert M. and Mick Couper (1998) *Nonresponse in Household Interview Surveys*. New York: Wiley.

Groves, Robert M. and Robert Louis Kahn (1979) *Surveys by Telephone: A National Comparison with Personal Interviews*. New York: Academic Press.

Groves, Robert M. and Lars Lyberg (2010) 'Total survey error: past, present, and future', *Public Opinion Quarterly* 74(5): 849–879.

Groves, Robert M. and Lou J. Magilavy (1986) 'Measuring and explaining interviewer effects in centralized telephone surveys', *Public Opinion Quarterly* 50(2): 251–266.

Groves, Robert M. and Emilia Peytcheva (2008) 'The impact of nonresponse rates on nonresponse bias: a meta-analysis', *Public Opinion Quarterly* 72(2): 167–189.

Groves, Robert M., Eleanor Singer and Amy Corning (2000) 'Leverage-saliency theory of survey participation: description and an illustration', *Public Opinion Quarterly* 64(3): 299–308.

Groves, Robert M., Don A. Dillman, John L. Eltinge and Roderick J.A. Little (2002) *Survey Nonresponse*. New York: Wiley.

Groves, Robert M., Stanley Presser and Sarah Dipko (2004) 'The role of topic interest in survey participation decisions', *Public Opinion Quarterly* 68(1): 2–31.

Groves, Robert M., Floyd J. Fowler, Jr, Mick P. Couper, James M. Lepkowski, Eleanor Singer and Roger Tourangeau (2009) *Survey Methodology*, 2nd edn. Hoboken, NJ: Wiley.

GSOEP (2008) 'Individual Question Form for the Living in Germany: Survey 2008 of the Social Situation of Households', available at http://www.diw.de/en/diw_02.c.238114.en/questionnaires_fieldwork_documents.html (accessed 12 September 2012).

Häder, Sabine, Michael Häder and Mike Kühne (eds) (2012) *Telephone Surveys in Europe: Research and Practice*. Berlin: Springer.

Hansen, Morris H. and William N. Hurwitz (1943) 'On the theory of sampling from finite populations', *Annals of Mathematical Statistics* 14(4): 333–362.

Harding, John (1944a) 'Refusals as a source of bias', in Hadley Cantril (ed.) *Gauging Public Opinion*. Princeton, NJ: Princeton University Press. pp. 119–123.

Harding, John (1944b) 'The measurement of civilian morale', in Hadley Cantril (ed.) *Gauging Public Opinion*. Princeton, NJ: Princeton University Press. pp. 232–258.

Hartley, H.O. and J.N.K. Rao (1978) 'Estimation of nonsampling variance components in sample surveys', in N. Krishnan Namboodiri (ed.) *Survey Sampling and Measurement*. New York: Academic Press. pp. 35–43.

Heberlein, Thomas A. and Robert Baumgartner (1978) 'Factors affecting response rates to mailed questionnaires: a quantitative analysis of the published literature', *American Sociological Review* 43(4): 447–462.

Heckathorn, Douglas D. (1997) 'Respondent-driven sampling: a new approach to the study of hidden populations', *Social Problems* 44(2): 174–199.

Heckathorn, Douglas D. (2002) 'Respondent-driven sampling II: deriving valid population estimates from chain-referral samples of hidden populations', *Social Problems* 49(1): 11–34.

Heerwegh, Dirk and Geert Loosveldt (2008) 'Face-to-face versus web surveying in a high-internet-coverage population: differences in response quality', *Public Opinion Quarterly* 72(5): 836–846.

Hippler, Hans, Norbert Schwarz and Seymour Sudman (eds) (1987) *Social Information Processing and Survey Methodology*. New York: Springer.

Hirodoglu, Michael A. and Pierre Lavallée (2009) 'Sampling and estimation in business surveys', in Danny Pfeffermann and C.R. Rao (eds) *Sample Surveys: Design Methods and Applications. Handbook of Statistics*, Vol. 29A. Amsterdam: Elsevier. pp. 441–470.

Höfling, Volkmar, Karin Schermelleh-Engel and Helfried Moosbrugger (2009) 'Analyzing multitrait-multimethod data: a comparison of three approaches', *Methodology* 5(3): 99–111.

Holbrook, Allyson L. and Jon A. Krosnick (2010) 'Measuring voter turnout by using the randomized response technique: evidence calling into question the method's validity', *Public Opinion Quarterly* 74(2): 328–343.

Holbrook, Allyson L., Melanie C. Green and Jon A. Krosnick (2003) 'Telephone versus face-to-face interviewing of national probability samples with long questionnaires: comparisons of respondent satisficing and social desirability response bias', *Public Opinion Quarterly* 67(1): 79–125.

Holbrook, Allyson L., Jon A. Krosnick, David Moore and Roger Tourangeau (2007) 'Response order effects in dichotomous categorical questions presented orally: the impact of question and respondent attributes', *Public Opinion Quarterly* 71(3): 325–348.

Holbrook, Allyson L., Jon A. Krosnick and Alison Pfent (2008) 'The causes and consequences of response rates in surveys by the new media and government contractor survey research firms', in James Lepkowski et al. (eds) *Advances in Telephone Survey Methodology*. Hoboken, NJ: Wiley. pp. 499–528.

Holleman, Bregje (1999) 'Wording effects in survey research using meta-analysis to explain the forbid/allow asymmetry', *Journal of Quantitative Linguistics* 6(1): 29–40.

Hox, Joop J. and Edith D. de Leeuw (1994) 'A comparison of nonresponse in mail, telephone, and face-to-face surveys: applying multi-level modeling to meta-analysis', *Quantity and Quality* 28(4): 329–344.

Hox, Joop, Edith de Leeuw and Harrie Vorst (1995) 'Survey participation as reasoned action: a behavioural paradigm for survey nonresponse?', *Bulletin de Méthodologie Sociologique* 48: 52–67.

Hyman, Herbert Hiram (1991) *Taking Society's Measure: A Personal History of Survey Research*. New York: Russell Sage Foundation.

Hyman, Herbert H. and Paul B. Sheatsley (1950) 'The current status of American public opinion', in J.C. Payne (ed.) *The Teaching of Contemporary Affairs: Twenty-first Yearbook of the National Council for the Social Studies*. pp. 11–34.

Jabine, Thomas B., Miron L. Straf, Judith M. Tanur and Roger Tourangeau (1984) *Cognitive Aspects of Survey Methodology: Building a Bridge Between Disciplines*. Washington, DC: National Academy Press.

Jäckle, Annette, Caroline Roberts and Peter Lynn (2010) 'Assessing the effect of data collection mode on measurement', *International Statistical Review* 78(1): 3–20.

Jasso, Guillermina (2006) 'Factorial survey methods for studying beliefs and judgments', *Sociological Methods and Research* 34(3): 334–423.

Jasso, Guillermina and Karl-Dieter Opp (1997) 'Probing the character of norms: a factorial survey analysis of the norms of political action', *American Sociological Review* 62(6): 947–964.

Jobe, Jared B. and Mingay, David J. (1991) 'Cognition and survey measurement: history and overview', *Applied Cognitive Psychology* 5(3): 175–192.

Jöreskog, Karl G. (1970) 'A general method for analysis of covariance structures', *Biometrika* 57(2): 239–251.

Jöreskog, Karl G. (1978) 'Structural analysis of covariance and correlation matrices', *Psychometrika* 43(4): 443–477.

Kahneman, Daniel and Angus Deaton (2010) 'High income improves evaluation of life but not emotional well-being', *Proceedings of the National Academy of Sciences (PNAS)* 107(38): 16489–16493.

Kalton, Graham and D.W. Anderson (1986) 'Sampling rare populations', *Journal of the Royal Statistical Society: Series A* 149: 65–82.

Kaminska, Olena, Allan L. McCutcheon and Jaak Billiet (2010) 'Satisficing among reluctant respondents in a cross-national context', *Public Opinion Quarterly* 74(5): 956–984.

Kankaraš, Miloš and Guy Moors (2011) 'Measurement equivalence and extreme response bias in the comparison of attitudes across Europe: a multigroup latent-class factor approach', *Methodology* 7(2): 68–80.

Katz, Daniel (1942) 'Do interviewers bias poll results?', *Public Opinion Quarterly* 6(2): 248–268.

Katz, Daniel (1944) 'The measurement of intensity', in Hadley Cantril (ed.) *Gauging Public Opinion*. Princeton, NJ: Princeton University Press. pp. 51–65.

Keeter, Scott, Carolyn Miller, Andrew Kohut, Robert M. Groves and Stanley Presser (2000) 'Consequences of reducing nonresponse in a national telephone survey', *Public Opinion Quarterly* 64(2): 125–148.

Kish, Leslie (1962) 'Studies of interviewer variance for attitudinal variables', *Journal of the American Statistical Association* 57: 92–115.

Kish, Leslie (1965) *Survey Sampling*. New York: Wiley.

Kish, Leslie and Martin R. Frankel (1970) 'Balanced repeated replications for standard errors', *Journal of the American Statistical Association* 65(September): 1071–1094.

Kish, Leslie and Martin R. Frankel (1974) 'Inference from complex samples', *Journal of the Royal Statistical Society: Series B (Methodological)* 36(1): 1–37.

Kohler, Ulrich (2007) 'Surveys from inside: an assessment of unit nonresponse with internal criteria', *Survey Research Methods* 1(2): 55–67.

Krauter, Frauke, Standley Presser and Roger Tourangeau (2008) 'Social desirability bias in CATI, IVR, and web surveys: the effect of mode and question sensitivity', *Public Opinion Quarterly* 72(5): 847–865.

Krosnick, Jon A. (1991) 'Response strategies for coping with the cognitive demands of attitude measures in surveys', *Applied Cognitive Psychology* 5(3): 213–236.

Krosnick, Jon A. and Robert P. Abelson (1992) 'The case for measuring attitude strength', in Judith M. Tanur (ed.) *Questions about Questions*. New York: Russell Sage Foundation. pp. 177–203.

Krosnick, Jon A. and Duane F. Alwin (1987) 'An evaluation of a cognitive theory of response-order effects in survey measurement', *Public Opinion Quarterly* 51(2): 201–219.

Krosnick, Jon A. and Stanley Presser (2010) 'Question and questionnaire design', in Peter V. Marsden and James D. Wright (eds) *Handbook of Survey Research*, 2nd edn. Bingley: Emerald. pp. 263–314.

Krosnick, Jon A. and Howard Schuman (1988) 'Attitude intensity, importance, and certainty and susceptibility to response effects', *Journal of Personality and Social Psychology* 54(6): 940–952.

Krosnick, Jon, Allyson L. Holbrook, Matthew K. Berent, Richard T. Carson, W. Michael Hanemann, Raymond J. Kopp, Robert Cameron Mitchell et al. (2002) 'The impact of "no opinion" response options on data quality: non-attitude reduction or an invitation to satisfice?', *Public Opinion Quarterly* 66(3): 371–403.

Krueger, Alan B. and David A. Schkade (2008) 'The reliability of subjective well-being measures', *Journal of Public Economics* 92: 1833–1845.

Kruskal, William and Frederick Mosteller (1980) 'Representative sampling, IV: the history of the concept in statistics, 1895–1939', *International Statistical Review* 48: 169–195.

Kühne, Mike and Michael Häder (2012) 'Telephone surveys via landline and mobile phones: mode effects and response quality', in Sabine Häder, Michael Häder and Mike Kühne (eds) *Telephone Surveys in Europe: Research and Practice*. Berlin: Springer. pp. 229–262.

Kuklinski, James H., Paul M. Sniderman, Kathleen Knight, Thomas Piazza, Philip E. Tetlock, Gordon R. Lawrence and Barbara Mellers (1997) 'Racial prejudice and attitudes toward affirmative action', *American Journal of Political Science* 41(2): 402–419.

Kuusella, Vesa (2011) 'Paradigms in statistical inference for finite populations up to the 1950s', *Statistics Finland Research Reports*, No. 257.

Lambert, Paul and Erik Bihagen (2011) 'Stratification research and occupation-based social classifications', DAMES Node, Technical Paper 2011–1.

Layard, R., G. Mayraz and S. Nickell (2008) 'The marginal utility of income', *Journal of Public Economics* 92(8–9): 1846–1857.

Lazarsfeld, Paul (1944) 'The controversy over detailed interviews – an offer for negotiation', *Public Opinion Quarterly* 8(1): 38–60.

Lazarsfeld, Paul and Marjorie Fiske (1938) 'The "panel" as a new tool for measuring public opinion', *Public Opinion Quarterly* 2(4): 596–612.

Leckie, Norm, Taylor Shek-Wai Hui, Doug Tattrie, Jennifer Robson and Jean-Pierre Voyer (2010) 'Learning to save, saving to learn', *Final Report of the Individual Development Accounts Project*. Ottawa: Social Research and Demonstration Corporation.

Leiulfsrud, Håkon, Ivano Bison and Heidi Jensberg (2005) 'Social class in Europe: European Social Survey 2002/3', NTNU Social Research Ltd, Trondheim, available at http://ess.nsd.uib.no/ess/doc/ess1_social_class.pdf (accessed 12 September 2012).

Lensvelt-Mulders, Gerty, Joop Hox, Peter van der Heijden and Cora Maas (2005) 'Meta-analysis of randomized response research: thirty-five years of validation', *Sociological Methods and Research* 33(3): 319–348.

Lessler, Judith T. and Forsyth, Barbara H. (1996) 'A coding system for appraising questionnaires', in Norbert Schwarz and Seymour Sudman (eds) *Answering Questions: Methodology for Determining Cognitive and Communicative Processes in Survey Research*. San Francisco: Jossey-Bass. pp. 389–402.

Levy, Paul S. and Stanley Lemeshow (2008) *Sampling of Populations: Methods and Applications*, 4th edn. Hoboken, NJ: Wiley.

Lin I-Fen and Nora Cate Schaeffer (1995) 'Using survey participants to estimate the effect of nonparticipation', *Public Opinion Quarterly* 59(2): 236–258.

Lipps, Olivier (2007) 'Interviewer and respondent survey quality effects in a CATI panel', *Bulletin de Méthodologie Sociologique* 95: 5–25.

Little, Roderick J.A. and Donald B. Rubin (1987) *Statistical Analysis with Missing Data*. New York: Wiley (2nd edn, 2002).

Loftus, Elizabeth (1984) 'Protocol analysis of response to survey recall questions', in Thomas B. Jabine, Miron L. Straf, Judith M. Tanur and Roger Tourangeau (eds) *Cognitive Aspects of Survey Methodology: Building a Bridge Between Disciplines*. Washington, DC: National Academy Press. pp. 61–64.

Loftus, Elizabeth F. and Wesley Marburger (1983) 'Since the eruption of Mount St. Helens, has anyone beaten you up? Improving the accuracy of retrospective reports with landmark events', *Memory and Cognition* 11: 114–120.

Lohr, Sharon L. (2009) 'Multiple-frame surveys', in Danny Pfeffermann and C.R. Rao (eds) *Sample Surveys: Design Methods and Applications. Handbook of Statistics*, Vol. 29A. Amsterdam: Elsevier. pp. 71–88.

Lohr, Sharon L. (2010) *Sampling: Design and Analysis*, 2nd edn. Pacific Grove, CA: Duxbury.

Lozano, Luis M., Eduardo García-Cueto and José Muñiz (2008) 'Effect of the number of response categories on the reliability and validity of rating scales', *Methodology* 4(2): 73–79.

Lozar Manfreda, Katja, Michael Bosnjak, Jernej Berzelak, Iris Haas and Vasja Vehovar (2008) 'Web surveys versus other survey modes: a meta-analysis comparing response rates', *International Journal of Market Research* 50(1): 79–104.

Lumley, Thomas (2010) *Complex Surveys: A Guide to Analysis Using R*. Hoboken, NJ: Wiley.

Mahalanobis, Prasanta (1946) 'Recent experiments in statistical sampling in the Indian Statistical Institute', *Journal of the Royal Statistical Society* 109(4): 325–378.

Malekinejad, Mohsen, Lisa G. Johnston, Carl Kendall, Ligia R.F.S. Kerr, Marina Raven Rifkin and George W. Rutherford (2008) 'Using respondent-driven sampling methodology for HIV biological and behavioral surveillance in international settings: a systematic review', *AIDS and Behavior* 12, Supplement 1: 105–130.

Malhotra, Neil (2009) 'Order effects in complex and simple tasks', *Public Opinion Quarterly* 73(1): 180–198.

Martin, Elizabeth (2004) 'Vignettes and respondent debriefing for questionnaire design and evaluation', in Stanley Presser et al. (eds) *Methods for Pretesting and Evaluating Survey Questionnaires*. Hoboken, NJ: Wiley. pp. 149–172.

Martin, Peter (2011) 'What makes a good mix? Chances and challenges of mixed mode data collection in the ESS', Centre for Comparative Social Surveys' Working Paper Series, Paper 02, City University London.

Mason, Robert, John E. Carlson and Roger Tourangeau (1994) 'Contrast effects and subtraction in part-whole questions', *Public Opinion Quarterly* 58(4): 569–578.

Matsueda, Ross L. (2012) 'Key advances in the history of structural equation modeling', in Rick H. Hoyle (ed.) *Handbook of Structural Equation Modeling*. New York: Guilford Press.

Maynard, Douglas W. and Nora Cate Schaeffer (2002) 'Standardization and its discontents', in Douglas W. Maynard et al. (eds) *Standardization and Tacit Knowledge: Interaction and Practice in the Survey Interview*. New York: Wiley. pp. 3–46.

McCarthy, Philip J. (1969) 'Pseudo-replication: half samples', *Review of the International Statistical Institute* 37(3): 239–264.

McClendon, McKee J. and Duane F. Alwin (1993) 'No opinion filters and attitude measurement reliability', *Sociological Methods and Research* 21(4): 438–464.

McClendon, McKee J. and David J. O'Brien (1988) 'Question order effects on the determinants of subjective well-being', *Public Opinion Quarterly* 52(3): 351–364.

Meyer, Bruce D. And James X. Sullivan (2011) 'Viewpoint: further results on measuring the well-being of the poor using income and consumption', *Canadian Journal of Economics* 44(1): 52–87.

Mills, C. Wright (1959) *The Sociological Imagination*. New York: Oxford University Press.

Mingay, David J. and Michael T. Greenwell (1989) 'Memory bias and response order effects', *Journal of Official Statistics* 5(3): 253–263.

Moore, Jeffrey C., Linda L. Stinson and Edward J. Welniak, Jr. (2000) 'Income measurement error in surveys: a review', *Journal of Official Statistics* 16(4): 331–361.

Mutz, Diana C. (2011) *Population-Based Survey Experiments*. Princeton, NJ: Princeton University Press.

Neisser, Ulric (1967) *Cognitive Psychology*. New York: Appleton-Century-Crofts.

Neter, John and Joseph Waksberg (1964) 'A study of response errors in expenditures data from household interviews', *Journal of the American Statistical Association* 59(March): 18–55.

Neyman, Jerzy (1934) 'On the two different aspects of the representative method: the method of stratified sampling and the method of purposive selection', *Journal of the Royal Statistical Society* 97(4): 558–606.

Neyman, Jerzy (1938) *Lectures and Conferences on Mathematical Statistics and Probability*. Washington, DC: Graduate School, US Dept of Agriculture (2nd edn, rev. and enlarged, 1952).

Nock, Steven L. and Thomas M. Guterbock (2010) 'Survey experiments', in Peter V. Marsden and James D. Wright (eds) *Handbook of Survey Research*, 2nd edn. Bingley: Emerald. pp. 837–864.

Oksenberg, Lois, Charles Cannell and Graham Kalton (1989) 'New methods for pretesting survey questionnaires', in Charles Cannell, Lois Oksenberg, Floyd J. Fowler, Graham Kalton and Katherine Bischoping (eds) *New Techniques for Pretesting Survey Questions*. Ann Arbor, MI: Survey Research Center. pp. 30–62.

O'Muircheartaigh, Colm (1999) 'CASM: successes, failures, and potential', in Monroe Sirken et al., *Cognition and Survey Research*. New York: Wiley. pp. 39–64.

O'Muircheartaigh, Colm and Pamela Campanelli (1998) 'The relative impact of interviewer effects and sample design effects on survey precision', *Journal of the Royal Statistical Society: Series A* 161(1): 63–77.

Ongena, Yfke P. and Wil Dijkstra (2006) 'Methods of behavior coding of survey interviews', *Journal of Official Statistics* 22(3): 419–451.

Osborne, Thomas and Nikolas Rose (1999) 'Do the social sciences create phenomena? The example of public opinion research', *British Journal of Sociology* 50(3): 367–396.

Payne, Stanley L. (1951) *The Art of Asking Questions*. Princeton, NJ: Princeton University Press.

Peffley, Mark A. and Jon Hurwitz (1985) 'A hierarchical model of attitude constraint', *American Journal of Political Science* 29(4): 871–890.

Petty, Richard E., Pablo Briñol and Kenneth G. DeMarree (2007) 'The meta-cognitive model (mcm) of attitudes: implications for attitude measurement, change, and strength', *Social Cognition* 25(5): 657–686.

Pew Research Center (2012) 'Assessing the representativeness of public opinion surveys', available at http://www.people-press.org/2012/05/15/assessing-the-representativeness-of-public-opinion-surveys/ (accessed 4 July 2012).

Presser, Stanley and Johnny Blair (1994) 'Survey pretesting: do different methods produce different results?', *Sociological Methodology* 24: 73–104.

Presser, Stanley, Mick P. Couper, Judith T. Lessler, Elizabeth Martin, Jean Martin, Jennifer M. Rothgeb and Eleanor Singer (2004) 'Methods for pretesting and evaluating survey questionnaires', *Public Opinion Quarterly* 68(1): 109–130.

Raghavarao, Damaraju and Walter T. Federer (1979) 'Block total response as an alternative to the randomized response method in surveys', *Journal of the Royal Statistical Society: Series B (Statistical Methodology)* 41: 40–45.

Rodgers, Willard L., Frank M. Andrews and A. Regula Herzog (1992) 'Quality of survey measures: a structural modeling approach', *Journal of Official Statistics* 8(3): 251–275.

Roper, Elmo (1940) 'Sampling public opinion', *Journal of the American Statistical Association* 35(210, Part 1): 325–334.

Roper, Elmo (1957) *You and Your Leaders*. New York: William Morrow.

Rosenberg, Morris J. (1968) *The Logic of Survey Analysis*. New York: Basic Books.

Rossi, Peter H. (1979) 'Vignette analysis: uncovering the normative structure of complex judgments', in Robert K. Merton et al. (eds) *Qualitative and Quantitative Social Research: Papers in Honor of Paul F. Lazarsfeld*. New York: Free Press. pp. 176–186.

Rossi, Peter H. and Andy B. Anderson (1982) 'The factorial survey approach: an introduction', in Peter H. Rossi and Steve Nock (eds) *Measuring Social Judgements: The Factorial Survey Approach*. Beverly Hills, CA: Sage. pp. 15–67.

Rothgeb, Jennifer, Gordon Willis and Barbara Forsyth (2001) 'Questionnaire pretesting methods: do different techniques and different organizations produce similar results?', *Proceedings of the Annual Meeting of the American Statistical Association*, Atlanta, GA.

Rubin, Donald B. (1976) 'Inference and missing data', *Biometrika* 63(3): 581–592.

Rugg, Donald (1941) 'Experiments in wording questions: II', *Public Opinion Quarterly* 5(1): 91–92.

Rugg, Donald (1944a) 'How representative are "representative samples?"', in Hadley Cantril (ed.) *Gauging Public Opinion*. Princeton, NJ: Princeton University Press. pp. 143–149.

Rugg, Donald (1944b) '"Trained" vs. "untrained" interviewers', in Hadley Cantril (ed.) *Gauging Public Opinion*. Princeton, NJ: Princeton University Press. pp. 83–97.

Rugg, Donald and Hadley Cantril (1942) 'The wording of questions in public opinion polls', *Journal of Abnormal and Social Psychology* 37(4): 469–495.

Saris, Willem E. and Irmtraud N. Gallhofer (2007a) 'Estimation of the effects of measurement characteristics on the quality of survey questions', *Survey Research Methods* 1(1): 29–43.

Saris, Willem E. and Irmtraud N. Gallhofer (2007b) *Design, Evaluation, and Analysis of Questionnaires for Survey Research*. Hoboken, NJ: Wiley.

Saris, Willem E., Albert Satorra and Germà Coenders (2004a) 'A new approach to evaluating the quality of measurement instruments: the split-ballot MTMM design', *Sociological Methodology* 34: 311–347.

Saris, Willem E., William van der Veld and Irmtraud Gallhofer (2004b) 'Development and improvement of questionnaires using predictions of reliability and validity', in Stanley Presser et al. (eds) *Methods for Pretesting and Evaluating Survey Questionnaires*. Hoboken, NJ: Wiley. pp. 275–297.

Saris, Willem E., Melanie Revilla, Jon A. Krosnick and Eric M. Shaeffer (2010) 'Comparing questions with agree/disagree response options to questions with item-specific response options', *Survey Research Methods* 4(1): 61–79.

Saris, Willem E., Daniel Oberski, Melanie Revilla, Diana Zavala, Laur Lilleoja, Irmtraud Gallhofer and Tom Gruner (2011) 'Final report about the project JRA3 as part of ESS Infrastructure', Universitat Pompeu Fabra (Barcelona) – Research and Expertise Centre for Survey Methodology: Working Paper Number 24, available at http://www.upf.edu/survey/_pdf/RECSM_wp024.pdf (accessed 8 September 2012).

Särndal, Carl-Erik and Sixten Lundström (2008) 'Assessing auxiliary vectors for control of nonresponse bias in the calibration estimator', *Journal of Official Statistics* 24(2): 167–191.

Schaeffer, Nora Cate (1991) 'Hardly ever or constantly! Group comparisons using vague quantifiers', *Public Opinion Quarterly* 55(3): 395–423.

Schaeffer, Nora Cate and Jennifer Dykema (2011) 'Questions for surveys: current trends and future directions', *Public Opinion Quarterly* 75(5): 909–961.

Schaeffer, Nora Cate and Douglas W. Maynard (2002) 'Occasions for intervention: interactional resources for comprehension in standardized survey interviews', in Douglas W. Maynard et al. (eds) *Standardization and Tacit Knowledge: Interaction and Practice in the Survey Interview*. New York: Wiley. pp. 261–280.

Schaeffer, Nora Cate, Jennifer Dykema and Douglas W. Maynard (2010) 'Interviewers and interviewing', in Peter V. Marsden and James D. Wright (eds) *Handbook of Survey Research*, 2nd edn. Bingley: Emerald. pp. 437–470.

Scherpenzeel, Annette C. and Willem E. Saris (1997) 'The reliability and validity of survey questions: a meta-analysis of MTMM studies', *Sociological Methods and Research* 25(3): 341–383.

Schneider, Silke L. (2010) 'Nominal comparability is not enough: (in-)equivalence of construct validity of cross-national measures of educational attainment in the European Social Survey', *Research in Social Stratification and Mobility* 28: 343–357.

Schnell, Rainer and Frauke Kreuter (2005) 'Separating interviewer and sampling-point effects', *Journal of Official Statistics* 21(3): 389–410.

Schober, Michael F. and Frederick G. Conrad (1997) 'Does conversational interviewing reduce survey measurement error?', *Public Opinion Quarterly* 61(4): 576–602.

Schober, Michael F. and Frederick G. Conrad (2008) 'Introduction', in Frederick G. Conrad and Michael F. Schober (eds) *Envisioning the Interview of the Future*. Hoboken, NJ: Wiley. pp. 1–30.

Schuman, Howard and Lawrence Bobo (1988) 'Survey-based experiments on white racial attitudes toward residential integration', *American Sociological Review* 94(2): 273–299.

Schuman, Howard and Stanley Presser (1981) *Questions and Answers in Attitude Surveys*. New York: Academic Press.

Schwarz, Norbert (2007a) 'Cognitive aspects of survey methodology', *Applied Cognitive Psychology* 21(2): 277–287.

Schwarz, Norbert (2007b) 'Attitude construction: evaluation in context', *Social Cognition* 25(5): 638–656.

Schwarz, Norbert and Seymour Sudman (eds) (1996) *Answering Questions: Methodology for Determining Cognitive and Communicative Processes in Survey Research*. San Francisco: Jossey-Bass.

Schwarz, Norbert, Hans-J. Hippler, Brigitte Deutsch and Fritz Strack (1985) 'Response scales: effects of category range on reported behavior and comparative judgments', *Public Opinion Quarterly* 49(3): 388–395.

Schwarz, Norbert, Fritz Strack and Hans-Peter Mai (1991) 'Assimilation and contrast effects in part–whole question sequences: a conversational logic analysis', *Public Opinion Quarterly* 55(1): 3–23.

Sheatsley, Paul B. (1983) 'Questionnaire construction and item writing', in Peter H. Rossi et al. (eds) *Handbook of Survey Research*. Orlando, FL: Academic Press. pp. 195–230.

Shih, Tse-Hua and Xitao Fan (2008) 'Comparing response rates from web and mail surveys: a meta-analysis', *Field Methods* 20(3): 249–271.

Singer, Eleanor (2011) 'Toward a benefit–cost theory of survey participation: evidence, further tests and implications', *Journal of Official Statistics* 27(2): 379–392.

Singer, Eleanor, John Van Hoewyk, Nancy Gebler, Trivellore Raghunathan and Katherine McGonagle (1999) 'The effect of incentives on response rates in interviewer-mediated surveys', *Journal of Official Statistics* 15(2): 217–230.

Singer, Eleanor, John Van Hoewyk and Mary K. Maher (2000) 'Experiments with incentives in telephone surveys', *Public Opinion Quarterly* 64(2): 171–188.

Sirgy, M. Joseph, Alex C. Michalos, Abbott L. Ferriss, Rickard A. Easterlin, Donald Patrick and William Pavot (2006) 'The quality-of-life (QOL) research movement: past, present, and future', *Social Indicators Research* 76(3): 343–466.

Sirken, Monroe G. (1970) 'Household surveys with multiplicity', *Journal of the American Statistical Association* 65(1): 257–266.

Sirken, Monroe, Thomas Jabine, Gordon Willis, Elizabeth Martin and Clyde Tucker (eds) (1999) *A New Agenda for Interdisciplinary Survey Research Methods: Proceedings of the CASM II Seminar*. Hyattsville, MD: Centers for Disease Control and Prevention, National Center for Health Statistics. Available in full at http://www.cdc.gov/nchs/data/misc/casm2pro.pdf (accessed 8 September 2012).

Skrondal, Anders and Sophia Rabe-Hesketh (2007) 'Latent variable modeling: a survey', *Scandinavian Journal of Statistics* 34(4): 712–745.

Smith, T.M.F. (1976) 'The foundations of survey sampling: a review', *Journal of the Royal Statistical Society: Series A* 139(2): 183–204.

Smith, Tom (2011) 'Refining the total survey error perspective', *International Journal of Public Opinion Research* 23(4): 464–484.

Sniderman, Paul M. and Douglas B. Grob (1996) 'Innovations in experimental design in attitude surveys', *Annual Review of Sociology* 22: 377–399.

Sniderman, Paul M. and Thomas Piazza (1993) *The Scar of Race*. Cambridge, MA: Harvard University Press.

Sniderman, Paul M. and Paul M. Theriault (2004) 'The structure of political argument and the logic of issue framing', in Willem E. Seris and Paul M. Sniderman (eds) *Studies in Public Opinion: Attitudes, Nonattitudes, Measurement Error, and Change*. Princeton, NJ: Princeton University Press.

Sniderman, Paul M., Perangelo Peri, Rui J.P. de Figueiredo, Jr and Thomas Piazza (2000) *The Outsider: Prejudice and Politics in Italy*. Princeton, NJ: Princeton University Press.

Snijders, Tom A.B. and Roel Bosker (2011) *Multilevel Analysis: An Introduction to Basic and Advanced Multilevel Modeling*, 2nd edn. London: Sage.

Snijkers, Ger, Joop Hox and Edith D. de Leeuw (1999) 'Interviewers' tactics for fighting survey nonresponse', *Journal of Official Statistics* 15(2): 185–198.

Squire, Peverill (1988) 'Why the 1936 *Literary Digest* poll failed', *Public Opinion Quarterly* 52(1): 125–133.

Stalker, Glenn J. and Lesley J. Wood (2013) 'Reaching beyond the net: political circuits and participation in Toronto's G20 protests', *Social Movement Studies* forthcoming.

Statistics Canada (2008) *Methodology of the Canadian Labour Force Survey*. Ottawa: Minister of Industry. Online at http://www.statcan.gc.ca/pub/71-526-x/71-526-x2007001-eng.pdf (accessed 6 November 2012).

Sterba, Sonya K. (2009) 'Alternative model-based and design-based frameworks for inference from samples to populations: from polarization to integration', *Multivariate Behavioral Research* 44(6): 711–740.

Stock, J. Stevens (1944) 'Some general principles of sampling', in Hadley Cantril (ed.) *Gauging Public Opinion*. Princeton, NJ: Princeton University Press. pp. 127–142.

Stoop, Ineke (2005) *The Hunt for the Last Respondent: Nonrespondents in Sample Surveys*. The Hague: Social and Cultural Planning Office of the Netherlands.

Stoop, Ineke, Jaak Billiet, Achim Koch and Rory Fitzgerald (2010) *Improving Survey Response: Lessons Learned from the European Social Survey*. Chichester: Wiley.

Stouffer, Samuel A., Edward A. Suchman, Leland C. DeVinney, Shirley A. Star and Robin M. Williams, Jr (1949) *Studies in Social Psychology in World War II: The American Soldier*. Vol. 1, *Adjustment During Army Life*; Vol. 2, *Combat and Its Aftermath*. Princeton, NJ: Princeton University Press.

Sudman, Seymour and Norman M. Bradburn (1973) 'Effects of time and memory factors on response in surveys', *Journal of the American Statistical Association* 68(December): 805–815.

Sudman, Seymour, Adam Finn and Linda Lannom (1984) 'The use of bounded recall procedures in single interviews', *Public Opinion Quarterly* 48(2): 520–524.

Sudman, Seymour, Monroe G. Sirken and Charles D. Cowan (1988) 'Sampling rare and elusive populations', *Science* 240 (May 20): 991–996.

Sudman, Seymour, Norman M. Bradburn and Norbert Schwarz (eds) (1996) *Thinking About Answers: The Application of Cognitive Processes to Survey Methodology*. San Francisco: Jossey-Bass.

Tarnai, John and Danna L. Moore (2004) 'Methods for pretesting and evaluating computer-assisted questionnaires', in Stanley Presser et al. (eds) *Methods for Pretesting and Evaluating Survey Questionnaires*. Hoboken, NJ: Wiley. pp. 319–335.

Thompson, Steven K. and Ove Frank (2000) 'Model-based estimation with link-tracing sampling designs', *Survey Methodology* 26(1): 87–98.

Tourangeau, Roger (1984) 'Cognitive sciences and survey methods', in Thomas B. Jabine, Miron L. Straf, Judith M. Tanur and Roger Tourangeau (eds) *Cognitive Aspects of Survey Methodology: Building a Bridge Between Disciplines*. Washington, DC: National Academy Press. pp. 73–100.

Tourangeau, Roger and Norman Bradburn (2010) 'The psychology of survey response', in Peter V. Marsden and James D. Wright (eds) *Handbook of Survey Research*. Bingley: Emerald. pp. 315–346.

Tourangeau, Roger and Tom Smith (1996) 'Asking sensitive questions: the impact of data collection mode, question format, and question context', *Public Opinion Quarterly* 60(2): 275–304.

Tourangeau, Roger and Ting Yan (2007) 'Sensitive questions in surveys', *Psychological Bulletin* 133(5): 859–883.

Tourangeau, Roger, Lance J. Rips and Kenneth Rasinski (2000) *The Psychology of Survey Response*. Cambridge: Cambridge University Press.

Tucker, Clyde (1983) 'Interviewer effects in telephone surveys', *Public Opinion Quarterly* 47(1): 84–95.

Turnbull, William (1944) 'Secret vs. nonsecret ballots', in Hadley Cantril (ed.) *Gauging Public Opinion*. Princeton, NJ: Princeton University Press. pp. 78–82.

Turner, Charles F. and Elizabeth Martin (1984) *Surveying Subjective Phenomena*, 2 vols. New York: Russell Sage Foundation.

Van der Zouwen, Johannes and Johannes H. Smit (2004) 'Evaluation survey questions by analyzing patterns of behaviour codes and question–answer sequences: a diagnostic approach', in Stanley Presser et al. (eds) *Methods for Pretesting and Evaluating Survey Questionnaires*. Hoboken, NJ: Wiley. pp. 109–130.

Vannieuwenhuyze, Jorre, Geert Loosveldt and Geert Molenberghs (2010) 'A method for evaluating mode effects in mixed-mode surveys', *Public Opinion Quarterly* 74(5): 1027–1045.

Volz, Erik and Douglas D. Heckathorn (2008) 'Probability-based estimation theory for respondent-driven sampling', *Journal of Official Statistics* 24(1): 79–97.

Wallander, Lisa (2009) '25 years of factorial surveys in sociology: a review', *Social Science Research* 34(3): 505–520.

Warner, Stanley L. (1965) 'Randomized response: a survey technique for eliminating evasive answer bias', *Journal of the American Statistical Association* 60(March): 63–69.

Weisberg, Herbert F. (2005) *The Total Survey Error Approach: A Guide to the New Science of Survey Research.* Chicago: University of Chicago Press.

Williams, Robin M. (1989) 'The American soldier: an assessment', *Public Opinion Quarterly* 53(2): 155–174.

Willis, Gordon B. (2004) 'Cognitive interviewing revisited: a useful technique, in theory?', in Stanley Presser et al. (eds) *Methods for Testing and Evaluating Survey Questionnaires* (eds) Hoboken, NJ: Wiley. pp. 23–44.

Willis, Gordon B. (2005) *Cognitive Interviewing: A Tool for Improving Questionnaire Design.* Thousand Oaks, CA: Sage.

Willis, Gordon B. and Judith T. Lessler (1999a) 'The question appraisal system: a guide for systematically evaluating survey question wording', Final Report submitted to the Centers for Disease Control and Prevention, National Center for Chronic Disease Prevention and Health Promotion. Research Triangle Institute, Research Triangle Park, North Carolina.

Willis, Gordon B. and Judith T. Lessler (1999b) 'Question Appraisal System: QAS-99', http://appliedresearch.cancer.gov/areas/cognitive/qas99.pdf (accessed 8 September 2012).

Willis, Gordon B., Susan Schechter and Karen Whitaker (2000) 'A comparison of cognitive interviewing, expert review, and behavior coding: what do they tell us?', American Statistical Association, *Proceedings of the Section on Survey Research Methods.* Indianapolis, IN.

Wunderlich, Gooloo S. and Janet L. Norwood (eds) (2006) *Food Insecurity and Hunger in the United States: An Assessment of the Measure.* Washington, DC: National Academies Press.

Yan, Ting, Roger Tourangeau and Zac Arens (2004) 'When less is more: are reluctant respondents poor reporters?', Paper presented to the American Statistical Association Section on Survey Research Methods, Toronto.

Ye, Cong, Jenna Fulton and Roger Tourangeau (2011) 'More positive or more extreme? A meta-analysis of mode differences in response choice', *Public Opinion Quarterly* 75(2): 349–365.

Yeager, David S., Jon A. Krosnick, LinChiat Chang, Harold S. Javitz, Matthew S. Levendusky, Alberto Simpser and Rui Wang (2011) 'Comparing the accuracy of RDD telephone surveys and internet surveys conducted with probability and non-probability samples', *Public Opinion Quarterly* 75(4): 709–747.

Zaller, John R. (1992) *The Nature and Origins of Mass Opinion.* Cambridge: Cambridge University Press.

Zaller, John and Stanley Feldman (1992) 'A simple theory of the survey response: answering questions versus revealing preferences', *American Journal of Political Science* 36(3): 579–616.

Index

This index is in word-by-word order. Page references in *italics* indicate figures.